Narcomania

How Britain Got Hooked on Drugs

MAX DALY &
STEVE SAMPSON

WINDMILL BOOKS

Published by Windmill Books 2013

2 4 6 8 10 9 7 5 3 1

Copyright © Max Daly and Steve Sampson 2012, 2013

First published in Great Britain in 2012 by William Heinemann

Windmill Books
The Random House Group Limited
20 Vauxhall Bridge Road, London SW1V 2SA

Addresses for companies within The Random House Group Limited
can be found at: www.randomhouse.co.uk/offices.htm

The Random House Group Limited Reg. No. 954009

www.randomhouse.co.uk

A CIP catalogue record for this book
is available from the British Library

ISBN 9780099538035

The Random House Group Limited supports the Forest Stewardship
Council® (FSC®), the leading international forest-certification organisation.
Our books carrying the FSC label are printed on FSC®-certified paper. FSC is
the only forest-certification scheme supported by the leading environmental
organisations, including Greenpeace. Our paper procurement policy can be
found at www.randomhouse.co.uk/environment

Typeset in Minion by Palimpsest Book Production Limited, Falkirk, Stirlingshire
Printed and bound by CPI Group (UK) Ltd, Croydon, CR0 4YY

For Hajra and Mikael

For Safia and Sidney

Contents

Preface

Drug stories often combine three key elements – money, sex and power. Drug stories not only sell newspapers, but are ever-present across the Internet, on television, in films and in music. Yet a lot of what we read, see and hear are half-truths, exaggerations and urban myths. For all the column inches and coverage dedicated to discussing the issue from afar, we know very little about the true shape of the drug industry in the UK.

It is an industry that is vast and ever-mutating, and one that is hardwired into this country's cityscapes – a hidden edifice, involving tens of thousands of workers and an army of law-enforcers and professionals; a realm which links the deeply emotional psychoactive world of intoxication with cut-throat economics; a world that affects us all.

As investigative journalists who have covered drugs and drug crime for over twenty years – reporting on the minutia of the trade, charting and uncovering trends and watching as drug stories emerge and are passed through a media prism – we found ourselves in a unique position to tell the true story of illegal drugs in Britain. We have attempted here to provide as full and detailed a portrait as possible, though the sheer scope of the subject meant we had to exclude some areas, and each chapter would undoubtedly benefit from a book-length investigation. Many of the names of those we have interviewed, on both sides of the law, have been changed to protect their identity and, in some cases, to protect them from harm.

What follows is a panoramic journey through Britain's drug landscape – from the streets to Whitehall, and back. We meet users, dealers, elusive middlemen, drug-squad officers and bankers, taking a ringside seat as the media and politicians hold forth on the drug industry and as new scare stories hit the news-stands.

Our aim has been to anchor the British drug trade in some sort of reality – to examine one of Britain's most prosperous, though illicit, economies through the real stories of those involved. If progress is to be made in reducing the harms to society of the drug trade, of making headway on this seemingly unsolvable problem, then one of the first steps has to be to remove the mask and see what lies beneath, to view the reality of the situation rather than rely on hoary tales and tired rhetoric.

Unfortunately for those who would rather we turned a blind eye to the drug trade, it is a living, breathing, powerful entity. And it is closer than you think.

Introduction

The Face Behind the Mask

The ketamine hit home about ten minutes down the path on the way to the main stage at Glastonbury. Lucy and her friends – James, Paul and Pete – had each snorted a thick line of the hallucinogenic anaesthetic drug in their tent before heading out into the night.

As they walked arm in arm, Lucy's feet started feeling heavy, as if someone had poured cement into her boots. Her legs began to slow. Then the visuals kicked in. She began to see in a kind of tunnel vision, darkness surrounding the dimly lit path, with hundreds of faces coming towards her and passing by. Who was that man and why did he look like a skull with a wig on? What was that granny doing with her boobs out? And who was that mad-eyed hippy frothing at the mouth?

Three cowgirls came up to them with a tray of vodka jelly. 'Look what we made for you,' they said, popping a cup of shimmering scarlet into their hands.

Lucy wasn't even sure if she knew where her mouth was. She turned to Paul and saw that his eyes were wobbling from side to side, his mouth tightly clenched. They looked at each other and crumpled in hysterics, bent over double, tears streaming from their eyes. They couldn't speak.

After a while, they continued their journey, stumbling into oncomers every few paces, but no one seemed to mind. More people streamed past. Who was that dressed up as the Queen Mum? And what were all those girls in tutus doing in that tree? Lucy had forgotten she had taken drugs: the world around her had gone mad – all she could do was laugh at it.

The next morning, sitting in the sunshine, they were piecing together the night before. 'Did we see Gorillaz?' said Paul. 'I don't know – did we?' said Lucy. 'I don't think we got to the main stage,' said James. 'I don't even think we got to the end of that path.'

Lucy and her friends are all in their thirties. One works for BP, another runs a flooring company, the third is a personal assistant and the fourth is an artist.

They had bought what Lucy called a 'well-planned package of drugs', alongside the usual camping supplies. Like many of the hundreds of thousands of festival-goers each year, they saw a few days listening to music in a giant field in British summertime as the ideal situation in which to get 'out of it'.

Two powerful human drives – to get high and to make easy money – have been constantly reshaping and reinventing the drug trade since the first global anti-drug laws were set in place over 100 years ago. And, despite a century of law enforcement, the trade has mushroomed to become not only the biggest earner for international organised-crime groups but also larger, globally speaking, than most legitimate industries.

In 1998 Britain added its support to a landmark UN declaration on global drug control with the slogan: 'A Drug-Free World: We Can Do It'. The stated aim was to rid the world of illicit drugs in ten years. But twelve years later, in 2010, the UN had changed its tune. It now acknowledged the existence of a drug world that had changed for ever. It not only admitted the defeat of its 1998 aim but said that the online proliferation of new synthetic drugs such as mephedrone had moved the goal-posts. So what role does the drug trade play in Britain today?

Your view of the drugs trade will probably depend on where you sit within, or in relation to it. For dealers it is a way of making easy money, for consumers a route to a good night out. For those outside the trade its creeping presence may well be a reminder of everything that is wrong with modern society. But is Britain really a nation, as some national newspapers would have us believe, of dope fiends? Perhaps the drug trade has Britain hooked in a more subtle, yet pernicious, way. How does an illicit billion-pound industry operate beyond the reach of law enforcers? Where does the money go? And why does the mention of drugs scare our politicians into silence?

Drugs are perhaps Britain's last taboo. A heady haze of morality swirls around this world of hard cash, criminality and intoxication. While great strides have been made in dealing with other Victorian-era bugbears like women's rights, racism, slavery, sex and homosexuality, the attitude of those in power to the business of drug selling and narcotic intoxication remains stuck in a world of evil street peddlers preying, like dope-dealing vampires, on helpless young drug fiends.

The cloud of moral panic and disinformation that shrouds the drug trade in Britain is nothing new. When a Canadian soldier stationed in Folkestone in the 1920s was arrested for selling cocaine, or 'snow' as it was then called, the press came up with some familiar headlines: 'London in the Grip of Drug Craze' and 'Cocaine Driving Hundreds Mad'. Britain exists in a perpetual state of moral intoxication on the issue of drugs: a marijuana-type inertia befuddled further by a trance-like reliance on purely symbolic policies, gift-wrapped as 'pragmatism'. It is a condition we call 'narcomania' and you will encounter countless examples of it throughout this book.

The term was first used by the eminent Victorian addiction specialist Dr Norman Kerr in 1865 to refer to a pathological craving for drugs. He saw addiction as a disease that 'infected' unfortunates in Britain's underclasses, as well as a more privileged set who devoted their lives to 'pleasure-seeking'.

But, as far as this book is concerned, the term characterises the deeply confused way in which drugs, drug users and the drug trade are seen by the state, the media and the wider society in Britain. It is a symptom of a century-old disease. It is a malady caused by the conflict of two irreconcilable forces: the drive for illicit intoxication and the drive to deny it. In the past four decades, while governments have sought ever-stricter regimes to prohibit the trade, the agents of globalisation and social change have combined to undermine their efforts. Today the two forces continue to clash in a never-ending, Treasury-sapping game of cat and mouse.

In this book, we step into the collective mind of drug Britain by stripping away the cartoon drug world created by the media and politicians, the distorted vision of substances invading people's minds, and indeed entire towns and cities, like some kind of alien horde, or of dealers selling drugs to eight-year-olds outside the school gates. Our intention is to reveal the real trade behind the line of cocaine snorted off a toilet cistern, the spliff burning in the ashtray and the wrap of heroin smoking on a piece of tinfoil.

In 1967, US drug pioneer and guru Timothy Leary delivered the mantra of 'turn on, tune in, drop out' to his followers. But what motivates today's British drug user? What is the buzz that keeps them coming back for more?

And what do we really know of the industry? Each year around twenty tonnes of heroin, thirty-five tonnes of cocaine (supplying the powder and crack-cocaine market), four hundred and twelve tonnes of cannabis and around sixty million ecstasy tablets enter the country in boats, planes, trains and automobiles. Beyond these statistics there has been little research into how Britain's modern drug industry works, from port to street, and how it cloaks itself from detection.

Our journey begins on the front line of the drugs trade: the street, where the exposed interface of the trade in crack and heroin exists in a blizzard of unseen cash-and-wrap transactions. We explore how Britain's Class A drug market, originally based on the pavements around Piccadilly Circus in the 1960s, spread to every corner of the country.

Transactions have been transformed by crack, a young, professionalised workforce, the mobile phone and the Internet. It is now an industry with tens of thousands of street vendors working for a distribution network with better coverage than Vodafone. It sells an array of products – on a plate, as it were – to an ever-widening, and younger, polydrug-using population. But who are the drug dealers, what is the job's allure, and, once sucked in, how easy is it to get out? Or move up?

Above the street-level trade sits Britain's burgeoning middle market, where the real money is and where the drug trade, as it has to in order to survive, has been increasingly blending into mainstream society. And it is a very different beast from the traditional world of Mr Bigs portrayed in popular media. We investigate how drugs changed the crime world to create pools of illicit wealth previously beyond the reach of the average British drug dealer, as well as a new ecosystem of small-time importers and kingpin moneymen. We examine the inside workings of the trade that has become a one-stop shop for a new generation of entrepreneurs and specialist operators – and that has turned Britain into a drug-producing nation.

Where the Internet put the world of adult entertainment into the living rooms and offices of the nation, and revitalised bingo and poker in the online gambling boom, it has also created an invisible but highly active 'virtual' drug market. The Web and people's seemingly insatiable desire to get high mean that with a click of a mouse a shopper in Croydon can order cannabis from Canada, ketamine from India and the latest legal high from China and have their purchases delivered to their front door within days.

Where does law enforcement figure in all this? Globalisation, domestic cannabis cultivation and the rise of the Internet have left police with another new set of problems to solve. We speak to police from the front line to the top brass, from those who chase the money and those who go deep undercover on the trail of the suppliers in this ever-changing game of cat and mouse.

Despite all the Victorian-era rhetoric about foreign drug peddlers, it was Britain that was in fact the world's first drug dealer when it pushed opium to China, backed with the threat of its fleet of gunboats. Indeed, many of our financial institutions and largest companies have their origins in the drug trade. We look at whether those organisations have managed to distance themselves from drugs since then. In the wake of the 100 year war on drugs and the recent credit crash, we explore how banks, businesses, manufacturers, retailers and consumers appear to be as susceptible to the appeal of the drug dollar as any young dealer setting out to sell their first stash.

Parliament has been in a muddle over how to deal with all this for decades. And this muddle has resulted in a virtual vow of silence as far as any kind of adult debate is concerned. Drugs is a subject MPs *ought* to talk about but rarely do, for fear of treading on a political landmine. What is the reason for this odd form of *omertà* that grips our politicians when it comes to anything drug-related? We talk to those in the know to find out.

Narcomania is a disease suffered – and fostered – by society as a whole. The drug trade's illegality, its sex-like aura of forbidden, salacious pleasure and its links to organised crime have made it a key player in modern culture.

The trade is never far from the headlines or from people's lives. It's on TV, in films and inside music. Whether it is a story about the death of a teenager at a party, a major drug bust or a celebrity caught snorting cocaine, psychoactive substances are always in the news. Are we a nation obsessed by drug porn? And what drives the propaganda, myths and lies?

By the time you have finished your journey with us we hope to have provided you with a 360-degree view of Britain's most taboo economy – and to have created a fresh gateway to a debate free from the stereotypes, myths and misinformation that form the backdrop for the public rhetoric about Britain's war on drugs. Enter *Narcomania* . . .

1

Intoxication

Into the Mind of Drug Britain

It all started when eighteen-year-old Finn was bundled wriggling and screaming into a police van in Cockfield, an isolated rural village in north-east England, on a crisp July morning in 2009. His mother, Debbie, had called 999 an hour beforehand after spotting Finn whirling around, arms outstretched in a field near the family home. 'He saw my car pull up and hid in a bunch of nettles,' said Debbie. 'I asked him what he was doing there and he just ran off screaming. I was so worried I called the police and the ambulance.'

She told officers she was certain the cause of Finn's strange behaviour was a drug called 'drone' that he had recently confessed to taking with his friends. She put up with Finn and his friends messing around in his bedroom – at least they weren't getting arrested. The drug smelled, she said, 'like one of those sickly air fresheners'. They had bought it with the money saved up from grouse beating during the shooting season.

When the police managed to get hold of Finn, he became abusive and violent. He started shouting at Debbie. The two officers pinned him to the ground. The paramedics tried to give him valium to sedate him, but he refused. He said it wasn't going to be strong enough. 'They'd been taking it non-stop for the last four days,' Debbie told one of the arresting officers. 'They say it's legal.'

Baffled, police arrested Finn for public disorder and drove him to the local hospital where, in his super-agitated state, he was soon ejected after threatening nursing staff and other A&E patients. He was taken to the cells at Bishop Auckland police station to cool off. CCTV footage from the cell showed Finn, slightly built for his age, writhing, convulsing and screaming uncontrollably for ninety minutes. At one point he stripped naked. It looked as though he was going through hell. When he was returned to hospital by a worried police doctor, forensic tests revealed that Finn had extremely high levels of a little-known drug coursing through his body: mephedrone.

What further puzzled police was that Finn hadn't bought this new and potent high from a street dealer. It was ordered via credit card over the Internet, delivered by DHL, and was, as Finn claimed, completely legal. A drug-taking revolution that had for a long while been simmering in cyberspace was now coming to the attention of the country.

Mephedrone, misleadingly labelled as 'plant food' and 'bath salts' by sellers to sidestep health and safety laws, is chemically similar to MDMA, the chemical name for the euphoric dance drug ecstasy, the powerful stimulant crystal meth and the East African plant khat, which when chewed gives an amphetamine-like high. To its growing army of devotees it was a bargain-basement cross between high-quality cocaine and ecstasy. Finn explained that it was cheaper than cocaine (approximately £10 a gram instead of £45), easier to get hold of, and more potent. The dealers who bothered coming to Cockfield often cut their cocaine with inert white powders, and while ecstasy pills were cheap, they often contained more caffeine, BZP and amphetamines than MDMA.

There was something kid-in-sweetshop-like about Finn's regular mephedrone binges. For jobless teenagers looking for kicks in an out-of-the-way village with only two shops, two pubs, a Chinese takeaway and a dilapidated working men's club, the sudden availability of cheap, powerful and legal highs was likely to lead to trouble. Mephedrone provided the boys with a new way of filling time.

'They started taking it at the weekend, then they were on it every day, snorting or swallowing it in their bedrooms,' said Debbie. Finn and his friends got so out of it, according to Debbie, simply because they had nothing else to do. They were just bored out of their minds.

Although Finn was one of the first people in Britain to be hospitalised through mephedrone, he wasn't the only teenager who ended up taking dangerously large doses of the drug. Police watched as mephedrone use spread from Cockfield to surrounding towns in County Durham – Barnard Castle, Bishop Auckland and Darlington. They started picking up more and more young people with bags of white powder that looked like cocaine, but turned out to be mephedrone.

Frustratingly for the authorities, not only were some people openly trading and taking mephedrone on the street and in pubs, but those arrested for possession of white powder were demanding their 'drone' back once it had been tested by forensics. The teenagers had discovered a substance that their elders knew little about, and were powerless to prohibit.

Mephedrone first surfaced briefly in Denmark and Sweden in 2008, when it was thought to be involved in the deaths of two teenagers. Until spilling so visibly on to Cockfield's streets, the drug had largely been the preserve of British Internet drug enthusiasts, who had been ordering 'meph' online, completely undetected, in significant quantities because it was cheap, potent and easily accessible.

Although mephedrone was made illegal in 2010, its popularity prompted the emergence of a slew of similar products, turning the online drug trade into a virtual alphabet soup of chemical formulas and names. Manufacturers of new drugs simply altered the chemical structure of substances to stay within the law. Now no one, other than chemists able to test the products in laboratories, has much idea what they are buying, or whether or not it is legal.

Available to anyone within a few clicks of a computer mouse, mephedrone and its analogues have become the latest additions to a burgeoning menu of highs readily available to a new generation of eager customers. Social commentators have described those born after 1990 as 'Generation Z': a group born into an era of globalisation and developed technology; highly connected 'digital natives' who believe that enjoyment is a right, not a privilege. They have witnessed, sometimes visibly, what effects drugs have had on an older generation, are aware of the range and effects of drugs, and are educated about the risks.

The increase in teenagers experimenting with drugs bought online represents just another shift in the drug-using habits of a nation which, since the dawn of the modern drug-using era in the 1960s, has become a vociferous consumer of narcotics.

Britain is a drug-taking nation. While the use of some illicit substances such as heroin and cannabis has fallen in recent years, the latest government and European statistics show the use of synthetic drugs is on the rise. Britain sits alongside some South American countries, Spain and the United States as one of the biggest per-head cocaine consumers on the planet: an average British citizen is twice as likely to have taken cocaine as the average European. This seemingly voracious demand for drugs has made the country a key destination for illegal substances from the far corners of the world. As the CIA's briefing puts it: 'Britain is a major consumer of south-west Asian heroin, Latin American cocaine, and synthetic drugs.'

Nobody knows exactly how many people take illegal drugs in Britain. We know that the average person drinks 775 pints of beer and 1,000 cups of tea a year, but, like most indiscretions, taking banned substances is not something people readily own up to. Official figures on drug use, compiled by doorknockers for the government's annual crime statistics, are accepted as being the lowest estimates. They show that around one in ten adults admits to taking an illegal drug in the last year. Cannabis is by far the most widely used, followed by powder cocaine, then ecstasy, speed, ketamine and magic mushrooms. But the engine room that drives the British drug economy is the estimated 380,000 persistent users of crack and heroin. Despite its relatively small size, this group accounts for approximately half of all the money spent on drugs in Britain.

Since the 1960s, drug taking has become part of normal life for a significant number of people. The generational shift is clear to see. Government drug-use statistics show a quarter of people now in their fifties and sixties have admitted taking drugs. This rises to a third of people in their forties, and more than half for those now in their twenties and thirties. Even these conservative estimates show there are more people who regularly take drugs (approximately 5 per cent of the population) than there are vegetarians (approximately 3 per cent).

Most drug users are young. The number of sixteen-to-twenty-four-year-olds who have used drugs is more than twice that of other age groups. All the statistics show that as people age through their thirties, forties and fifties, their drug use severely reduces or stops completely.

Drug users are unlikely to be in a long-term relationship. Single adults are nearly six times more likely to have taken a drug in the last year than those who are married. Students, the unemployed and those earning under £10,000 a year are more than twice as likely to use drugs than those with a full-time job. However, drug use does not necessarily decrease as the wage packet thickens: a higher proportion of people earning over £50,000 a year had taken drugs in the last year than those on more modest salaries.

Men are twice as likely to be users than women. White people are twice as likely to have taken drugs in the last year than black or Asian people. The more alcohol people drink, and the more they socialise, the more likely they are to take drugs. The area with the highest proportion of drug users in the country is the north-west of England.

As the official statistics would have it, if you're a young, single, white student who rents a flat in Liverpool and regularly visits pubs and clubs, the statistical chances of you *not* having taken an illegal drug in the last year would be slim to none. Conversely, if you're a retired, teetotal, married Asian female who owns a detached house in rural West Midlands, you would be something of a statistical quirk if you were a regular user of illegal substances.

It is easy to generalise about drug users – and people often do – but there is no homogeneous group. Drugs used to be associated with specific youth cultures: punks sniffed glue, hippies took LSD and speed was the drug of choice on the northern soul scene. But for such a small, relatively well-connected country, Britain hides an intriguing array of drug-using enclaves.

Britain's drug-using population cannot be clearly categorised. People take different drugs to achieve different results: from everyday encounters of pub-goers snorting cheap cocaine off cisterns and crack addicts smoking in Soho phone boxes, to confessions made to us by students opening a bag of vacuum-packed mephedrone delivered by recorded post, and an all-night grocery worker taking a quick dab of speed to enable her to get through a long night.

Michael Linnell, who has spent twenty-five years working in the drugs field in Manchester, says there is a simple logic to drug taking. 'If you want to go out dancing all night, stimulants will keep you awake. If you are suffering from physical and emotional pain, you take a painkiller like heroin, and if you want to go on an adventure in your head, you take hallucinogens.'

Where you live also has an influence on what drugs you take. In Bristol and Nottingham ketamine is one of the most popular drugs available. But you would be hard pushed to seek out a bag of it if you live in Belfast. London's gay clubbing scene is one of the few parts of Britain where crystal meth can be found, and in some parts of the north of England hashish is virtually unattainable.

Hidden communities of drug users have been forged from the diverse number of ethnic groups settling in Britain. There is, for instance, a growing number of Nepalese heroin users in the Aldershot area, often the children of retired Gurkhas who have moved to live near the town's British Army base. In the quiet north London suburb of Barnet there exists a pocket of opium smokers, drawn from the area's Iranian community.

Khat is used by around half of all Somali men in the UK, sold in £4 bundles in greengrocers, halal butchers and special chew-rooms called *mafrishes* in East African communities. Despite containing cathinone, the active ingredient in mephedrone, and being banned in most Western countries, khat is legal in the UK.

Near Stockwell in south London, close to the Underground station where Jean Charles de Menezes was shot and killed by police, the babble of Portuguese dialect can be heard above most other languages. Portuguese-owned restaurants, bars and delis, decked out in the national colours of red and green, are commonplace. In 2000, outreach staff from the local drug service started to discover large groups of homeless Portuguese heroin and crack addicts in the area. They lived together in huge squats, a disused factory or an old launderette, sleeping, and 'speedballing' – injecting heroin and crack simultaneously. Most of them were without passports, unable to get benefits and scratching a living by 'mini-cabbing', delivering street drug deals. Mysteriously, over 80 per cent of this group were from small villages on the Portuguese archipelago of Madeira. Most had arrived with a heroin problem, but had taken up crack while in London.

The discovery of the Madeiran speedballers resulted in the setting up of a sophisticated system of treatment and housing that has now become the template for dealing with non-English drug users in the area. But every winter sees a surge in Portuguese drug users who arrive in Stockwell when the seasonal work in Portugal dries up.

Out on the high seas, trawlermen have for many years taken amphetamines to cope with long hours in fishing boats. 'The longer they stay out at sea, the more money they can earn,' says a drug worker based in Penzance. He has seen dozens of trawlermen, some of them in their twenties, seeking help for amphetamine addiction. 'It's a tough job – physically and mentally gruelling, so some of the guys find that taking speed is a good way of keeping the money coming in. Many of them are fishing to survive.'

Cornwall has for decades been connected with amphetamines, a cheaper, longer-lasting, but less palatable drug than cocaine. It has been popular with the 'alternative' communities that have settled in the area since the 1970s. The county has nearly three times the proportion of people seeking treatment for the drug than anywhere else in southern England.

But fishermen are not the only workers using drugs to cope with long hours. While long-distance lorry drivers have traditionally been associated with amphetamine abuse, a shake-up of working practices has largely removed the habit from their ranks, although one firm carrying out tests for a major haulage company found 10 per cent of drivers tested positive for illegal drugs. Now drug workers report a new generation of people such as shift workers, teachers, taxi drivers, twenty-four-hour shop staff and students writing dissertations, who use speed (as well as illegally obtained prescription equivalents like Modafinil, Ritalin and ephedrine), to remain alert for long stretches.

Drugs' capacity to keep people awake was harnessed by the government long before it became commonly used by civilians. British Army troops in World War One were issued with pep pills containing cocaine as part of their regulation kit, and in World War Two, army physicians prescribed British troops with amphetamines to alleviate battle fatigue. Cocaine's ability to bestow feelings of alertness, exhilaration and physical strength is utilised in many settings and situations. For self-confessed

Nottingham Forest FC hooligan Tony, taking cocaine is a regular part of getting ready for a match.

'You've got to have a swagger, and a few lines of coke will help you along,' says the thirty-two-year-old mobile-phone executive and family man. 'Coke enhances the feeling, the arrogance and the bravado. You feel you can take anyone on.

'On the coach, you will see lads snorting off the tables, bags or wraps of coke will be passed around with everyone taking a dab. Cocaine keeps your thought processes alive; too much alcohol deadens them. The last thing you want is not to be able to function properly. You need your wits about you. With the natural adrenaline of meeting your rivals, it's a powerful thing.'

Football thugs snorting cocaine will not be a surprise to many. But behind the respectable veneer of Middle England lies a treasure trove of illicit intoxication. In December 2008, an undercover police unit discovered seventeen pensioners, including a ninety-two-year-old, regularly buying cannabis from their milkman. Residents in Burnley, Lancashire left notes for Robert Holding, himself a pensioner, detailing how much milk and cannabis they required. The drugs were left for the customers in egg cartons. Holding, who was given a suspended sentence, said most of his elderly customers smoked the drug 'to ease aches and pains'. One question not addressed during the court case was why an expensive, time-consuming police surveillance operation had been set up to catch a milkman selling small amounts of cannabis to pensioners.

For those who take up key roles in government, drug-taking is a double-headed taboo. Few people knew that while he was working as Margaret Thatcher's senior adviser on NHS reform, Dr Clive Froggatt was hiding a secret addiction to heroin. For years the charming, smiling Cheltenham man, at the time the most powerful GP in the land, had been faking prescriptions of pharmaceutical heroin to feed his habit. 'I was taking it every day,' he later said, 'and shooting up before meeting ministers. I don't know if you want to call it an addiction, but no one in Whitehall noticed anything wrong.'

He was forced to resign from his role when he was discovered in 1995, and was given a twelve-month suspended sentence. He gave the required interviews to the press about his 'destructive double life' and advised Nicole Kidman on how to play a heroin addict in *Eyes Wide Shut*, a Hollywood film shot in Britain in 1996.

If you do not look like a stereotypical junkie, it's less likely you will be caught out, but not impossible. Take the case of Hans and Eva Rausings, a married, middle-aged couple who lived in a £10 million mansion in Chelsea, one of the most expensive residential areas in Britain. Eva, who later died of a suspected drug overdose in 2012, was caught and arrested at the US Embassy with wraps of heroin and crack in her bag when she went to renew her passport. After arresting Eva and her husband Hans, who is heir to the multibillion pound Tetrapak empire, police found more crack and heroin and £2,000 worth of powder cocaine at their house. To the surprise of many, the couple walked away with a caution.

The police themselves accept that drug use is not unheard of within the force. Only a handful of officers subjected to random testing are found to have traces of illegal drugs in their system, although according to one serving WPC in her forties, it is more common than the statistics show. Susan, who works in the West Midlands force, lives a manageable double life. What the police did not know when they hired her was that she had spent two years as a professional LSD dealer in the 1990s, selling a hundred trips a night, four nights a week at a London nightclub. She was also caught and deported from America for trying to smuggle in two suitcases crammed with khat. She uses her drugs of choice, cocaine and mephedrone, while she is partying over a two- or three-day break between shifts. She isn't overly concerned with getting caught, mainly because cocaine, unlike cannabis, disappears from the body quickly and is therefore less likely to be detected in random drug tests. 'I know of many other officers who take recreational drugs. I've been to the same parties as them. A lot of officers are young and they want to have a good time, so if they have a line or two at the weekend and get away with it, then why not?'

Claire, a former WPC, incredibly hid a £500 a week crack and heroin habit in the early 2000s. While she was on duty, she smoked heroin in her police station's toilets, bought drugs from her unmarked patrol car and sparked up her crack pipe at home while watching daytime TV. For years she was too scared to admit her addiction to her bosses, who were aware she was struggling to cope with her job, but decided to own up after the Met modernised their drug and alcohol policy and made it easier for employees to come forward and get help.

The bizarre and tragic case of PC David Pilling, nicknamed 'Robocop' for his determination to chase down north London's drug dealers, remains a mystery to many of his friends and colleagues. PC Pilling was found dead from a heroin overdose at his Regent's Park home. An investigation revealed that the forty-seven-year-old had been looking up how to inject the drug on the Internet. Traces of cocaine and ecstasy were also found in his system. None of his friends, colleagues or family had any idea he took drugs. An inquest suggested the popular officer, who once chased a dealer down a flight of steps on his motorbike, may have been experimenting and died from an accidental overdose.

In a sweaty basement in Manchester's old industrial quarter, the DJ cranks the trance tunes up a notch. The dance floor is heaving, the bass shakes the floor and the crowd is lit by flickering strobes. Amy, a thirty-six-year-old teacher, along with most of those in the club, is coming up on ecstasy. She floats through the crowds that seem, to her, to part like the Red Sea. Smiles and chats are exchanged with strangers, and encounters become infused with a sense of fun. The music becomes more euphoric, and the beats get harder and faster, until the whole room reaches a crescendo of dancing, grinning, human happiness.

'I can't imagine not doing it. It's a part of me,' says Amy in a thick Lancastrian accent. 'When I'm on ecstasy I feel profoundly content. I start smiling even more broadly than usual. One minute it's 11 p.m., the next people are shouting "one more tune" and it's six in the morning.'

Amy grew up in a loving working-class family and her childhood was spent 'swotting' and competing in county long-jump championships. She is intelligent, pretty and full of energy, with bright bleached blonde hair. Every other weekend she goes out dancing 'on pills' at one of Manchester's famous trance nights. 'You need to be able to balance the hedonism with periods of hard work,' she laughs. 'I work a sixty-hour week so I think I'm allowed a little indiscretion.'

Amy has been going to clubs and taking ecstasy for seventeen years. She estimates she's had around 1,000 pills, but she's never had a bad experience on one, never been arrested and never missed a day of work. 'I only buy pills from people I know.

I've been using the same person who sells on the Manchester trance scene for the last four years.'

For Amy, ecstasy and clubbing are inseparable. 'For me the pills, the dancing, the music and the atmosphere at clubs are one entity. Ecstasy and dance music are made for each other. It wouldn't work if you took ecstasy out of that equation.'

She feels far more at home with strangers in a trance club than she does drinking in a regular pub or bar. 'I wouldn't feel comfortable on my own in a bar or pub, you get hassled all the time. I'm quite shocked at how bad it is. In the clubs I don't feel like I'm under siege. I talk to lots of men and have a good chat but there is no other agenda. There is an unwritten rule: it's all focused on the music, people are there to hear their favourite DJ, not to chat anyone up. I guarantee as a woman you are safer taking ecstasy in a club than you are drinking in a pub.'

During the Victorian era, Manchester's manufacturing district was a patchwork of burgeoning industry, and the major employer of the city's population. Now, many Mancunians owe their living to what is called the 'night-time economy', an industry that has thrived while the others have withered, and whose pubs, bars, music venues and clubs now inhabit the old warehouses, factories and mills. Instead of being divided into zones centring around the textile, engineering and chemicals industries, the area can be split into a variety of clubbing zones to suit all tastes of drug consumption.

'This one's popular with students,' says Amy, pointing at a club venue not far from Manchester's central Piccadilly train station. 'Depending on the DJ, it will be either really boozy or really pilled-up. It's sold as Manchester's underground warehouse party night, but it's very corporate.'

Nearby, in the heart of the old industrial zone, there is a

proliferation of trendy bars. 'This is the cocaine zone,' she says. 'It's mainly people in media and IT buying expensive drinks and snorting in the toilets.' Five minutes away is a large underground techno and trance venue. 'The entry fee is expensive, the clientele is middle class and there is lots of ecstasy,' says Amy. 'The police never go anywhere near it.'

The 1960s marked a key shift in the emergence of widespread recreational drug use in Britain. Until then, the use of opiates and cocaine was largely restricted to people over thirty. Of the 2,139 convictions for possession of opiates and cocaine between 1926 and 1945, the average age of offenders was forty, and only 13 per cent were under thirty. In the 1960s, cannabis, LSD, amphetamines and barbiturates became synonymous with a counter-cultural challenge to the system on all fronts. With the exception of the use of various amphetamine and barbiturate-based pills, such as 'bombers', 'blues' and 'purple hearts' by working-class Mods, the British drug scene could still be largely summed up as 'bohemian' in social orientation. Cannabis use, in particular, became widespread – introduced to Britain by first-generation Caribbean immigrants, who had themselves been exposed to 'ganja' in the nineteenth century by colonial migrant labourers from India. The means, opportunity and the relaxing of social controls that otherwise may have held people back, combined to create the conditions for an expansion of drug taking.

In 1967, during the San Francisco-inspired hippy Summer of Love, Paul McCartney became the first British pop star to admit to taking LSD. He told *Queen* magazine: 'It opened my eyes. We only use one-tenth of our brain. Just think of what we could accomplish if we could only tap that hidden part! It would mean a whole new world if the politicians would take LSD. There wouldn't be any more war or poverty or famine.'

When McCartney was interviewed by ITV over his admission, and whether it would encourage fans to take drugs, he replied, intelligently: 'The whole bit about how far it's gonna go and how many people it's going to encourage is up to the newspapers, and up to you on television. I mean, you're spreading this now, at this moment. This is going into all the homes in Britain. And I'd rather it didn't. But you're asking me the question – you want me to be honest – I'll be honest.'

In his 1971 book *The Drugtakers*, the first serious analysis of the new culture of drug use in Britain, criminologist Jock Young documented young cannabis smokers in Notting Hill. He noted that although they were regarded as being antisocial, law-breaking deviants by mainstream society, they had more in common with everyone else than was initially apparent.

'The demand for psychotropic drugs is part and parcel of everyday life, ingrained in the average respectable citizens as it is in the most way-out hippy,' he wrote. The only difference between illicit highs and the use of nicotine, caffeine, alcohol and prescription pills, he argued, was related to what had been deemed publicly and legally acceptable.

The rise of recreational drug use led to the introduction of a succession of anti-drug laws in the 1960s and 1970s, with President Nixon's 'War on Drugs' – which reverberated across the Atlantic – launched in 1971. The dangerous nature of drugs was there for all to see: between 1969 and 1971 Rolling Stones guitarist Brian Jones, Jimi Hendrix, Janis Joplin and Jim Morrison all suffered drug-related deaths. The 1970s witnessed a rise in drug use in Britain, with the percentage of young adults who had tried an illegal drug jumping from under 5 per cent in the 1960s to 10 per cent in the 1970s. They picked from a drug menu that consisted largely of cannabis, amphetamine, LSD and other hallucinogenics such as peyote and mescaline, barbiturates and heroin. The decade, thick with the rise of heavy-metal and punk bands such as Motorhead that openly boasted and sang about their use of speed, ended with the fatal heroin overdose of Sex Pistol Sid Vicious, signalling what seemed to be the final nihilistic nail in the coffin of the political idealism that had grown up around drugs such as LSD and cannabis since the 1960s. But by the mid-1980s an entirely different drug began to attract the attention of London's in-crowd and it was one that would change drug use in Britain for good.

By 1985 ecstasy was the must-have drug of the capital's elite. Music journalists, models and pop stars such as George Michael, Marc Almond and Boy George were some of the privileged few who were able to get hold of bubble-wrapped, US imported pills that had been part of the New York club scene since the start of the decade. First synthesised in 1912 and patented as an appetite suppressant by German pharmaceutical firm Merck, MDMA was re-synthesised by the pharmacologist and psychedelic drug pioneer Alexander Shulgin in California in 1976 for use in psychotherapy. Shulgin, known as the 'Godfather of ecstasy', published two books covering his research into ecstasy and other compounds – and crucially how to manufacture them.

As Britain entered its third consecutive term of Conservative rule and headed towards the precipice of Black Monday and recession, the clique's chosen drug high was becoming democratised. Suburban Londoners began gathering on the Balearic holiday island of Ibiza to take ecstasy and dance all night. What became known as the 1988 'Summer of Love' was effectively the year that ecstasy turned into a dance drug. The use of ecstasy, as well as other recreational drugs such as speed, LSD and cannabis spiralled, and would fundamentally reshape Britain's drug-using landscape.

'It is difficult to overstate the impact that ecstasy had on young people's perception of drug taking,' says Matthew Collin in his seminal book on ecstasy culture, *Altered State*. 'It was, many believed, not only an alternative to alcohol and tobacco, but a less harmful alternative, an axiom that was then extended to justify drug consumption across the board. To the thousands of people who had never taken illicit substances ecstasy's innocuous appearance was the opposite of everything they had ever been told about drugs. It came packaged . . . as the ultimate entertainment concept, with its own music, clubs, dress codes.'

The growing movement around the drug mirrored the counter-culture, 'one love' vibes of the 1960s. But, whereas the 1960s bohemian drug culture of LSD, speed and cannabis was limited to a relatively small group of middle-class bohemians, hippies and rebels, the ecstasy movement in Britain soon gathered pace and went corporate. 'Madchester' was born at the Hacienda nightclub in Manchester, 'Ebenezer Goode' by the Shamen and its thinly veiled 'Es are good' refrain hit number one in the charts in 1992 and superclubs opened in all the major cities.

Rave culture went mainstream in the 1990s and by 1994 government statistics revealed around 2 million young people had taken the drug in the last year. Ecstasy, 'rave' music and the venues, such as London's Ministry of Sound, became industries in their own rights.

It was also an era when the perception of drugs radically changed. Drug use began to become defined in a very different way. When the daughters of police, politicians and journalists started to take ecstasy, drug users began to be seen in an entirely new light by those in authority; they were not drug fiends, they were just teenagers having fun.

Arena-capacity superclubs and festivals sprang up across Britain, and despite rumours of its demise, Britain's clubbing scene today remains stronger than ever. 'We've interviewed 600 people at festivals about their drug use and most people still love ecstasy,' says Dr Fiona Measham, who has carried out fieldwork among drug users at clubs and festivals for more than twenty years. 'If they can get hold of it, that's what they want – it is always everyone's favourite drug.'

Despite the media scaremongering over the death of Leah Betts in 1995 (it was later found that she died from drinking too much water), ecstasy proved to many people that getting high on illegal drugs was not instantly addictive, highly lethal, nor the preserve of deviants. Now, with nearly one in three, around 10 million, of Britain's adult population saying they have tried an illegal drug, it is widely accepted that taking the most popular drugs, such as cannabis, cocaine, amphetamines and ecstasy, is not an extreme sport. While it is not something that the majority of people do, taking illegal drugs is seen by many as fairly normal behaviour.

Today there exists a living, breathing population of drug users for whom getting high is one of a range of lifestyle choices. Unlike their predecessors in the 1960s and 1970s, they are unlikely to be hidebound by a specific youth culture, or see themselves as outcasts, in the minority. While the law of the land states that drugs are illegal to buy, to most of the hundreds of thousands of people who use them, taking drugs does not herald a rite of passage, an act of wild abandon, a surrender to peer pressure or a sign of broken innocence, it's another form of consumption, no less self-indulgent or meaningless than going to a restaurant, going to the cinema or shopping for clothes.

Twenty-seven-year-old Luke is a 'psychonaut': someone who uses drugs to explore the mind, spending time researching and recording the effects of new substances. He lives with his partner and young family in a picturesque village just outside Brighton. He was buying mephedrone for two years before the events in Cockfield.

'When you know where to look the vastness of the Internet becomes much more interesting than visiting your local dealer, it's a far more varied, and well-stocked marketplace to find your wares. I went for analogues of drugs such as mescaline and acid: if you change a few molecules, you get slightly different effects,' says Luke. 'But they can be far harsher on the body and mind than coke or ecstasy, and take some effort – so they are not for everyone.'

He and his partner juggle their recreational use of drugs and their responsibilities as parents with 'ultra precision'. But their passion for experimentation influences every aspect of their lives – literature, movies, music, socialising and sex.

'If we get a chance in the week we'll have few lines of ketamine with a movie,' says Luke. 'While you might be slumbering away at 2 a.m. on a Tuesday night I'll often be stretched out, watching a documentary on my newly extended widescreen monitor, feeling like I'm falling at high speed.

'If I'm playing music or painting I might take some Moxy [a banned Class A psychedelic and hallucinogenic drug known as a tryptamine] which is also great if you're in bed – everything becomes so sensual. Sex on drugs is different, you tend to lose yourself in the experience more. Without drugs you won't have experienced those volcanic orgasms, those delightfully delirious moments of intense pleasure.'

Luke first started buying drugs over the Internet in 2001 when he was studying for a degree. 'It was to a certain extent out of necessity. The sort of drugs I wanted, research chemicals, weren't available from friends or street dealers. It was all about experimenting – taking a trip, exploring your mind – and it was all there on the Internet. It's just about knowing where to look. I joined community groups, started chatting with people, exchanging contacts and building up trust. It was like being part of a private members' club.'

He was so enthused by trying out and documenting his experiences on different substances he spent a month travelling in South America experimenting with a range of natural hallucinogens.

'It was brilliant. I'd always taken a very scientific approach to drugs, but I wanted to find out if there really was a spiritual side to this, a shared experience. I was very sceptical. But I met a Christian shaman in the back of a shanty house, I'm sitting there in total darkness high on drugs. I'm on my own, a man's killing pigeons outside and the shaman was talking in tongues and throwing stuff at me. I had to work hard not to panic, but I overcame the fear. I had to do so much work in my head sorting out the things that were bugging me. I don't think it had anything to do with spirituality – I think the drugs were a great tool for therapy and self-healing.'

Luke's experience is only one part of the endless ebb and flow of drug trends over the last fifty years. But using natural or synthetic substances to venture into an alternate state is not a recent invention. From stoned, smashed and bombed to tipsy, tanked and plastered, there are reportedly more synonyms for being intoxicated than any other word in the English language. In his 1989 book *Intoxication: Life in Pursuit of Artificial Paradise*, American pharmacologist Dr Ronald K. Siegel concluded that after the basic desires of hunger, thirst and sex, comes the 'fourth drive' – an instinctive drive to change the ordinary state of awareness, whether through spinning around in circles to produce a state of dizziness, by eating sugar, drinking coffee or taking illegal psychoactive drugs. Research carried out by Dr Siegel, whose 'fourth drive' theory remains a respected one more than two decades later, found that the urge to become intoxicated is in evidence all around us:

'After sampling the nectar of certain orchids, bees drop to the ground in a temporary stupor, then weave back for more. Birds gorge themselves on inebriating berries, then fly with reckless abandon. Cats eagerly sniff aromatic "pleasure" plants, then play with imaginary objects. Cows that browse special range weeds will twitch, shake, and stumble back to the plants for more. Elephants purposely get drunk on fermented fruits. Snacks on "magic mushrooms" cause monkeys to sit with their heads on their hands in a posture reminiscent of Rodin's *Thinker*.'

In 2009, scientists in Australia dropped liquefied cocaine on bees' backs, so that it entered the brain and circulatory system. The scientists found that bees react much like humans do: cocaine alters their judgement, stimulates their behaviour and makes them exaggeratedly enthusiastic about things that might not otherwise excite them.

It is certainly the case that drugs are used by humans across the globe, and in virtually every society. Their power is such that for some people, intoxication becomes the dominant aspect of their lives – more so than family, food or survival. And humans have been intoxicated since prehistoric times.

In the 1970s two chillum-style pipes made out of hollowed-out puma bones were excavated from a cave in the Andes mountains in north-west Argentina. Radiocarbon-dated to 2000 BC, the chillums were found to contain the residue of a mountain shrub, *Anadenanthera*, a source of the powerful hallucinogen, DMT – a drug which has experienced a resurgence in popularity with buyers in cyberspace.

Civilisations such as the Egyptians, Chinese and Aztecs had been getting high on alcohol, cannabis and hallucinogens for thousands of years before Britain was introduced to alcohol, in the form of mead, beer and wine, around AD 400. For centuries it was alcohol that was Britain's sole drug of choice.

By the Victorian era, alcohol was joined by opium, cocaine and cannabis. All were available legally and were sold in grocers, chemists and by street peddlers as a cure for afflictions ranging from insomnia, depression, diarrhoea, hunger, shyness, cowardice and indolence. The major pharmaceutical companies Merck and Parke-Davis marketed cocaine as a powder, a solution, in throat lozenges, tablets, toothache drops – even cocaine-impregnated cigars and cheroots. The product range included pocket-sized injecting kits containing cocaine, morphine and miniature needles.

'By the 1890s high-street pharmacies had become places of wonder,' says Mike Jay in his 2010 compendium of drug history and culture, *High Society*. 'With exquisitely machined tablets in all the colours of the rainbow, their shelves were compared to sweet shops. Among this exotic pharmacopeia, opium, cocaine and cannabis, the three plant drugs that would become the mainstay of the twentieth century's illicit trade, were all well represented.'

But towards the end of the century the attitude towards these 'miracle' drugs was already beginning to harden, amid tales of working-class babies dying from high doses of opium cough suppressants and of people becoming afflicted with what was termed 'narcomania'. Arthur Conan Doyle's fictional detective Sherlock Holmes's cocaine-injecting habit mysteriously disappeared as the tide began to turn against the high-street drugs.

The growing fear of what the media was calling 'the drug menace' did not dampen the enthusiasm of everyone. In 1902 the *British Medical Journal* reported a new fashion among upper-class ladies – tea and morphine parties:

> A number of ladies meet at 4 o'clock every afternoon, tea is served, servants are sent out of the room, the door is locked, the guests bare their arms and the hostess produces a small hypodermic syringe with which she administers an injection to each person in turn. It is only too true that alcoholism, morphinism, cocainism and other supposed means of getting beyond a monotonous daily life are becoming increasingly prevalent among women.

Contrary to the common perception that all illegal drugs are merciless enslavers of the innocent, arbiters of false joy and will lead the 'victim' to inevitable ruin, a long line of studies carried out among recreational drug users has revealed the vast majority see taking drugs as a positive, pleasurable lifestyle choice.

There is a large group of recreational drug users that exist under the radar of the authorities, but who are, compared to the average person, far more prolific drug takers. These people are rarely arrested, convicted and, even if they do get into problems with drugs, seldom register with statutory drug treatment clinics. A unique insight into this group was provided by the Global Drugs Survey, an online survey of 15,500 largely young, white, employed, well-educated, middle-class people carried out in conjunction with the *Guardian* and clubbers magazine *Mixmag* in 2011. It found drug use was far more prevalent in this group of Web-savvy, club-going respondents than the general population. Two-thirds had used cannabis in the last year, more than half had used MDMA, 41 per cent cocaine and 25 per cent ketamine, figures that in some cases are fifty times the national average according to the British Crime Survey. Of those interviewed for the Global Drugs Survey, 91 per cent had used cannabis in their lifetime, three-quarters had taken MDMA, 69 per cent cocaine and nearly half had used ketamine.

One in ten respondents said they had been stopped and searched for drugs in the past twelve months. Just under half of those found with cannabis, and just over a third of those found with MDMA, were released with a verbal warning.

Niamh Eastwood, chief executive of the drugs charity Release, said the findings suggested the police might be reluctant to criminalise this demographic group for carrying drugs. 'If you sent the same survey to different groups – young black males in inner-city areas, say – it would tell a different story. The survey probably does represent the experience of middle-class people who use drugs.'

According to a 2011 survey of mainly private-educated students at the University of Cambridge, 63 per cent admitted to have taken illegal drugs, with half of them having experimented before they turned sixteen. 45 per cent of those who take drugs admitted to buying illegal drugs for their friends and 14 per cent also admitted to having sold drugs for a profit.

A survey of 500 London-based managers carried out in 2011 found more than one in ten admitted taking illegal drugs at work or a work social event. Class A drugs were the most widely used, with 90 per cent of those who admitted taking drugs admitting to using cocaine and ecstasy. Cocaine was the most popular drug for London professionals, with 40 per cent of workplace drug users admitting to snorting lines at work.

The modern drug user wants drugs that do not eat up too much of their time. Rather than mould their way of life around a particular drug, they will fit the drug into their lives. It is ironic that, considering the fact that being intoxicated is linked with the desire to 'let go', drug users have gravitated towards using substances over which they have more control.

Paul, a manager at a high-profile international digital marketing firm, says: 'At one point I tested to see if I could take a line of ketamine at the start of my lunch hour and be able to function in the afternoon. And I could. That's why it was difficult to stop – because it didn't interfere with my working life – much less so than a pint at lunch or a hangover the next day.'

Despite the happy veneer, 'party' drugs can also lead to serious addiction, illness and death. They can be more problematic for users to deal with than substances that attract more stigma. Whereas most heroin addicts will be fully aware they have an addiction, if you are habitually using recreational drugs then it is easier to deny you have a problem. Sigmund Freud was one of the original cocaine addicts in denial. In 1884, when he was a young neurologist, Freud ordered a sample of cocaine, at the time a 'research chemical'. He dissolved a tenth of a gram in water, noting 'a sudden exhilaration and feeling of ease'. He put his feelings of increased energy to the test by measuring his muscular force. Later that year he published his paean to the new drugs, *Uber Coca*, in which he described 'the most gorgeous excitement' and 'lasting euphoria' that cocaine gave him. But he had failed to notice the drug's addictive qualities. He continued to use the drug for another twenty years.

Specialist services and individual clinics, such as the Club Drug Clinic at Chelsea and Westminster Hospital in south-west London, have begun springing up across the country aimed at young professionals battling with drug addiction. In the last few years drug treatment services started to see a marked rise in teenagers coming for help with sometimes life-threatening addictions to drugs such as the liquid anaesthetic GHB and ketamine.

Emily, a twenty-one-year-old Sussex woman who started taking ketamine at sixteen with her friends in the local park, came out of hospital in 2011 after a five-year addiction to the drug. She weighed only 33 kg, suffering severe damage to her kidneys and bladder.

An unpublished study of long-term cannabis users carried out by researchers at the University of Kent found that although most could go for long stretches without using cannabis while only suffering mild irritation, the pull of the drug remained too strong to cut it out altogether. Most admitted the drug had a negative impact on their jobs. Some had even lost their jobs, after being caught out by colleagues or arrested by the police.

Drug taking is increasingly a game of lucky dip. Because of the expansion of substances now on the market, someone offered a white line of powder to snort in a club could be about to inhale anything from cocaine, heroin, ketamine, speed, MDMA, crystal meth, mephedrone, CK1 (a mix of cocaine and ketamine), naphyrone or Mexxy, to name the most common substances. The Global Drugs Survey found one in five drug users has taken a drug with no real understanding of what it was. Duncan, an events organiser from Cheshire who has been taking recreational drugs for twenty-five years, spent most of his fortieth birthday in a hospital bed after being offered a line of white powder at a club. But despite the element of risk in today's recreational drug market, the emphasis is on having fun. More then two-thirds of people who fed back to the Global Drugs Survey agreed strongly with the statement that 'drugs can make a good night out better'.

In the spring of 2007, sixteen-year-old Carly Townsend was released from a secure unit and returned to her family home. She had been using heroin since she was fourteen. A week after her return, she asked her older half-sister Gemma Evans, twenty-five, a long-term addict, to buy her some heroin, which she then injected. She died of an overdose while her mother and sister were watching a TV soap.

The subsequent court case prompted a public outcry. In a television interview recorded before the sentencing, Gemma said: 'I'd seen Carly so many times like that, it was nothing unusual. On her sixteenth birthday we had to phone an ambulance . . . she was much worse [than the night she died]. She wasn't even taken to hospital, she was taken to the police station. I genuinely thought she was going to be OK. Her last words to me were "eff off, leave me alone" so I thought just leave her to sleep it off, she'll get up and be happy.'

The conviction and jailing of the two women for manslaughter was to some in the media yet more proof of the inhuman depths to which 'evil junkies' will sink. But, far more interesting, the case illuminated, albeit briefly, the hidden world of inter-generational drug addiction.

Gemma and Carly were exposed to drugs and the damage of drug abuse from birth, at the family home in a rural hamlet on the outskirts of Llanelli on Wales's south coast. Stephen

Townsend, Carly's father and Gemma's stepfather, died of a drugs overdose after a life of unemployment and heroin addiction. Andrea, a long-term amphetamine and heroin user, admitted in court that at least twenty of her friends had died of heroin overdoses. To Gemma and Carly, taking heroin and 'sleeping off' the effects of high doses had, by their mid-teens, become as normal an act as making a cup of tea.

'It's hard to explain to outsiders, but heroin was part of the furniture in this family,' said Alan Andrews, a local drug worker, after the trial at Cardiff Crown Court. 'They would have been taking heroin as an everyday thing, like some families sit round the table and eat an evening meal. Like any kids, these girls were just repeating a pattern of behaviour they had seen all their lives. It's difficult to break out of, because it's all they've ever seen. They have nothing to compare their life to.'

Andrews says the Townsends were 'not untypical' in parts of Wales which have lost key local industries. 'I know of one family in Llanelli,' said Andrews, 'where drug addiction spanned three generations – from a granddad in his sixties to his grandson in his early twenties. None had jobs. The granddad used to take heroin, methadone, barbiturates and sleeping pills with his son and his grandson. They all supplied it to each other. You could write a family tree based on who takes what drugs.'

There are an estimated 350,000 children in Britain living with parents who have a drug addiction. An in-depth study into intergenerational drug use in the south-west of England, carried out among 144 children, parents and care professionals, found many of the children interviewed – average age twelve – had already started using drugs themselves, some at 'worrying' levels. Several said they were introduced to heroin by their parents. The research, undertaken by social-work experts

Brynna Kroll and Andy Taylor for the Department of Health, found that children's drug use was often in direct response to their parents' use, through learned behaviour and as a way of coping with a chaotic childhood.

A significant majority of the parents identified by services as problematic users with child-welfare concerns, had also experienced their own parents' substance misuse. Fear of disclosure and a culture of denial was one of the major barriers to helping these families, according to the sixty professionals interviewed for the study. Both parents and children were scared of the perceived consequences of owning up to drug problems. Family members viewed the police and social workers with fear and suspicion.

'If drug use is endemic in a child's family and social setting – if their uncles, aunts, grandparents, parents are all using something or other – then the amount of change that is required to stop it is mind-boggling,' said one of the study's authors. 'This is why the problem often remains hidden.'

On the morning of 15 September 2005, the *Daily Mirror* featured a grainy photo of supermodel Kate Moss snorting what looked like cocaine. The media was in a fit of moral outrage: reprinting the images of 'Cocaine Kate' for all to see, while in the same breath expressing shock that Moss's alleged drug taking would encourage her fans to do the same.

That same day in Liverpool, a wholly different drug story was hitting the streets; one that would provoke far less outrage. When Lyn Matthews, a local drug worker, spotted a headline in the local paper about the body of a woman being found in bushes in the middle of Liverpool's red-light district, she silently hoped it wasn't someone she knew. By the early evening she had found out it was Anne Marie Foy. Matthews was familiar with many of the city's sex workers, but she had known Anne Marie more than most.

'She was someone whose hand I had held when she gave birth to her last child,' wrote Matthews shortly after the murder, in an article about her friend, who had been addicted to heroin for most of her forty-five years. On the night she was killed, she was on the streets, homeless and selling her body to get money for drugs and a bed for the night. 'She was a woman who had suffered profoundly all her life, a woman who would never have hurt anyone, only herself. She had been left in bushes, discarded like an old tin can.'

There have been at least 140 murders of sex workers since 1990 – a killing every nine weeks. In terms of the human cost of addiction, the lives lived by the estimated 30,000 street sex workers in Britain exposes it in its rawest, most tragic form.

A report into street sex workers in Tyneside found drugs were enmeshed in the trade. Drugs and drug debts were the most popular routes into sex work: 80 per cent were addicted to heroin, and half to crack. Most engaged in sex work for money to buy drugs, although some directly exchanged sex for drugs. More than eight in ten spent all their money from sex work on drugs, with an average daily drugs spend of £137. Most said that if they could stop taking drugs, they would stop sex work.

Many street sex workers use drugs in order to cast a shroud over a difficult past. But the drugs exact a heavy price – death, disease and often poor mental and physical health. One of the most torturous problems they face is that many have children they love, from whom they have become separated, and may never see again. 'Drug addiction is the consistent thread, and remains the driving force behind why so many women resort to prostitution,' says Brian Tobin, head of Ipswich drug project, Iceni.

Tobin, who knew all five victims of the Ipswich serial killer Steve Wright, sometimes resorted to giving them cash to buy drugs in order to keep them off the streets and out of danger. 'Unless we as a society learn to deal with drugs more effectively, we will never see an end to what is a desperate and dangerous activity that destroys lives. Without exception, all the women I have worked with expressed an intense hatred for what they did and disliked the men they did it with. I cannot recall one woman ever stating that she would be involved in prostitution, if it wasn't for her addiction.'

There were 2,182 drug-related deaths reported in the UK in 2010 (a figure which has doubled since 1996), and heroin and other opiates such as methadone and morphine accounted for nearly three-quarters of them. Cocaine accounted for around one in ten deaths. That the cities with the highest numbers of drugs deaths have for several years been Brighton and Blackpool, paints a depressing image of social deprivation existing side by side with family fun days out at the beach. Drug addiction is far more deadly than being involved in drug gangs: research carried out by the Home Office into the 696 non-terrorist murders in England and Wales between 2005 and 2006 found just 6 per cent were linked to any level of organised crime.

Half of all injecting drug users, chiefly people who inject heroin, crack or both, have the hepatitis C virus, which can cause life-threatening liver disease. A third suffer from infected needle wounds. The level of HIV/AIDS among injecting drug users is relatively low compared to many countries, although 5 per cent of injecting drug users in London have the virus, far higher than the figure of 0.14 per cent for the general population. Around half of problem drug users are thought to suffer from some form of mental illness. So-called recreational drugs also exact their toll on the human body. Stimulants such as mephedrone, speed and cocaine put pressure on the heart and cardiac system increasing the risk of heart attacks, cannabis and LSD have links to mental health problems, ecstasy can cause lethal overheating in the body and ketamine can severely damage the bladder resulting in users having to use catheters.

Many problem drug users live in a limbo-like state, trapped in a revolving door: from halfway house to arrest to court to jail to detox to rehab to halfway house and back again. It's a game with many snakes and very few ladders. Between a third and a half of new receptions into prison are estimated to be problem drug users. A quarter of all women and 15 per cent of men in jail are there for either drug possession, dealing or trafficking. A much wider group of prisoners are inside after committing offences directly related to their drug use. But prison is no place to be if you are addicted to drugs. Some inmates, who previously had no problem, come out of jail with a drug addiction, because the drug market in prisons is as thriving as the one outside.

Today, drug use spans the social divide. The only difference is that those who become addicted to drugs more often come from deprived backgrounds and unhappy childhoods. It is not surprising, with an existence far tougher and depressing than most, that homeless people and street sex workers have incredibly high rates of drug addiction. Heroin use among young people is falling, so does this mean Britain has turned a corner, away from the blight of serious drug addiction? 'As long as there are people with shit lives,' says Gary Sutton, head of drug services at Release, a charity specialising in drugs and the law, 'there will always be people using drugs such as heroin and crack.'

From heroin's rise within those economically deprived working-class communities, such as Glasgow, Manchester and Liverpool that were located within the drug's distribution system (unlike Belfast and Newcastle) in the 1980s, it has always been a drug linked with unemployment. But one of the key misunderstandings about the mindset of jobless heroin users is it is done simply to get into a state of oblivion, to blot out the past and to escape the present. This is only half the story.

Researcher Geoffrey Pearson discovered during a series of studies into heroin use in northern England in the mid-1980s that heroin addiction was also about filling empty, boring days with some kind of structure.

'Their behaviour is anything but an escape from life. They are actively engaged in meaningful activities and relationships seven days a week,' said Pearson in *A Land Fit for Heroin*. 'The brief moments of euphoria after each administration of a small amount of heroin constitute a small fraction of their daily lives. The rest of the time they are aggressively pursuing a career that is exacting, challenging, adventurous and rewarding. They are always on the move and must be alert, flexible and resourceful.

'Dependence on heroin, quite literally, imposes its own rigid time structure involving a necessary cycle of events if withdrawal sickness is to be avoided.' He described how addicts' days were taken up by a never-ending cycle of 'hustling' (obtaining money illegally), 'copping' (buying heroin) and 'getting off' (taking heroin).

'This same cycle of events was described to us repeatedly, albeit in less formal language, in interviews with heroin users and ex-users in northern cities. The rhythm of a heroin user's day was often described as if it were dictated by the beat of a metronome, of getting up, hustling for money, buying heroin, smoking it, and then hustling for the next bag.'

Pearson pointed out that because these busy cycles of activity were such all-consuming preoccupations, getting off the drug was all the more difficult. 'The question of how to break from the routine and replace it with a new and different pattern of daily activity could be experienced as a more difficult obstacle to overcome than actually withdrawing from heroin. In common with many other accounts of ex-users, "coming off" was seen as relatively easy compared with "staying off", and it was sometimes felt that the problem of "staying off" was made all that more difficult by the absence of employment possibilities which would be able to supply both alternative routines and rewards.'

Yet even some people who do use heroin are perfectly able to control their use of the drug if they are living relatively contented lives. This was the conclusion of a study by the Institute for Criminal Policy Research, which received short shrift in the media because of its controversial findings. It revealed that contrary to public perception, not all heroin users were addicted to the drug, and that significant numbers of them were engaged in what the authors called 'non-problematic use'.

Drugs temporarily rewire the mind and body to trigger feelings of pleasure. But they are just chemicals. Much of the public discourse on drugs puts the substances themselves firmly in the driving seat, with the person who has taken them as the helpless passenger. To suggest otherwise is heresy. Newspaper reports give drugs lifelike qualities usually associated with devils and diseases. So a bag of chemicals is given the powers of possession or to become the scourge of a nation.

Drugs are incredibly pleasurable, personal and specific. Opiates induce a feeling of detachment from pain and anxiety, crack is compulsive, and cannabis a sticky habit that even social users find it hard to abandon. No two drug experiences are the same, but neither are they always good. In fact drugs have been described by one ex-user as being 'like indoor fireworks – sort of good, but actually a bit naff'. Few people would suggest developing penchants for hard drugs. Yet to deny the fourth drive appears only to make it more pernicious – fuelling in the case of heroin addicts a physical craving or in the case of the recreational drug user, an ever wider menu of unregulated drugs.

To journey into the mind of a drug-using nation it is important to accept that intoxication is not just about the chemical effects of drugs. It is also about the drug taker, their motivations, the buzz, the setting, and the environment in which they live.

For some, the pleasurable part of drug taking begins in planning a night out, purchasing the substances, and preparing them for use – whether that be the careful rolling of a spliff, the process of injecting heroin into a vein or racking out perfectly equal lines of cocaine with a credit card. Alone in a remote field, indoors with your best friends or surrounded by strangers in a noisy club, the drug user's surroundings add an additional element to a drug's physical effects. People's circumstances and the environment in which they live have a huge effect on their propensity to become addicted to drugs.

If the allure or the stark desperation that draws people into using drugs, and the vast array of drug-using cultures that make up Britain, is not understood, then you have only half the story.

But what makes the drug trade such a unique industry is that it is one where hard cash, and sometimes brutal illicit market economics, mix with people's intensely personal desire to become intoxicated, to alter their state of mind.

2

Transaction

The Frontline of the Drug Trade

'In Stapleton Road you can get anything you want,' says Vernon Blanc as we motor down the M32 through east Bristol. 'Drugs, guns, girls . . . It's become the new front line for the crack and heroin trade.'

As we walk on to Stapleton Road, superseding St Paul's as the drug hub of the city, Vernon points to the side of the road. 'Look, it's turning into the OK Corral.' He motions to the week-old tributes to an eighteen-year-old boy, stabbed to death in a fight between rival gangs feuding over drug turf.

Blue neckerchiefs, the colour of the High Street gang from Easton, lie next to flowers and notes of condolence. 'The week before Abdi was stabbed, another kid was gunned down in the middle of the day. The gunman didn't even wear a hood or mask; he just stood there shooting. Some of the kids round here think they're untouchable.'

The rain-stained cards and flowers mark the start of an unremarkable 150-metre strip of inner-city suburb, one of the most deprived parts of Bristol. It's easy to forget the chic city centre with its luxury bars, shops and restaurants lies just under a mile to the south-west. Decaying Georgian town houses provide a reminder of the area's former glory as a grand eighteenth-century shopping district. Stapleton Road is today known as 'Junkie Street', according to one national tabloid: 'a moral cesspit where the pavements are heaving with killers, addicts, hookers and their pimps'. One local councillor, John Kiely, dubbed Easton 'the drug supermarket of the south-west of England'; and the M32 cutting Stapleton Road in two its front door.

The tension is palpable: youths with faces half-concealed by hoods loiter, eyeballing a police car cruising the main drag; shoppers clasp their bags and walk with purpose. The likelihood of being caught in a crossfire is very small, but no less real. The only thing missing from the scene is the tumble-weed.

Vernon nods to three houses that mark the start of this new front line. Paint peeling from brick and bay windows plastered with the faded pages of super-hero comics, these are known drug dens – houses where dealers sell heroin and crack cocaine twenty-four hours a day in exchange for cash or stolen goods.

One bears the hallmarks of a police raid – its windows and front door boarded with sheets of steel. Next door, however, business is brisk. A group of people dressed in waterproofs are gathering at a nearby bus stop. When there are enough punters to make it worth his while, a dealer leaves the crack house, quickly checks for police, then distributes wraps of heroin and rocks of crack, collecting cash. The crowd rapidly disappears.

'Over there, on the church steps, that's where all the street dealers gather, most days and most nights,' Vernon says, as he acknowledges the eye of a shopper. 'Further down, the Yardie gangs sell drugs from the tables outside the pubs. They just move in – the pubs have no choice. Once somewhere gets a reputation as a spot to score the people just come. Cars will pull up, a punter will buy what they want and drive off.'

'Everyone knows the rules of the game. It's cops and robbers. If I can stay out of the clutches of the cops and I'm making money – all good. You get caught – you go to jail. End of. I was in and out of jail at one time. I was a junkie, and carried on selling and using inside. But you have to do a cold turkey to pass the prison drugs test. I'd done it so many times I just got fed up with it. The last sentence I got was the end of it for me. I stopped.'

Vernon stands around six feet tall, has long dreadlocks and the physique of a boxer. Today he's dressed in the urban chic of fresh white trainers, blue jeans and a bright red tracksuit top. A London-born Jamaican, Vernon walks a fine line among the turmoil. He is no longer a street dealer and has been clean of drugs for more than a decade. Nor is he an undercover informer – he has no contact with the police; they know him but ignore his comings and goings.

He is a guardian angel, not for drug users, but for drug dealers. Through his charity, Switch, he offers them a lifeline to get out of a game that is becoming increasingly complex, competitive and violent. Several times a week, Vernon enters the 'no-go' corners of the city in search of dealers, leaving his calling card at bars, cafés and crack houses. As we walk down the street, he stops and talks to passers-by, touches fists and shakes hands.

'Like the drugs they sell, the job sucks you in and it's difficult to let it go. Some of these guys are earning £5,000 a week. They are not going to give it all up to go and work in

Sainsbury's. Dealers get used to the money, the way of life, their position on the street. It's well paid, but it takes its toll,' says Vernon, stamping his feet on the pavement. 'When you're on the street you're constantly aware of danger. It's not just the cops you want to evade, there's always someone who wants to steal your stash. You take on a lifestyle, a routine. You become paranoid, isolated, you don't trust anyone. When you arrange to meet someone you're always a little early or a little late. You check the location out, see who's waiting. It's a way of life that sticks with you.'

Ralph, now approaching fifty years of age, is one of the dinosaurs of the Bristol street drug scene. A dealer in the 1980s and 1990s, he used to make £500 a week selling Class A drugs. Still struggling with addiction, he is one of many street dealers Vernon has helped walk away.

Ralph's drug journey began aged fifteen when he became a small-time dealer on the streets of Soho, King's Cross and Notting Hill. Selling cannabis, LSD and speed to hippies and bohemians, he managed to pay his rent, but started dabbling in opiate-based medicines. The high gave him a warm feeling he had never experienced before, it made him feel safe.

'I woke up one morning feeling sick with my eyes streaming and nose running. A mate came up to me and said "You're rattling," and I thought what's rattling? I'd never heard of it. He said "Get some gear and you'll be all right."'

So he did. Ralph became a drugstore cowboy – breaking into chemists to get his hands on the 'Dangerous Drugs' cabinet of medicinal opiates. But as chemists tightened up security, Ralph turned to street heroin, and his dabbling became a daily routine. Small-time dealing could no longer fund his habit. He and his friends resorted to street robberies, thieving, burglaries, heists and shop robberies.

Ralph's friends warned him against trying crack when it first emerged on to the Bristol scene in the early 1990s. They knew he would like it, and he did. 'I met this American guy who taught me how to wash up cocaine into crack properly, in bulk, an ounce at a time,' Ralph says. Making crack was simple – all you needed was a microwave, a couple of glass dishes and a few high-street products. 'What you get afterwards is one huge lump of pure crack – I tried one pipe and didn't stop.'

Sold alongside heroin, crack's moreish nature ramped up dealers' profits and turned the street heroin market from a disorganised jamboree into a cut-throat, money-minded business. Ralph's old-school generation of user-dealers was increasingly elbowed aside by teams of managed foot soldiers, lookouts, stash holders and servers who have turned Stapleton Road into such a busy narcotics thoroughfare.

The national drug economy is part of a giant $322 billion worldwide narcotics industry that constitutes the third biggest global commodity in cash terms after oil and the arms trade. Drug dealers, in turn, are the public face of a vast, diverse and highly enigmatic UK industry with a turnover of between £7 billion and £8 billion a year that looms large, yet invisible, behind its army of front-line workers.

Britain's drug market has often been described as having a pyramid-like structure of large importers operating at an apex, filtering down to street dealers who work on the lowest tier. In turn, each drug-dealing organisation has its own pyramid-like structure, with the boss at the top, supported by trusted lieutenants and a multitude of street runners. It is a structure that means those at the peak of the pyramid are well removed from the visible side of the trade, the customers and the thousands of daily transactions that feed the industry.

As with the legitimate trades, the illegal drug market has an importation, a wholesale and retail level. But what makes the drug trade so lucrative is the dramatic mark-up along the supply chain of the product, from farms in Colombia, Bolivia, Afghanistan and Pakistan, to the streets of Croydon, Belfast, Aston and Plymouth. The farm gate price of heroin per kilo in Afghanistan starts at approximately £450, for example, rising to £8,150 in the hands of Turkish middlemen, £20,500 on entering the UK and £75,750 on UK streets.

The closer the product gets to the user, the more valuable it becomes. Most of the drugs imported into Britain pass through the major drugs hubs of London, Liverpool and Birmingham, and are then filtered down across the country, often through a network of middle-market 'brokers', to street dealers.

Packages are broken down and passed along a supply chain that typically has between four and seven links. Some drugs, particularly cocaine and speed, are progressively cut to the bone with bulking agents as they near the street. Networks may trade at middle-market level in more than one product, but at street level the sale of crack and heroin, commonly £10 per rock of crack or £10 per bag of heroin, remains largely distinct from the market in drugs such as cocaine, cannabis and ecstasy.

But it's a structure that police and academics have found hard to pin down. The more you look at it, the less regimented it appears. In an attempt to map out the trade, a 2001 Home Office study could only conclude: 'It is like a large jigsaw – but a jigsaw in which each particular piece comes from a different set.'

Research published in 2007, also for the Home Office, estimated that the domestic drug trade was one of 'considerable complexity and diversity', encompassing around 300 major traffickers, 3,000 middle-market wholesalers and 70,000 street dealers. A wide-ranging review of all the police and academic intelligence to date on the drug trade, published in 2008 by the UK Drug Policy Commission, concluded that 'the lines between the different levels in the supply chain are far from clear ... the various roles within them are often fluid and interchangeable'.

But research *has* shed light on one key aspect of the drug trade's make-up: the traditional 'pyramid' model is collapsing into a more fragmented, non-hierarchical, entrepreneurial model, of loosely interlinked local and regional markets. The roles and the levels at which drug outfits operate are far from static. It's not yet a free-for-all, but compared to the way the drug market was structured in the 1980s and 1990s, when it was widely agreed the trade had a pyramid structure and was maintained by a handful of 'Mr Bigs' who had a stranglehold on importation, it's verging on anarchy.

But perhaps the biggest shift in the structure and modus operandi of Britain's drug trade has occurred on the front line, among the tens of thousands of street drug dealers who form the human shield for the upper echelons of the trade.

The outdated yet prevailing image of a street dealer is of a shifty-looking man preying on innocent teenagers. But today it is much more likely to be a teenager on a bicycle than an older local villain. A quarter of all people convicted of supplying Class A drugs in Britain are twenty-one or under, and the number of teenage drug dealers arrested, charged and locked up for drug dealing is rising every year.

In the new business-like era of crack cocaine, front-line distribution has been reorganised to maximise sales and minimise the risk of arrest and imprisonment. It is not so much about who you know or how pure your drugs are, but instead about speed of delivery, availability and manpower.

Many of the new breed of dealers are not addicts, but are selling to fund a lifestyle. Their aim is not to escape their grim surroundings amid a haze of heroin smoke or on the end of a crack pipe, but at the steering wheel of an expensive car. For a new generation of dealers, the substitute economy of the drug trade offers a route out of poverty and a chance at the jackpot or at least a taste of the good life.

Gangland criminologist Professor John Pitts, director of the Vauxhall Centre for the Study of Crime, has been investigating the changing face of youth crime in Britain since the 1980s. He says the drug trade is now the dominant paradigm for aspiring young offenders. 'For someone quite young, being asked by someone with a high status in the neighbourhood to take a package for them for a small reward gains them kudos,' says Pitts. 'It appears to be a glamorous world, people seem to do well out of it. To someone who is struggling at school, who has a cold, hard home life with few prospects, it's dangerous, it's exciting, and it's a step up the ladder. In many urban street cultures, you hope to be a football star, or a villain.

'In the past you could offer offenders an apprenticeship in plumbing, for example. You could say to them "Use your loaf, why turn to crime when you could earn a fortune by learning a new skill?" and it was a genuine option. Now, you have escalating youth unemployment and a lack of those opportunities. In today's drug business you could be earning, with relatively little effort, £500 a week. The old ways of reasoning with young offenders – all that is now gone.'

Teenagers often enter the drug trade at the lowest level of the food chain, either delivering the drugs from the dealer to the buyer (runners, or 'shotters') or as lookouts, watching for police or rival dealers. The more the labour is split among the runners, the less evidence the police will have against them if they are searched. Rarely will any street runner or dealer be in possession of more than one of the three basic components of the street drug deal: the phone, the drugs and the money. When they are carrying bags or rocks, dealers will store them in their mouths, ready to swallow if the police turn up, or hide them inside bras or pants, throw them away or even insert them elsewhere. Under-sixteens know too well that police cannot conduct full body searches of them unless a responsible adult is present.

Most are recruited by friends, family members, or local dealers looking for new employees. At the lower end of the drug trade, even as lookouts and runners, the financial rewards compare well with legitimate employment. While there are a number of people who are exploited and paid pitiful amounts for working long hours (court cases and research studies have shown low-level employees earning as little as £60–180 for a six-day week), runners, lookouts, carriers and dealers can expect to earn on average £450 a week.

Despite the risk of arrest and violence, even at a relatively junior level of the drug trade, on that basis these people are earning the take-home equivalent of £31,000 a year, the same salary as the average police constable, and more than the average UK salary of £25,000.

The drug trade operates a kaleidoscope of sales techniques. One of the most in-depth studies into local drug markets carried out in the UK was undertaken by criminologists Dick Hobbs and Gavin Hales, who investigated the numerous dealing scenes revolving around council estates, parks and hostels in an anonymous London borough.

The study found up to seven different teams working within the borough, each with unique set-ups and target audiences. On one estate there appeared to be a group of fifteen-year-olds trying to take it over, carrying out drug dealing, undeterred by police. 'Go back into your fucking house,' they were recorded shouting at residents. 'We're busy out here.' In another part of the borough 'a seventeen-year-old was running what was in effect a protection racket in his neighbourhood, demanding that the local youths either dealt drugs for him, or paid him protection money'.

In another neighbourhood, a police officer told of a set-up, again based on an estate, involving a small group of young men who dealt crack in their local park to clientele mainly drawn from a nearby hostel and drug treatment service. They managed to confuse the local drug squad by all using the same street name, 'Jonny'. When they realised that mobile phone texts were being used as evidence to convict their foot soldiers, they made sure that their phones were locked (BlackBerrys are the hardest for police to unlock) and that only short phone calls using coded conversations were made. They ordered sellers to wear gloves, to avoid leaving fingerprints and DNA on drugs and cash. The police were unable to confirm the identity of a single member.

The ubiquity of the crack cocaine market in London posed two key questions for Hobbs. What is the economic reality of involvement in the drugs economy for a fifteen-year-old, and to what extent are communities complicit in the persistence of the illegal economy?

An analysis by Pitts of a relatively small east London outfit called the Oliver Close Gang estimated that the gang sold crack and heroin to around 150 people, each of whom was spending a minimum of £50 per week. Thus the weekly residential drug spend was £7,500 a week: £390,000 a year. This income formed the basis for a weekly bonanza for the gang and their affiliates: in terms of crack, a wholesaler will buy per week at £1,500, and sell at £2,500, pocketing £1,000; an 'Elder' or 'Face' buys at £2,500 and sells for £5,000, making £2,500; while a team of five 'shotters' will buy at £5,000 and sell at £7,500.

Depending on their role and the crew they work with, runners and dealers are paid either a fixed rate or on commission. Either way they will be under pressure from above to sell a set number of bags of heroin and rocks of crack per week. A twenty-month investigation into local drug markets by a team of researchers from King's College London and published in 2005 by the Joseph Rowntree Foundation, discovered that three-quarters of street drug runners were male, half had been excluded from school or had no qualifications, and two-thirds had been in jail. Most continued to sell drugs because they had become reliant on the money and the lifestyle. Many street-market dealers were not outsiders, but from local communities.

The study also unearthed two teenage brothers who were required between them to sell 200 bags of heroin and 200 rocks of crack each week in order to receive their £150 wage. The boys' employer, an established drug dealer, paid them out of his own £3,000–4,000 weekly proceeds. He was their father.

Weighed against the high cash rewards are the inherent risks faced by those working on the front line of the drug trade – arrest and jail, violence, intimidation, robberies, addiction, competition from run-ins with rival sets of dealers.

The rising number of street runners reflects the fact that the lowest standing in social status are often forced into a choice between minimum wage jobs or working in alternative economies – and the drug trade is the biggest employer of them all. Caught at the sharp end of society, the drug trade offers to lift people from obscurity to positions of influence, instant celebrity (albeit on a local level), and wealth. But drug dealing does not come with a pension scheme. Instead, wary of the chance of jail, many have a 'spend as you go' attitude to the money they make. Most earnings go on family, partners and friends, as well as on luxury items such as designer clothes, trainers, cars, gambling, nights out and holidays. While even low-level dealers will have more cash in their pockets than their peers working in legitimate jobs, the vast majority end up caught between a rock and a hard place, between the crack and heroin dealers who see them as expendable cannon fodder, and the police, who see them as low hanging fruit, to be harvested at will to boost arrest figures and media headlines. Ultimately, the daily reality for the tens of thousands of young foot soldiers who people the front line of Britain's narco-economy is one of hardship, threat, and little reward.

Britain was first warned of the potential of crack cocaine to stir up the street drug market in dramatic fashion when Robert Stutman, an officer of the US Drug Enforcement Agency (DEA), crossed the Atlantic in 1989 to lecture a gathering of senior British police officers.

Stutman described how the highly addictive cocaine derivative had devastated US neighbourhoods and produced a generation of 'crack babies' – children born addicted to the drug because of their mother's habit. Stutman claimed that 'three-quarters of people who take crack get hooked after three tries' and predicted that within two years the 'deadly rocks' – which were smoked rather than snorted – would result in the collapse of British society.

Stutman also warned that producers of cocaine in Latin America and traffickers in the traditional trans-shipment islands in the Caribbean would turn their attentions to Europe.

To some UK drug experts, the warnings seemed outlandish and sensational. Britain's drug-taking culture was different, they said, and there was little likelihood that our more moderate society would succumb to a product that was clearly so destructive.

In his paper 'The Menace of the War on Crack in Britain', published in 1990, Richard Hammersley of the Behavioural Sciences Group at the University of Glasgow dismissed the DEA's warnings that the drug was instantly addictive, saying the chronic comedowns would deter users. Hammersley argued the crack epidemic that had swept the US was due to its geographic proximity to the large cocaine-producing countries of South America and high levels of recreational cocaine use, not just among the poor neighbourhoods, but among the professional middle classes. He added that the British at the time were not 'poly drug users', people who took a variety of substances, as the Americans were.

'None of these conditions apply to the UK. Nor is there evidence that cocaine or crack use is increasing epidemically in the UK,' wrote Hammersley. 'The main menace of crack is the intense rhetoric used against it.' The potential for a crack-cocaine epidemic appeared to be a purely academic argument. In 1990 the total amount of crack seized in the UK was less than one kilogram. The Met's Crack Intelligence Unit, launched in response to Stutman's warnings, was disbanded due to lack of work. Crack was an American thing.

The doubters, it appeared, had been right. But in the end, it came just as Stutman had warned. 'Crack in the UK was like a firework that fizzled, died and then exploded when you were least expecting it,' says Mark, a drug-squad officer in Liverpool in the 1990s. 'In the first half of the decade we would hear the odd bit of news about crack being sold, but heroin was always the main street-dealing drug. Within the space of a few years crack was all over the place. Crack twisted the market and changed the consumer and the dealer for good.'

The explosion of crack on to the British scene was made possible by the increasing availability of powder cocaine, primarily trafficked into the UK from South America, via the Caribbean and Spain. With this, came knowledge from America about how to mass-produce crack, alongside the economic reality that a gram of crack is worth double a gram of powder cocaine.

While billed by Stutman as a 'black' drug, Home Office research carried out in 2002, a decade after crack hit Britain, found that many users where white, as the drug had found favour in established heroin-using communities. It was used as a balance to the daily sedative effects of heroin, or in combination, injected in the same syringe as what became known as a 'speedball' or a 'snowball'. The cocktail magnified the dopamine high of a heroin rush, but left users plummeting in its wake to a new kind of low.

Dealers realised that the demand for the two drugs were inextricably linked and started to sell the two together. 'Crack and heroin started to become one drug,' says Gary Sutton of Release. The two markets merged, with dealers offering 'two for one' deals of brown and white. Crucially for the dealers, crack's short, powerful highs and nerve-jangling lows left users wanting more – it was the ultimate repeat-buy drug. Aware of crack's profitability, many dealers refused to sell heroin without crack, and as a result the number of crack users escalated, and so did the number of crimes committed to fund their new habit.

It sent a shockwave through communities. 'You lose your moral compass with that stuff, it's so compulsive,' says Sutton. Previously managing the largest needle-exchange project in London and a former crack and heroin user himself, he witnessed first-hand how crack changed the street trade. One user described a crack high 'as a hypersensitive state, like a cat on a hot tin roof' with a rush so beguiling that people would smoke until their money ran out.

'On crack, you are forever caught on the spike of trying to obtain that incredibly euphoric high and of avoiding the crash that follows it. What are people prepared to do to try and retain that? One lad I knew sold his Ford Escort Cabriolet worth £3,000 for £200 to get another hit. Because it's so compulsive there's so much money in it for dealers, their customers just kept coming back for more.'

But for the first time hard drug use became feminised in a way never previously seen in Britain. Where heroin had always been an antidote for the working girls of Britain's red-light districts, crack transformed the vice world. The increase in the amount of crack cocaine being used by sex workers reduced the price of sex on the street, which in some areas dropped to as little as £10, the price of a rock. Crack became so intertwined with the sex trade that the Home Office began to use the size of a red-light district as an indicator of the scale of its crack market.

'A heroin addict can get by on a £30 a day habit. You introduce them to crack and they're suddenly spending £500 a day,' says Sutton. 'No one used to give a shit if you were selling a bit of gear to support your habit, but I don't think it would be as easy to do that now, and that's because of crack. It turned drug dealing into a highly profitable business that people did not want to relinquish.'

To dealers, crack was an irresistible moneymaker. In his 1994 book *Crack of Doom*, the journalist Jon Silverman gave an account of one of the UK's first crack dealers, the Brent-based gangster Sammy da Costa Lewis. By 1991, at a time when crack was first making inroads into Britain's inner cities, he was making up to £12,000 a week by converting powder cocaine into crack using baking soda and a microwave. Lewis, taught how to convert cocaine to crack by a family friend in Trinidad, based himself at a flat in the Stonebridge Estate in Harlesden, a poor, north-west London district. It was there he converted the cocaine into rocks. He developed a loyal street-dealing crew who were making £1,500 a week selling crack on the streets and to residents on the estate. Lewis was arrested in a bungled undercover police operation that ended with one officer shot in the heart. Calling him a 'scourge of society' an Old Bailey judge sentenced Lewis to twelve years for attempted murder and drug supply. Police learnt their lesson; never again would they go unarmed to bust a major drug dealer, and to this day the Stonebridge Estate remains a focal point for drug crime in north-west London.

Because of the 'dirty' image of crack, its close links to acquisitive crime, its lucrative nature and its highly addictive qualities, crack dealers face higher penalties than those caught in possession of the powdered cocaine required to make it. The process of converting cocaine to crack takes place as close to the street as possible, with dealers and distributors wary of being caught in transit with large amounts of the drug. And by the nature of local crack markets, where customers are often tied to dealers and desperate for a hit, the quality of the drug appears secondary to the need for a hit. Silverman reported: 'They [street dealers] recoup their stake from the punters, who will keep buying rocks even if they are only 75 per cent pure, until there is nothing in their wallets – and then they start stealing for more.'

As John Pitts observed, the 1980s was an era in which working-class areas of Europe became the shop floor of the drug economy. As the drugs business grew, so too did the size and the number of drug-dealing street gangs. It was the birth of the white urban hustler – where drug dealing not only provided rewards, but filled otherwise vacuous days of unemployment. Dressed in sportswear, trainers and baseball caps, the white urban hustler was not alone in defining the new legion of dealers for whom the drug trade offered opportunity where legitimate business appeared to fail.

In London, Birmingham and Bristol, black and Caribbean gangs entered the crack-cocaine trade. Crack changed the way in which race defined the British street market. Where once white and Asian gangs dominated the heroin trade and black gangs the cocaine trade, now gangs started to work together, forming alliances to ensure their ability to source both drugs and heroin and crack were dealt by white, Asian and black alike.

Importantly, black gangs were not reliant on British cocaine smugglers for the supply: Jamaica had for a long time been the preferred Caribbean trans-shipment point for South American cocaine en route to the US, and Jamaican and British Caribbean drug barons soon sought to exploit their ability to supply in the UK. Hundreds of drug mules carrying cocaine were flown into drug factories in British cities that became hubs of supply.*

With increasing profit came increasing competition, but not of the 'healthy' kind imagined by free-trade theorists. The issue of 'turf' and postcode wars came increasingly into play and the violence associated with the drug trade increased, both within individual ethnic communities running local markets and between them. The Yardies, as the gangs originating from Jamaica became known, didn't just bring with them their own supply of product, they also brought a level of violence previously unseen on Britain's streets.

Operation Trident was set up by the Met Police in 1998 to investigate 'black on black' shootings, with special attention to gun crime relating to the illegal sale of drugs. The next year it was claimed Yardie gangs were linked to more than thirty murders in the capital.

The trade swamped small city markets like Bristol with devastating effects, that are perhaps best summed up in the words of Steve Wilks, the owner of the Black and White café at the heart of St Paul's, widely dubbed 'Britain's most raided drug den'. Speaking at a court hearing in a bid to prevent the café being closed on the grounds that it was a thinly disguised crack-dealing HQ, Wilks protested his innocence: 'For thirty years we have provided black food for the black

---

* Turkish, Kurdish, Bengali, Pakistani and Tamil gangs exploited their links to the heroin producers in a similar way, turning north London and much of Humberside into countrywide distribution hubs.

community. I don't sell drugs. Closing the café is not going to change the drug situation in St Paul's. Crack cocaine has mashed up the community. We have all suffered, myself included.'

But long before the police closed in on violent hotspots, drug markets had started to slip from view. Intense policing had sought to drive the trade from the street, but in the mid-1990s the mobile phone had effectively decoupled the retail drug trade from a central geographic location. Where once street markets offered a very public snapshot of the trade, mobile phones freed buyers and sellers to arrange transactions in less visible locations: a council-estate stairwell, subways, bus stops, park bench or alleyway, with a runner dispatched on foot or on a bicycle to carry out the transaction.

For the first time drug gangs were less reliant on drug users to distribute the product at street level. Dealers who were efficient, businesslike and weren't tempted to adulterate or cut the product for their own use, took up the baton, and as they reached more customers, they could make a proper living.

Drug Markets and Distribution Systems, a study by criminologists Mike Hough and Tiggey May published in 2004, charted the partial disintegration of London's internationally known heroin market of King's Cross, as the technology made the street deal a more elusive transaction for police to observe. And as time went on the possibilities for avoiding detection proliferated; stolen phones could be unlocked or numbers cloned. And the Hough–May study hinted at the future: 'Smart cards can be bought which provide a set amount of phone time, which can be accessed from any phone; in the US, there are 1,800 companies which pre-sell airtime for cash.

These systems all make it increasingly hard to maintain effective surveillance.'

And as drug gangs became more mobile they sought to move ever closer to the consumer, away from the busy, city-centre markets that had characterised street drug dealing from the 1970s, and which were reaching saturation point. Gangs turned their sights on smaller rural markets, which crack had now made profitable, following the demand the length and breadth of Britain.

Located on a latitude north of Moscow, three hours' drive up Scotland's north-east coast from Edinburgh, lies the harsh, granite cityscape of Aberdeen. Still surfing on the boomtown wave created by the first oil strike in the North Sea in the late 1960s, Aberdeen is a rich city, teeming with offshore workers, many of whom use it as a base and watering hole before going out to sea again. Surprisingly, one of Britain's most isolated cities is also Scotland's crack capital, and home to two-thirds of the region's crack users.

One of the reasons for this is the bizarre, underworld twinning of Aberdeen with the nondescript Midlands town of Wolverhampton.

One summer in the mid-1990s, while the weather was bearable, a pair of sex workers from Wolverhampton decided to take the train up to Aberdeen to investigate what a friend had told them: that the city was home to a booming sex trade fuelled by the thousands of multinational oil and seaport workers that use Aberdeen as a base for spending their wages and getting drunk. Their friend was correct. It was at the time a dedicated 'free zone' for independent prostitutes, a local trial in a city that had no organised sex trade. Inspired by the prices the offshore workers were willing to pay for sex, they stayed. Word quickly spread, and more sex workers followed.

Police say it was drug-dealing pimps, who had worked with the girls in Wolverhampton, that first sniffed a chance to double their profits, and joined the caravan up north, soon dubbed the 'Wolverhampton run'. Drugs were hard to come by in the isolated city, and users were willing to pay for quality. A rock of crack worth £10–20 in Wolverhampton could sell for up to £50 in Aberdeen. Until the West Midlands invasion, local dealers had travelled to Liverpool to buy their crack, needing to sell it high on their return to make the dangerous trip worthwhile.

Unopposed by Aberdeen's low-level drug gangs, the visitors from Wolverhampton muscled in, introducing crack to the local heroin market by offering 'two for one' deals. When Aberdeen's heroin users had got a taste for crack, they ramped the prices back up. 'By the late 1990s we saw an influx of professionally made, high-purity rocks of crack on the streets of Aberdeen,' DI Willie Findlay, head of Grampian Police's drug squad, told *Druglink* magazine.

The area's heroin users, as their counterparts were doing across England, began to add crack to their daily diet, and Aberdeen's crack problem spiralled. The local detox unit, the Alexander Clinic, started treating air hostesses, housewives, road-sweepers, fishermen and oil workers for addiction to the drug.

But as soon as police dismantled one English gang, another would take its place. Learning from the mistakes of their prede-cessors, and as the dulcet tones of the Wolverhampton accent began to raise eyebrows, new firms realised they had to 'go native' and use local people as cover.

One such firm, the 'Flava' gang, sent four dealers at a time on the seven-hour train journey to Aberdeen to provide a twenty-four-hour drug service. They buried stashes around the city: in a garden centre, the grounds of a local hospital and in residential streets. They used customers' homes as dealing shops, rigged up CCTV cameras at each house they occupied, and used scanners to listen into police communications. The Flava gang made as much as £6,000 a day in Aberdeen, and were caught only after a four-month surveillance operation.

Gangs from Wolverhampton are still being busted in Aberdeen on a regular basis. The drug expressway has lost none of its appeal. In January 2012 Wolverhampton dealer Daniel Sterling was jailed for eight years after he was found guilty of masterminding a crack- and heroin-selling outfit in the city. The judge said: 'The word must go out that those who come to Aberdeen and the surrounding area to deal in drugs face long prison sentences.' Grampian Police DI Chris Lawrence, of the major investigation team, said Sterling was part of the biggest organised-crime group from England yet to be busted.

'In cities across the country, young lads would be given a set of car keys by their bosses,' says Mark, a former drug-squad officer. 'They'd be given the name of a town, a mobile phone, a bag of white [crack] and a bag of brown [heroin], and told "I want £1,000 from that and £1,000 from that, and anything you make on top is yours. If you lose the money you owe me, if you lose the car, you owe me, and if you get arrested, I don't give a shit." It was happening right across the country.'

The established gangs of Liverpool, Birmingham and London were the first to flex their muscles in regional markets, working a very basic rule of thumb: the further they travelled from the established markets the greater the profits they could achieve, driving the trade ever deeper in Middle England. They called it 'going country'.

Norfolk, Sussex, Suffolk and Dorset were not immune, nor Devon and Cornwall. All reported the influx of drug gangs with Scouse, Brummie or south-east accents. Liverpool dealers spread across Lancashire and Wales. England's traditional holiday resorts, such as Margate and Blackpool, had long lost their former glory, B&Bs had become bedsits popular with drug addicts who ended up in seaside towns after literally getting off at the end of the line and staying there.

Police claimed the gangs were treating towns like training grounds for street dealers: those who could blend in, win influence and develop a market would then be moved on to bigger and better opportunities.

Gavin, now in his mid-thirties, was part of that generation of mobile dealers who found new lives in the country. Growing up in a town on England's north-east coast as heroin swept the country in the wake of recession, the arrival of crack brought fresh options to communities where choices were largely limited to using heroin, as his cousins did, spending their days nodding off on the sofa, or making a good living by dealing.

For Gavin it was a chance to escape, but it wasn't what he'd expected; the south was a new world. 'It was amazing to just travel around and see England, it was a world away from the shithole in which we grew up – the high streets had shops and people had jobs. But what we couldn't believe was the demand. Everyone we knew at home took drugs because they had nothing else to do – the people down south just took drugs for fun.'

To Gavin, the towns and cities of Britain's 'sunshine strip' – Gloucester, Cheltenham and Swindon – appeared in the daytime as bastions of Middle England, populated by 'rosy faced country folk and day-trippers'. But after dark in alleyways, subways and secluded parks, crowds would line up for his services. Some of his customers were prostitutes and the homeless, but many were local weekend bingers seeking an ever more evasive high. For a decade Gavin lived on a cocktail of cash, crack and prostitutes, travelling non-stop, and meting out a mixture of coercion, exploitation and extreme violence daily. It was a brutal, roller-coaster existence that he describes as an addiction in itself. In the space of ten years most of his friends ended up either in prison or hospitalised – the victims of near-lethal assaults. But Gavin was a success, and emerged unscathed, a fact he puts down to an ability to fit in.

Integration is seen as the biggest challenge faced by mobile drug gangs – who are still operating effectively across the country. But many are now able to slip into towns virtually unawares, using local drug addicts and dealers to carry out the transactions while lying undercover in rented flats or the homes of local drug users. The successful, and ongoing, expansion of drug-dealing gangs across the country led to the establishment in 2007 of the police's Organised Crime Group Mapping database, which for the first time analysed drug gangs working across regional borders within the UK. While Hobbs found a ubiquity of crack across London alarming, today Class A drug markets can be said to be the lifeblood of many housing estates across Britain and embedded in communities.

Embedded on a large, neglected Humberside housing project for six months, two documentary makers found themselves in an unprecedented position to witness at first hand the daily activities of the local drug firm. What they witnessed, the brazenness of how the drug firms operate, was what thousands of council-estate tenants across Britain see day in, day out. Along with blue plastic bags stuck in trees, vandalism and joyriding, the drug trade is part of life on many run-down estates across Britain, and this one was no different. They got to know the firm's characters, from the thirteen-year-old street runner to the violent Glaswegian gangster at the top of the pile.

'It wasn't long before the dealers began to make themselves apparent,' says one of the directors. 'We'd be interviewing these teenagers about life on the estate and they'd be pulling out and counting wads of notes from their socks, and arranging meet-ups on their mobiles every ten minutes. They didn't admit what they were doing, but it was so blatant.' Gradually a picture emerged of the drug firm that was responsible for running the entire drug trade on the estate, an area of long-term social exclusion and concentrated crack and heroin use.

Crack and heroin transactions are openly carried out, as if the dealers are selling ice creams from a van, unhindered by residents or police, from a wall in the centre of the 1970s housing project's tatty shopping precinct. 'It's a bit like a crappy, English version of *The Wire*,' says the director, who filmed on the estate between 2011 and 2012 for a TV series about life on Britain's run-down housing projects.

The firm employs two young teenagers, both around thirteen years old, to work as runners and lookouts. One of them, Joey, whose family are well-known local criminals, is permitted to buzz around the estate on his stolen motorbike, selling bags of skunk cannabis from his tracksuit trouser pockets.

In the layer above, earning around £600 a week, are a constantly changing group of around eight or nine front-line dealers. They provide drug users living on or nearby the estate, where many families have been unemployed for two or three generations since the area's steel industry was dismantled in the 1980s, with crack and heroin.

'Apart from the odd show of force when a motorbike gets stolen or something, the police don't give a shit,' says the director. 'If one of them dressed as an undercover tramp for a week on this estate they'd get everyone, but they obviously can't be bothered.'

Crack dealer Jason, a cocky eighteen-year-old 'Danny Dyer' wannabe, is hyperactive, always up for a fight, and loves the position of power his job gives him on the estate. Tall and handsome, he goes out with the best-looking girl on the estate, although they hate each other, and last year he was jailed for beating her up.

Teenager Ryan, a heroin dealer, is a bit dopey, scruffier and more prone to errors than the others. Whereas Jason spends his profits on new trainers and tracksuits, Ryan's supermarket-brand trainers and scruffy sweatshirts and sweatpants are an indication of the fact most of his profits go on his own addiction to heroin.

Like many low-level drug dealers around the country, Ryan bears the scars of a punishment beating by his superiors. The directors turned up at the estate one day to find Ryan sitting on the wall nursing a gaping, bloody hole in his lower lip and some missing teeth. 'He found it hard to talk, but he told us he had been "keyed" by one of the firm's upper-level dealers. His boss had gripped a key in his knuckles and punched it through his lower lip, creating the hole and smashing his lower teeth.' It was over a debt of just £50.

Further up the estate's drug firm are the two 'managers', Rob and Nate, who keep the dealers in line, check out the safe houses on the estate ('friendly' flats where the drug stashes are kept) and administer violence if needed. Both in their late twenties, they earn around £60,000 a year, the basic salary of the average British MP, and have been working under the auspices of the same boss for several years.

Rob, a muscle-bound steroid user with a love of superbikes and ultra-thick gold neck-chains, is the public face of the firm on the estate. No one is aware of anyone else above him. His presence is enough to scare people. He punches homeless people at random, he looks like the kind of guy whose violence is out of control. The front-line dealers are terrified of Rob, with even Jason barely daring to speak on camera if his boss is present. From a family of Glaswegian gangsters, Rob makes a living selling cocaine on the estate, and in bars and clubs across town.

Nate, the other 'manager', is quick-witted, funny, but also malevolent. An ex-boxer who has been in and out of jail most of his life, he has a low tolerance of mistakes and is the one who 'keyed' Ryan for losing £50. Nate, who is always accompanied around the estate by a small terrier dog, uses heroin but lightly enough to remain 'savvy' about exactly what is going on in the estate. Jason, Ryan and the other dealers dread being asked to look after Nate's dog, because they know that if it gets lost, injured or killed on their watch, they may well be crippled in return.

The directors first bumped into the head of the firm by accident, during their second week filming on the estate. 'We came round the corner with our cameras and suddenly there was this guy with Rob, stocky with tattoos, just staring at us. He had the look of violence and the look he was giving us was saying without doubt "turn that camera off now otherwise I'll smash it to pieces", so we turned it off and went,' says one director.

The documentary makers had no idea who he was but a

few weeks later were approached by him in the estate's pub, asking for £10,000 protection money to be able to film on the estate. After a few days the documentary makers and the head of the firm, Doug, came to a more amicable agreement. Doug would allow the filming to go ahead on 'his' estate, as long as none of the firm would be identified and that he was able to have his say.

Doug, who like Rob has connections with Glasgow's crime families, likes to see himself as an old-school gangster, with morals. To all intents and purposes, he is a local businessman, who enjoys a round of golf and taking his wife and friends out to dinner at expensive restaurants. He gave £2,000 to a local football team so they could afford their own strip.

But he is also the figure behind most of the crack, cocaine and heroin sold in the town in which the estate sits and who sanctions the violence carried out as part of that trade. He has contempt for most of his underlings, and for the drug addicts who buy his product. It became apparent that Doug, as head of the local drug firm, has a far more powerful influence on the day-to-day lives of those living on the estate than the head of the residents' association, the police or the local council.

'I pop into the estate a few times a week, to keep things under control, to see if there are any problems and make sure my dealers are not getting too rowdy with the coppers [attracting too much attention with the police],' says Doug, who we meet in one of east Humberside's most expensive restaurants. 'But the police usually leave us alone.' He says the use of violence by drug dealers is a myth, but quickly admits that around once a month violent acts become a necessity 'because people get ripped off or someone comes into your area'.

He has little respect for those involved in the business end of his firm. 'Drug addicts are feeble-minded, they are weak. I've had lots of tragedies in my life but I'm not a drug addict. A lot of the dealers are imbeciles. Once a month I'll sack one of them, and every six months I'll make sure I change them even if they are good, because they start getting greedy. I don't trust anyone.'

Doug recycles his work mobile phones every two weeks. He talks about specific drugs and meeting points on the phone in coded language.

'My biggest fear? Two things: one of my people getting caught and turning; and a confiscation order.'

The directors, who pulled back from filming the activities of the drug firm after the channel which commissioned the programme decided against including the drugs angle, says the recession is having a palpable effect on people's lives. 'Derek, a scaffolder who lives on the estate, who has never broken the law in his life, is so short of money with a family to support he has asked for a job in the firm selling cocaine. There are prostitutes having sex for £20 – the equivalent of two low-purity rocks of crack – who will set up their punters to be robbed by a bunch of thirteen-year-olds.

'Life on this estate is desperate and drugs is a big part of it all. Some residents see drug dealing on the estate as abhorrent, and they want to ban kids from the precinct, but some see it as part of the fabric of life, they see it as better than moneylending, for example. People don't sign on, purely so they can stay off the radar and live from the alternative economy.

'A lot of the crime here is neighbours robbing off each other. There was a woman who ran the bookmaker's and she used to look after one of the local heroin addicts and give him tea every day, but he ended up robbing the place. There are sixteen-year-olds saying that the new generation of ten-year-olds are crazy compared to their day.'

The street market in heroin, crack and cannabis is the only visible section of the drug trade, but the drug hubs of our cities serve far larger consumer bases.

Such are the rewards offered by the student market, for example, that heroin and crack dealers have been known to enrol for degrees to get closer to their customers. Hampshire Police uncovered three such cases in Southampton in 2009. As students, the dealers also enjoyed the benefits of cheap accommodation in prime city locations, discounts and exemption from tax. One dealer described the allure: 'Students can rely on mummy and daddy's credit card to pay the bills when things go wrong. They are a reliable source of cash, once you apply a little pressure. Now the money is flowing back our way; from the haves to the have-nots.'

On the street, brawn, muscle and backup are key. But most street dealers find it hard to blend into mainstream society to sell their wares. Being street smart and having an air of violence are qualities required on the street, but are more likely to cause attention in the world inhabited by the socially accepted, where the transaction takes place behind closed doors.

*

The black BMW glides to a halt on a side street in the swanky London district of Knightsbridge. Behind the wheel is Kareem, a working-class boy from north London who earns a living selling high-purity powder cocaine to London's privileged set. Underneath the driver's seat is a pouch containing sixteen wraps of cocaine – enough to cover the morning shift: two five-star hotels and a luxury penthouse in Chelsea.

Scanning the street for police, Kareem slips the wraps into his jacket pocket. As he steps on to the pavement, he almost bumps into a woman balancing a large Starbucks coffee in one hand and a tiny dog in the other. She says something in Italian and struts off in the direction of Hyde Park. Kareem bleeps his car doors shut, but can't help noticing that his prized motor looks a bit shabby next to the Bentleys and Maseratis surrounding it.

The call for the Knightsbridge drop had come earlier that morning from Louise, an escort girl. The majority of Kareem's calls came from girls working at an escort agency run by a family friend. Kareem's job was to provide the cocaine that the girls' super-rich clients demanded. More often than not, the rendezvous was a hotel room costing more per night than most people earn in a month. This time it was a £2,000-a-night suite in one of London's most exclusive hotels, located minutes away from Buckingham Palace and Harrods.

Kareem walks round the corner and sees a team of bellboys dressed in top hat and tails, ferrying suitcases between the hotel's entrance and a waiting fleet of taxis and luxury cars. His half-Japanese, half-British parentage, smart-casual clothes and trendy oversized glasses give Kareem, named after a sheikh his mother once knew, something of the international jet-setter look. He fits in well.

The lobby is lavishly decorated in mahogany and mirrors and buzzing with tourists checking in and out. Piles of designer suitcases cover the lobby floor. Kareem walks through the throng and notices a young girl in a uniform putting out some fresh white orchids for the day and a sign for the hotel's famous bar, a former haunt of Madonna, Leonardo DiCaprio and the young Russian spy Anna Chapman. With a nod and a brief smile to one of the concierges, he gets into the lift and the doors close.

Up on the fourth floor, the carpeted corridors are relatively tranquil. But then Kareem notices a strange, hollow clanging sound. It gets louder as he gets nearer the room number Louise gave him. He knocks twice and the door opens an inch, revealing a petite and pretty blonde girl with blue eyes wearing lingerie. 'Kareem?' she asks. He nods and steps into the reception area of an elegantly furnished suite. He is immediately struck by the heavy odour of sweat and tobacco. To the left is a bathroom clad in Italian marble and on the right is a closed door, behind which Kareem can hear the clanging sound. 'Lou, Kareem's here,' the girl says.

Louise emerges through the door in see-through lingerie. She is followed by a large man in his fifties, naked apart from a huge cowbell hanging from his neck. The bell clangs with every step the clearly intoxicated man makes as he stumbles, dazed and confused, towards Kareem. 'Is this the gentleman with the coke?' he says in a posh London accent, cocking half an eye at Kareem. 'Yes it is,' says Louise, 'and he'll need £360.'

As he takes the cash, Kareem can't help thinking the man looks like an overweight version of the TV newsreader John Suchet. But to his friends and family, his customer is better known as a successful criminal barrister. The cocaine has been ordered to celebrate the halfway period in what has turned into an extended champagne, cocaine and sex session, complete with surreal cowbell fetish. The girls, who the barrister has paid £2,500 each for their company, are used to clients with odd tastes: their previous booking had been a tickling and wrestling session with a blind millionaire for six hours.

Shutting the door on the bizarre scene, Kareem catches the

sound of a sharp slap of hand on buttocks. He takes the lift down to the lobby. Finely dressed Italian, Japanese and American hotel guests are getting ready for a day in the capital. Kareem smiles to the concierge on his way out and pulls up on his phone the next destination on his Saturday morning delivery: a penthouse in Chelsea Harbour.

For Kareem, selling coke was a dream job with perks. It was a passport to a secret world filled with opulent debauchery and exotic characters straight out of a 1970s Playboy Mansion party.

There was the Israeli politician who had a fondness for hiring out two suites at another five-star hotel in Paddington, filling them with naked escort girls and mounds of the drug; the seventy-year-old Lebanese banker who loved to walk Kareem round his north London mansion pointing out photographs on his wall of himself smiling with the likes of Yasser Arafat and Saddam Hussein, before using Kareem's coke to fuel a weekend of gambling; the cocaine-loving gang of young suits at the private members' bar in Soho who boasted they were government economic advisers; the senior analysts in the City who furnished him with a pass card to the exclusive members' lounge at a swanky hotel in Mayfair, where they would meet weekly to discreetly swap cocaine and cash over cocktails.

Although illegal, Kareem saw the trade as a legitimate way to improve his lifestyle. It was a victimless crime, and proved a good living. He averaged £4,000 a month tax-free, close to £50,000 a year, twice the average UK annual salary. His previous job, as an assistant surveyor on the Channel Tunnel, had been fine, but it wasn't enough. He wanted a plush flat, the money to take his girlfriend to the top nightspots and to mingle with the capital's moneyed movers and shakers. Cocaine offered a fast-track route.

'I used to go to clubs and see a group of guys in the VIP sections ordering endless bottles of champagne,' Kareem says over a double cheeseburger and fries. 'I wanted what they had.'

It began with a job at an escort agency run by a family friend. Kareem earned extra cash at weekends taking credit-card payments on a swipe machine and passing to his bosses punters' requests for extras, such as ecstasy, cocaine and Viagra. Kareem, who had always had an interest and an aptitude for finance, eyed a chance to earn some real money. Maybe, he thought, he could be the guy who provided the psychoactive substances that the escort girls and their clients needed. He asked around to see if there was anyone within his family's circle of friends who sold cocaine. Driven by an entrepreneurial spirit, his business quickly expanded, as news of his reliability and quality supply spread.

'All I wanted to do was make money. I wanted everything, and I had all the work I needed. Some of the bankers were doing business with people in Abu Dhabi until 4 a.m., they led stressful lives, and they used cocaine as part of their jobs. Some of my customers could only make it into work after a big night out if they had some coke to set them straight. It felt like I was greasing the wheels of big business, feeding the economy.

'The more cocaine people snort,' says Kareem, 'the more money they spend: in bars, clubs, casinos, lap-dancing joints, hotels. My deliveries often made the difference to whether bar bills were £20, £200 or £2,000. There were never any suspicions or restrictions. It was so easy. I could walk past thousands of concierges or security guards and never get eyeballed.'

To some extent, hotels are the crack houses of the privileged set, where rich people go to take drugs in relative comfort and away from prying eyes. But it is a truth that is kept under wraps with the collusion of hotels, a fact backed by Miles Quest, spokesman for the British Hospitality Association, the umbrella body for hotels.

'Guests taking drugs and hiring escort girls is never talked about openly in the industry. But I would not deny some of this goes on, more than anywhere else, at the top-flight hotels. To a certain degree they turn a blind eye. If you are paying £1,000 a night you can do pretty much whatever you want. Hotels don't want to impinge on their guests' privacy. A lot of our customers are extremely wealthy people, so managers are wary of upsetting them in any way.'

The tendency for wealthy businessmen and the night-time industries to collide was neatly exposed following a police raid on the Capricorn Club in London's West End. Before the 2009 raid it was better known for being the place where Rolling Stone Ronnie Wood met his teenage Russian former girlfriend, Ekaterina Ivanova. But a six-month undercover operation by police had found that it was also a venue where rich clients could buy sex and cocaine. Another establishment where dealers like Kareem were not required was the Bar 9 club in Christopher Street on the edge of the Square Mile – a members-only bar, where customers were buzzed in on a video entryphone, and cocaine was served to City workers alongside their cocktails. During a raid in July 2010 police found £7,500 worth of cocaine, neatly portioned in wraps ready to be handed out with drinks. Four City workers drinking in the bar were arrested for possession.

In the first decade of the millennium, barely a day passed without a story in the media about the spread of middle-class cocaine culture. On his first day as Britain's most powerful policeman, Sir Ian Blair could not hide his disgust at the perceived loose morals of Middle England: 'People are having dinner parties where they drink less wine and snort more cocaine,' he said. 'I'm not interested in what harm it is doing to them personally,' he continued, 'but the price of that cocaine is misery on the streets of London's estates and blood on the roads from Colombia and Afghanistan.' But the Met chief was behind the times. Cocaine's price and availability meant it had already been taken up in droves, not just by the middle classes, but by teenagers and blue-collar workers. Its suitability with alcohol was key. It became the hidden mixer in Britain's drinking culture, it was a sociable drug that could be snorted in cubicles and enabled users to carry on partying into the late hours. Despite falling purity and publicity over the cocaine trade's links with both human and environmental damage, the cocaine brand remained a powerful one.

Alan McGauley, a senior lecturer at Sheffield Hallam University who has advised the government on social policy and drugs, says cocaine, like ecstasy, turned traditional perceptions of Class A drug use on its head. 'Cocaine currently occupies a unique position in the UK. Most users do not see the drug in the same rank as other Class A drugs such as heroin and crack cocaine. It is seen by users as occupying a space close to ecstasy and cannabis. It is not seen as problematic, and users are not seen as victims. Instead it is identified with success. This can explain some of the mixed messages which blight the attempts at harm reduction in relation to cocaine use.'

The pervading atmosphere that cocaine was a clean drug, and one wrapped in commerce, celebrity and creativity, meant that the doors of the City were opened to dealers like Kareem for whom the crime of drug supply offered a taste of the good life: expensive meals, designer clothes, treating his friends, many of whom were at university or unemployed, to nights out.

Kareem's family members were enjoying similar success. His mother and brother both had their own group of customers, and they often worked together. With the rising number of competing escort agencies, many of Kareem's contacts in that world moved on to other things, and Kareem's business shifted to some of those he had been hanging out with at glitzy parties, clubs and hotels, mainly what he described as 'Chelsea Girls', who were 'rolling in cash, had nothing to do all day but take coke'.

But while Kareem was nipping in and out of London establishments with wraps, the 'family business' was being investigated by a team of detectives from the Clubs and Vice Unit at the Metropolitan Police. His double life was soon to become headline news. Kareem and his family were arrested for running what police told reporters was a lucrative highly organised, cocaine-dealing racket. But Kareem got lucky. While they had caught his mother and brother red-handed selling cocaine to undercover officers posing as clubbers in the West End, Kareem's side of the business had not been investigated, because they took down one digit of his mobile number incorrectly. He was only implicated because of the work he took on for his mother when she was abroad.

'As soon as they arrested us they were looking for offshore bank accounts and properties, but they didn't do their homework. My mum leased a Mercedes and lived in a Housing Association property. All they took from me were two iPhones and £1,000. I spent what I earned, and actually had overdrafts coming out of my ears.'

Kareem was sentenced to more than two years in prison and his mother and brother were jailed for three years. He kept to himself in jail and was released in June 2010. 'I met lots of middle-class dealers inside, but what I was doing seemed minuscule compared to them. When I got out it was hard finding a job, I was unemployed for a year. I was tempted to go back to selling cocaine but I didn't want to put my older relatives through that again, so I decided to start from the bottom and begin again.'

Kareem got a job as an estate agent. 'I'm enjoying it. I have targets to hit, incentives. I drive around and meet people all day, in fact it's very similar to what I did. I'm still in the sales business.'

Someone who is able to supply their friends with drugs such as cocaine, ecstasy and cannabis is unlikely to be viewed within their social circle as they would be by the press and politicians. The ability to source and sell drugs has a certain social cache, on a par with getting their friends on the guest list to an exclusive party or getting hold of some knock-down designer clothes.

Some dealers will buy drugs for clients in the entertainment industry or act as personal shoppers for party organisers, sourcing and buying an array of high-quality drugs for a premium so their client does not have to get their fingers dirty. Tour managers, TV runners and personal medics are all in danger of becoming entwined in supplying a demanding celebrity's needs. But beyond VIP rooms the widespread recreational use of drugs has spawned a generation for whom their dealer is their 'friend'.

The middle-class drug dealer is perhaps where cannabis and LSD markets started, but the shift to cocaine markets was a path laid by the ecstasy era, according to Jennifer Ward, author of *Flashback: Drugs and Dealing in the Golden Age of the London*

Rave Scene. It was not only significant in normalising cocaine use, but also in giving the role of the new breed of middle-class dealer a social legitimacy against the fluffy 'loved up' club scene that accompanied it.

'Whether those people thought of themselves as dealers is hard to say, but essentially they were making substantial amounts of money by selling drugs,' says Ward. 'For some it was paying not only for their drugs, but their party lifestyle: the clubs, alcohol, taxis, clothes, it was an expensive way of life; for others it was their job. Suddenly a decade had gone by, and selling Class A drugs became acceptable.'

But even middle-class and ivory-tower markets are not without their elephant traps – their relaxed nature masks real risk. Patrick, a librarian who moved to the Midlands from Ireland as a child, started his ill-fated foray into selling drugs when he was a sixteen-year-old schoolboy. Using money saved from doing odd jobs, he decided he wanted to make his smoking habit more affordable, as well as dip his toes in the forbidden drug world, and bought a £120 ounce of cannabis from his older brother's friend, packaged it into eight bags and sold them at school for £20 each, leaving him with a free £40 bag to himself. He continued selling cannabis to his friends and acquaintances, around three ounces a week, using the profit to pay for his own share. Despite smoking lots of weed and popping the odd ecstasy pill, Patrick was a keen sportsman and academic, and secured a place at the University of Sussex to read English Literature.

During Freshers' Week he found a local supplier of cannabis and ecstasy and continued selling to his new university friends. They had been paying £10 for low-quality pills and Patrick, happy to help out, sold them good ones for as little as 50p. As before, money was not the object in his drug dealing, as long as he made sure he was not out of pocket and that the sales funded his own stash. But it was not just about the drugs.

'I suppose I was a bit of a nerd as a teenager,' says Patrick, ten years on. 'It gave me a buzz, another persona. I was the person who could sort out the pills. It was a social thing, a coolness, a way to relate to people, especially girls. It was easier to integrate, to talk to people and it was great – I found myself plugged into this amazing social network. We would all go to drum and bass clubs, take pills and dance.'

He had just started to buy larger batches from his supplier, taking 200 pills at a time and selling them on, when he was awoken at dawn by a sharp rapping at his front door. The next day Patrick was in a cell in a young offender's institute. Five police officers had found a hundred pills and dealing bags in his top drawer and charged him with intent to supply Class A drugs. At his trial, Patrick denied he was a drug dealer, but his academic record was used as a stick to beat him with. He was an 'intelligent lad' who knew exactly what he was doing. With his parents staring on, Patrick stood in the dock expecting a non-custodial sentence. During the trial he had read about a case in his native Ireland where a dealer had avoided jail after being caught with 700 pills. But the judge sentenced him to two and a half years.

'I had to train myself to be alone,' he says. 'The worst thing about prison was the constant threat of violence. It was a hyper-tense atmosphere. Most days someone would get badly beaten, and I was attacked twice. I can't help but be paranoid. I'm a self-preserver.' His conviction, and the emotional impact of his time in prison remains with him, a phantom from the past. 'Social dealers', as they have been termed by criminologists, are today the most common suppliers of recreational drugs. A 2007 study published by the Joseph Rowntree Foundation into how

182 eleven-to-nineteen-year-olds obtain cannabis found that nearly all of them bought the drug from a friend, with only 6 per cent having ever bought from an unknown seller. Half of them had been involved in cannabis transactions – whether by brokering access for someone or selling cannabis. A study among more than 500 adult cannabis users published in 2012 found only 8 per cent bought drugs from a street dealer. Just over 40 per cent bought their drugs from a friend and one in ten grew their own. During their time as cannabis users, 31 per cent had sold for profit; 32 per cent had sold to fund their own use; 46 per cent had sold for no profit; 67 per cent had bought as part of a large group; and 61 per cent had given cannabis as a gift. Drug sellers, far from the street-corner hustler, are more prevalent than we think.

The 'old school' cannabis dealer, for example, is still active in Britain today. Take Brian, a dealer for over thirty years. He stocks an array of authentic strains of cannabis – from Afghanistan, Morocco, West Africa, Thailand and Cambodia. From the outside his flat looks like every other in a pleasant low-rise estate in Putney, but inside he has recreated the perfect smoking environment: his living room features a shrine to the Hindu god Ganesh, with big cushions, bean bags and Indian patterned throws littering the space. Brian is a ganja connoisseur, and in the era of the profit-driven, mass-market cannabis farms, a rare breed of dealer.

The line between user and dealer is a fine one. Many drug users are also de facto dealers. Heroin and crack users are able to afford their own doses for free if they are willing to sell on the streets to others. For many people social dealing becomes a sideline to pay for holidays or tuition fees, but for others the hobby becomes an obsession and expands into a viable occupation.

Until 2012 with the arrival of new sentencing guidelines,

courts did not formally distinguish between 'for profit' dealers such as Kareem and the street hustlers of Stapleton Road, and those involved in buying and distributing drugs to their friends, often for no financial reward, like Patrick and Brian. Under new guidelines, supposedly, social dealers will avoid prison sentences, while 'for profit' dealers selling heroin or crack can expect at least five years in jail.

The guidelines retreat from prescribing precise amounts of each drug to gauge how serious an offence is. Instead, quantities of drugs are classified into four broad categories, with sentencing determined by whether the offender played a leading, significant or lesser role. The lowest category includes up to 100 g of cannabis, 5 g of heroin or cocaine, and twenty tablets of ecstasy.

Of all the drug market, it is the street dealers, those in daily contact with the public, about whom most of the urban myths about the drug trade have been generated over the past hundred years. From the bare-faced racism of anti-drug campaigns in the US and Britain in the 1920s and 1930s, where the blame for the spread of drugs was firmly placed at the feet of 'Negroes' (cannabis and cocaine) and 'Chinamen' (opium), drug dealers became the modern folk devil. Why else would they sell their wares at the school gates, impregnate children's tattoos with LSD, cut their drugs with brick dust and rat poison, or sell cannabis laced with crack cocaine?

In reality drug dealers do none of these things. These are all examples of real-life scare stories that received widespread media attention before being disproven, yet have remained urban myths to be repeated ad nauseam by journalists and politicians. The fact these myths are allowed to flourish masks a fundamental lack of knowledge about who and what a drug dealer is. One of the main misunderstandings about dealers is that they are out to harm their customers, a major mistake in any business. As one dealer reportedly said: 'Happy addicts come back, unhappy ones buy elsewhere.'

For criminologist Dick Hobbs, there has been a seismic shift in Britain in the way in which the drugs industry is perceived. Drugs are no longer part of an illicit black economy but part of a wider 'grey' economy with which we all interact, knowingly or not – one that has spread from its roots in the inner cities into the suburbs and out into Middle England.

The huge demand for recreational and hard drugs since the 1960s means that drug use has become normalised. Where once people were fearful of drugs, ongoing exposure to drug culture has numbed them; where policing once had impact, now it can merely shape the market.

It is an industry that welcomes all. By no means all drug dealers are the dispossessed, junkies or gun-toting teenagers. As the cases going through the British court system have revealed, they are also students, housewives, middle-class professionals and upper-class hobbledehoys. In 2007, Aurelien Goldstein, an account manager for Quintessentially, one of the world's most exclusive and largest concierge clubs, owned by Ben Elliot, the nephew of Camilla Parker Bowles, was caught by an undercover *Sunday Times* reporter offering to provide 30 g of cocaine. The firm, which boasts that it can supply its wealthy members with just about anything they require, has airlifted elm tea bags to Madonna and found a dozen albino peacocks for Jennifer Lopez's party. Cocaine, however, was most definitely not on their menu, and they offloaded Goldstein after he was caught offering a Quintessentially member, who he believed to be a wealthy businessman holding a party, the cocaine at a pricey £68 a gram.

With the rise in recreational drug use there are now many more people aware of the huge profits that can be harvested from street markets and social-supply circles. They also know about the apparent ease with which the transaction can be carried out and fortunes made. Low-level street dealing, which has become widespread among urban teenagers, has effectively become a 'school for scoundrels' and a fast-track escalator to the middle market of the UK drug industry, a market that operates above street level.

3

Network

From Underworld to Virtual World

Marco's office looks like many other small businesses: a couple of desks, swivel chairs, PCs and telephones – nothing to reveal the true nature of his enterprise. If you were to see him in the street, the likelihood is that you wouldn't give him a second's thought. In his mid-thirties, tanned, and dressed in the anonymous urban outfit of jeans, trainers and a Fred Perry shirt, he looks like the young dad next door who needs to get more sleep. But that is how he likes it. In Marco's world, little is how it appears.

Entering his zone is not easy and is only ever achieved by degrees. Marco's life is hidden behind a one-way mirror of charm, a number of identities and the ability to disappear into a crowd at any moment. Much of the time he is softly spoken, happy to hold court in conversations on topics ranging from world events to local politics, but at other moments he speaks in a tone of menace that can leave a shiver running down your spine.

His public persona is that of a struggling small businessman, but behind this thin veneer he lives a very different and more lucrative life. Marco runs an audacious hashish-distribution service that makes on average £3,000 a day. He is a seasoned importer and a broker of bulk consignments to other dealers, operating under a number of assumed identities while disguising his activities by channeling his profits into apparently legitimate business interests while conducting his projects from seemingly innocent premises.

At times his office is a processing and packaging plant. Kilos of warm hashish and sticky skunk are divided and weighed into hundreds of 'deals' by casual staff wielding kitchen knives. The deals are laid out on a mile of cling film that is sliced into tiny squares to form wraps, then dispatched to teams of waiting dealers.

At others it is a meeting place bristling with adrenaline, crowded with hired muscle awaiting a bulk delivery. All present would be acutely aware that this is when the operation is at its most vulnerable – to police and to ambush by rivals. The chatter among the hired muscle is nervous – a motley crew comparing past conflicts. Meanwhile Marco steers a courier to a middle-market exchange by telephone.

He describes the appearance of the man his courier is to meet and the location and the colour of the hire car in which 30 kg of cannabis sits in cardboard boxes waiting to be driven back to Marco's office. After confirming the exchange of cash and contraband the tension drops, the deal is done and Marco nervously awaits the safe delivery of the merchandise to his door. No one wants the delivery to be punctuated by a raid from rival dealers before the product is split into bags and boxes and dispatched.

It is a bipolar world of intense rushes of activity followed by mind-numbing boredom and for much of the time the office is empty. Marco is a go-to dealer, with the skills and contacts that place him at the heart of a new generation of narco-entrepreneurs.

On his desk sits a copy of *Stop the Ride, I Want to Get Off: The Autobiography of Dave Courtney*, part of a library of what Marco calls 'old war stories'. To the modern breed of drug trafficker, tales like these are now viewed as a slice of ancient history.

Courtney's colourful autobiography spans three decades – from the East End's Kray twins and family firms in the 1960s; their evolution to the crime syndicates of bank robbers in the 1970s; and their transition in the 1980s to the Mr Bigs of the drugs trade that formed the foundation for what was to become known as British organised crime.

Perhaps last in the line of the Great British drug barons is 'Cocky' Warren, who epitomised the get-rich-quick philosophy, pouring drugs into the UK and his profits into a real-estate portfolio valued at some £300 million. Paradoxically, while Cocky is perhaps one of the final Mr Bigs, his mode of operation helped to open up the fluid middle market in which Marco now works to a whole generation of British criminals. But his brazen approach was also to be his downfall.

Cocky, from Toxteth in Liverpool, learnt his trade first in heroin and then cocaine, before usurping traditional lines of supply by flying out to Colombia in person. He became a trusted client of Colombian cocaine cartels, as well as opening up lines of credit with Turkish heroin suppliers that allowed him to flood markets countrywide, seizing the opportunities opened up by the bulk shipping methods of containerisation that transformed global trade by offering concealed transport in a way never utilised before.

But his notorious reputation and very public criminal identity have led him into a war of attrition with the authorities, which has kept him behind bars for more than a decade and won him a status on release which will mean a life of virtual house arrest that makes him an unlikely role model.

For Marco the measure of a successful criminal is time served *outside* prison. While he has had a go at getting rich quick, he is more interested in his long-term goal: of owning enough legitimate businesses and rental properties to keep him in his old age. He seeks to avoid violence, police attention and dealing in Class As in his bid to stay off the radar. For Marco the drug market may have started on the street but it has spanned an ever-evolving market.

He undertook his own internship and his experience and know-how make him a go-to man in the new social order. In the late 1980s, when Marco found himself in west London at the age of fourteen and the breadwinner in the family, hustling hashish seemed the obvious vocation for a 'third-generation immigrant who had to put food on the table'. He has been successful. His career has spanned Marbella, Amsterdam and London, switching between illicit trade in drugs and legitimate enterprises. For three years he lived in Marbella, working behind the scenes trafficking cocaine and cannabis from Morocco into Europe.

From there he moved to Amsterdam where he managed shops selling magic mushrooms and legal psychedelics for two years. And when he became 'homesick for Blighty' he returned, joining the gold rush of seed sales, fresh magic mushrooms and commercial cannabis cultivation in the East End.

With each stage of his career he has built connections and trust that are the foundations for his current profession, a career criminal who is in a favoured position. He is what police refer to as a money man, capable of paying hired staff to handle the product every step of the way, and in case of arrest he can furnish his charges with a well-informed solicitor, references and counselling for that all-important court appearance, and what police protection can't provide: the promise of a job in the future.

But while much of his turnover is tied up in firewalling himself so that he appears as little more than a bystander in the business – hiring couriers, muscle and runners – after a good couple of decades Marco is capable of funding ventures where he wishes. Strip joints, escort agencies, pubs and cafés all find favour in a world where daily profits have to be hidden and each investment could lead to an eventual jackpot situation where he makes the transition from criminal to legitimate businessman.

Marco doesn't see *Stop the Ride* as an executive self-help book, or Cocky as a professional role model. 'In those days it was all being known, about having a public reputation, but these days it's about staying off the police radar, blending in,' he says. 'Many of the old family faces are still involved as money men or perhaps sitting in retirement thinking about their next big deal. But everyone I deal with is a generation on. The days of the Mr Big are over.'

As an aspiring career criminal Marco's ascent to Britain's middle market would not have been possible two decades ago, but as the UK drug market has extended its reach from the coast to the street it has flung open its doors to a new raft of opportunistic 'businessmen', enthusiastic amateurs and would-be kingpins. The UK's middle market is now a 'sweetspot' in the global drug market that delivers premium profits. Sharing the market with Marco are the criminal corporations of the drug industry that are constantly recruiting to maintain a steady flow of drugs washing over Britain's borders, with the ability to turn civilians into small-time kingpins overnight.

Duncan, a stocky, tattooed Glaswegian in his early forties, describes himself as a 'businessman'. He is a broker in Britain's port-to-street cocaine trail. He buys expensive, high-purity cocaine from traffickers in London, dilutes it to breaking point with cutting agents, repackages it and passes it on down the line to the street, creaming off a healthy £100,000 profit from an annual £2 million turnover. Like many small-time gangsters, he enjoys milking the notoriety that goes with the territory, but is planning on getting out of the game while his luck is still with him.

As we drive through the countryside of England's bleak east coast, he wearily undertakes a series of manoeuvres – U-turns, driving down dead-end streets and repeatedly going around roundabouts – designed to spot and shake off anyone trying to follow him. He has the paranoid, violent air of a gangster and, as he tells us, two machetes in the boot of his car. On the back seat sit his tax returns for the legitimate business that acts as the front for ill-gotten gains.

Six years ago, Duncan was working as a delivery driver for a coffee company. He says he was earning enough to get by, but he was not content. His connections in Glasgow's gangland world threw up an opportunity. In 2006, he heard on the grapevine that a Colombian gangster from his home city was recruiting 'super couriers': trustworthy people prepared to fly to South America and bring back large amounts of cocaine. The deal on the table was that he would fly to the island of Margarita off the coast of Venezuela, pick up 15 kg of cocaine (worth £750,000) and bring it back. He would be paid the equivalent of £160,000: £10,000 in cash and 3 kg of the cocaine, worth £150,000.

In what he calls 'a moment of madness' Duncan decided to take up the offer. As he drove to the airport he remembers being in floods of tears, crying out of sheer fright at the task that lay before him. He turned round and started driving back home before realising that the Colombian gangster had paid £2,500 up front for his trip, and there was *no* going back.

Duncan arrived safely and followed his instructions. On the return plane journey, he was on crutches, a ruse he thought would deflect suspicion. He befriended the woman sitting next to him and it was she who ended up wheeling the suitcases packed with three-quarters of a million pounds in high-purity cocaine through Customs, as Duncan hobbled along behind her. They both got through undetected. He has been distributing drugs ever since.

'It's a stressful life,' says Duncan. 'After an hour in the gym in the morning the phone starts ringing at 9 a.m. and it only stops when I turn it off. I don't condone using drugs myself, I get my buzz off money, respect and power.'

Duncan is typical of the thousands of middlemen: he is able to short-circuit the usually multi-layered route between smugglers and the street because he has contacts who can provide him with 'off the boat'-purity cocaine.

He is sent samples of new shipments of the product in small bullet-shaped packages. He tests its purity by using ammonia to wash away any cutting agents. Four out of five deliveries are below par, but when he sees a product that is above 90 per cent purity he sends a courier to Islington in north London to pick up a kilo, for which he pays half of the £58,000 up front and half once he has sold it all.

The firm that supplies Duncan, usually on a monthly basis, sometimes invites him to London for meetings, where he is put up in a hotel room and provided with a driver. The organisation, which has Colombian connections but is run by a Chinese man, is, according to Duncan, a big global outfit with heavy investments in trafficking drugs, capable of selling on hundreds of kilos of cocaine at a time.

Every minute that Duncan is in possession of his kilo of high-purity cocaine is a window of opportunity for the police.

But it is at this stage where the real money-spinner comes in. Using an ordinary kitchen blender, he expands his 1 kg of real cocaine into 10 kg of street-ready 'cocaine' by mixing 900 parts of benzocaine with every 100 parts of cocaine.

Benzocaine, a harmless dental anaesthetic that numbs the tongue but gives no drug high, is the most common chemical used by British gangs to adulterate cocaine. It is available on the grey market in drums for £2,000 a kg, and its price has been rapidly increasing. Although it is a legal substance, those found in possession of large amounts of benzocaine can be prosecuted for intent to supply drugs. Duncan says he has to be careful where he buys benzocaine these days because police are selling drums of it on eBay to try and root out cocaine dealers.

Once he has his kg of ten-per-cent-pure cocaine (the average purity of cocaine seized on Britain's streets is around 25 per cent) he repackages it to make it look like it has just come off the boat. He uses a small strong-arm press to pack the cocaine into slabs, which are then wrapped and stamped with a false mark of authenticity. He will then sell the product on to a small group of upper-level dealers at £10,000 a kg, making a profit margin after buying his original kilo and the benzocaine of £24,000. His dealers will make their own profit, merely by filtering down the kg to the street dealers in 36 ounce-weight packages at between £800 and £900 each, at a profit of around £20,000 per kg.

'The biggest change in the drug trade since I've been involved has been people's willingness to buy poor quality cocaine,' says Duncan. He admits that most dealers know repackaged cocaine slabs have been tampered with and are not genuine, but that they buy it anyway because 'it's a psychological thing' and 'they are all thick as fuck'.

Duncan, who has met the infamous Liverpool drug trafficker and uber-gangster Curtis 'Cocky' Warren, who he describes as 'too cool for school', admits the old-school gangster era is now at an end because he believes that the old moral code of politeness and friendship is being eroded. But Duncan has clung to some of the old-school habits. He says he plays pool regularly with a police detective, and the two get on like old friends.

'They'll give me a few steers every now and again, who's hot [who is being watched by police], and they don't ask for any money. They tell me that the police will sometimes find £100,000 worth of drugs, declare £70,000 of it and pocket the rest.'

Marco and Duncan are members of Britain's burgeoning middle market. Sitting one level above the street where the transaction takes place, they are part of a growing number of players – importers, regional wholesalers and brokers – who do not fit neatly into any pyramid of supply that has traditionally been used to cement the structure of the UK drug market.

While Marco and Duncan serve very local communities, they have global reach and are able to take a large slice of the profits that were once the sole preserve of a criminal elite known as Britain's Mr Bigs. They reflect the rise of the little man and the 'amateur' drug criminal in the UK drugs market, a shift in the balance of power away from the generation of crime families that first took hold of the drugs trade.

In the past, the UK drug market was largely a closed shop with the big names of crime controlling importation and holding the supply contacts. They were family firms that recruited from within the criminal fraternity, whom they trusted to maintain the 'code of silence' that insulated them from law enforcers. Colombian cartels and Turkish heroin suppliers would ensure delivery to Spain or to British waters, and British criminals would then organise the consignments' safe entry into the UK and their distribution through the UK's middle market where it would be broken down in distinct stages on its way to the street.

But when the UK Drug Policy Commission revisited the traditional pyramid model in 2008 it found that the new entrepreneurial sector was beginning to turn the traditional monopoly inside out.

The UK market is open to all, said the report, and while partly shaped by policing, is highly resilient when it comes to enforcement and economic change. There was no mention of Mr Bigs. New networks, players and means of supply had created a near-free market. But what had happened to Britain's colourful criminal elite? Who now runs UK Drug Plc? And how does the middle market operate and cloak its operation?

To understand how the British market above street level has evolved, one needs to step back in time to an age when crime and drugs existed in different worlds.

Until 1970 the illicit drug trade rarely raised comment among UK criminals. It was run by hippy adventurers, shady entrepreneurs and immigrants seeking a better life. The British criminal had focused first on neighbourhood crime – extortion, burglary and robbery – before giving way to a generation of armed robbers epitomised by the Great Train Robbers. Unlike their counterparts in the US and Italy, British criminals had been too conservative to enter the drug trade. And before the Summer of Love there had been little demand.

Where US and Italian criminals had enriched their coffers through their involvement in the alcohol and drug trades and had bought influence in institutions and a cloak of respectability, the British criminal had no alternative identity, it was visible to the eye and locked into local communities. Crime was cooped up in the inner cities. The East End of London is perhaps the best-known example of an area synonymous with the criminal underworld and a generation of bank robbers active across the capital.

Echoes of the old underworld where cops, journalists and gangsters drank together in the same pubs from mid-morning still existed in the mid-1980s when Dick Hobbs started studying the crime world in east London. 'It was incredible, a separate world and probably the only time when the police – although wildly corrupt – had a handle on what was going on,' says Hobbs. 'It was like being in an episode of *The Sweeney*. The mystique around criminality, the private drinking clubs and late-night bars that you could loosely call the underworld as we knew it then have now largely disappeared,' he says, almost with an air of disappointment. 'In part, that is down to drugs and Bertie Smalls.'

The late Derek Creighton 'Bertie' Smalls was a slightly over-weight North Londoner who sported a Mexican moustache. He was a member of the Wembley Mob, a 'blagger' who terror-ised victims by shooting a sawn-off shotgun into the air. Like others of the time, he was prolific. But he was also Britain's first supergrass whose evidence would play a part in bringing together the British drug and crime cultures.

Smalls was arrested in his underpants during a dawn raid after a £138,000 robbery at a Barclays Bank in Wembley in August 1972. Fearing that he could be jailed for up to twenty-five years, Smalls produced a sixty-five-page statement naming more than thirty robbers and identifying twenty raids between 1968 and 1972, which had yielded nearly £1.5 million. In return he was pardoned for all his previous crimes and he and his family were moved to a safe house and given new identities.

For Hobbs, who wrote Smalls' obituary in the *Independent*, this was a defining moment for British crime, the fallout from which would not only cross-pollinate the relationship between drugs and crime in Britain but would propel local crime lords onto the international stage. But it also undermined the traditional 'code of silence' that had bound the criminal underworld together.

'Perhaps the most significant aspect of Smalls' life was the way in which he broke for ever the myth of an underworld code of silence . . . other "supergrasses" followed in his wake. Armed robbery in London increased during the following decade, before gradually giving way to drug dealing as the felony of choice for career-minded villains.'

Following the Smalls case, many of London's most notorious criminals were split into two camps: one serving time in prison, the other on the run in Spain. Those in prison came into contact with a new generation of mainly middle-class criminals, students who knew about drugs and were serving time for importing cannabis or manufacturing LSD. The bank robbers realised that there was serious money to be made on the back of the new drug culture and, as the maximum sentence for drug trafficking was increased to life imprisonment in 1985, it was only natural that criminal gangs would inherit the trade from the hippy adventurers or entrepreneurs put off by the risk of being locked up for good.

Those who had fled to the Costa del Sol, chiefly as a result of the collapse of the extradition arrangements between Britain and Spain, were looking across to Morocco and considering their futures: they had ill-gotten gains from their bank robberies to invest. Spain had long been established as the entry point into Europe for North African hashish. But it wasn't just boatloads of cannabis that the former bank robbers had their eyes on – while Spanish police tolerated their cannabis capers, British gangs were beginning to forge links with a new breed of South American cocaine traffickers.

Until the mid-1980s the Colombian cocaine industry had been dominated by the Medellin and Cali cartels that trafficked huge amounts of the drug to America. When this monopoly fragmented, thanks to successful efforts to halt the trade into the US, smaller gangs were forced to seek fresh markets. One of these turned out to be Europe and it was a change of strategy that fuelled the rapid expansion of the cocaine market in many parts of the Continent during the 1990s and 2000s.

British criminals sunning themselves were perfectly placed to take advantage. The increased availability of cocaine turned it into a viable commodity for British gangs, and the floodgates to the UK market were effectively opened. Suddenly, British criminals were richer than they had ever been and former bank robbers became notorious international celebrities cocking a snook from sunnier climes at the British authorities. But their time at the top was to be limited.

A Customs campaign in 1998, Operation Extend, uncovered a supply network of shipments from Colombia, Mexico, Brazil and Panama. The Mr Big behind the operation was Brian Brendan Wright. 'The Milkman' – nicknamed thus because he always delivered – is said to have smuggled three tonnes of cocaine worth £1 billion into Britain. Although he escaped the reach of Operation Extend, Wright was eventually sentenced to 30 years in jail.

Light aircraft dropped drugs to offshore speedboats that in turn passed the drugs to yachts based in the Caribbean, Venezuela and South Africa, which then made the 3,500-mile voyage to UK waters. Locally registered British vessels then rendezvoused to pick up the contraband before putting into port several days later. Those onshore awaiting delivery would be informed of the pick-up point at the last minute by mobile phone. Operation Extend was one of a number of major busts that would change the drug industry and undermine the status quo, clearing the way for today's 'open market'.

In part, this police obsession with the Mr Bigs of the industry was highly effective. Major losses hit British gangs and their suppliers hard. To avoid detection, methods of distribution, supply lines and how drug deals were brokered all changed.

Cocaine and heroin suppliers reacted by easing out Britain's Mr Bigs, choosing to send large consignments through a supply chain of 'clean-skin' representatives, many of whom operated behind a screen of legitimate businesses running established import-export agencies.

Africa has superseded Jamaica as the natural trans-shipment point for the UK from South America, spawning drug hubs in Cape Verde, Mali, Benin, Togo, Nigeria, Guinea-Bissau and Ghana. In West Africa alone, the UN puts the value of the business at $900 million annually with between 30 and 35 tonnes arriving in the region each year.

Edging ever closer to Britain, cocaine cartels have co-opted the Balkan Route, the established route from Afghanistan and Central Asia for heroin entering first western Europe and then Britain. With its anchor point in Turkey, routes through the Balkans span Greece, Albania, Italy, Turkey, Bulgaria, Serbia, Montenegro, Bosnia and Herzegovina, Croatia, Slovenia, Italy, Austria, Romania, Hungary, the Czech Republic, Poland and Germany.

With the opening of the Channel Tunnel and the arrival of super-cheap long-haul air travel and last-minute flight-booking services, suppliers have unleashed a daily wave of couriers as the industry has moved towards moving smaller but more frequent consignments to avoid putting – and losing – all their eggs in one basket.

These changes, alongside the introduction of cutting agents, have created a global open market, where the profits reaped from the middle-market players can now match those made previously by traffickers. It is a sweetspot that has made the fortunes of previously local small-time players and drawn the global cartels ever deeper into the UK drug economy.

Spain and Holland remain key hubs where UK criminals broker deals but, since the old family firms no longer hold a monopoly, many of the brokers of Europe that once refused to deal with smaller UK players have opened their doors. The shrinking effect on lines of supply in the market was described in 2011 when the Scottish Crime and Drugs Enforcement Agency outlined how the new market worked. 'Previously Scottish criminals would go to Manchester, Liverpool or London. Now they're flying to Amsterdam and dealing direct.'

London, Birmingham and Liverpool, and other cities throughout the country have become home to the representatives of the heroin and cocaine suppliers, enabling small-time players such as Duncan access to bulk prices and purity.

The UK now ranks as the second-largest drug market in the world after the US. It is a perfect example of the ridiculousness of current drug policy: the harder law-enforcement agencies make it for people to smuggle and distribute drugs, the more profit there is to be made. So as with the smuggling of drugs into Category A prisons, the ultimate in enforcement lockdowns, the harder it is, the higher are the rewards for those prepared to take the risk.

'Drug dealing is profitable, or better compensated, in the UK today precisely because it's risky,' says Peter Reuter, professor in the Department of Criminology at the University of Maryland and an expert on global trafficking who has played a key role in informing the UN of the scale and size of the industry. 'You have a higher chance of going to prison but, if you're willing to get higher returns, it attracts perhaps different people and generates higher incomes, which is why drug dealers appear to make more money in the UK [than elsewhere in Europe].'

Britain's burgeoning middle market has developed in a 'blind spot' of the authorities that had their sights set on the elite of the British crime scene. Studies of drug supply were rare in comparison with studies of drug consumption, and the authorities held a stereoscopic view of drug crime – it existed at street level and in the form of a foreign threat from importers that included the UK's Mr Bigs, but the mechanics of how the home market worked had remained an area of little research.

'The police were very specific – they knew all about the guys at the top, the "level one" criminals that controlled the drugs at the point of production in Morocco, Turkey, Amsterdam; and the "level three" criminals selling on the street, but it was the middle market – level two – they didn't understand,' says Hobbs, whom the Home Office charged with producing a profile of the UK drug market in 2001. 'It was as if it was the missing link. I told them that was where the market was converging, the middle-market dealers were the ones driving the market.'

It is a study that helped to form the foundations of how the authorities now look at crime. In one section of this research – *King Pin? A Case Study of a Middle-Market Drug Broker* – Hobbs put flesh on the workings of a small but extremely busy middle-market drug distribution network. He revealed a very different side of the market from that previously assumed to exist, one that Hobbs says puts the anchor of the drug trade not in a criminal underworld but in mainstream society, in a grey zone where legal activities serve to hide the true nature of middle-market players.

His case study focused on a legitimate small business with one employee who acted as a delivery boy and who was paid £450 a week to deliver bulk orders of Class A drugs. There were no overt criminal trappings to the business. Drugs were exchanged in cardboard boxes in the car parks of high-street shopping centres. The business dealt in a variety of drugs, dipping in and out of the market where the dealer saw an opportunity.

It is not so much that Britain's crime families just disappeared as that they dropped off the radar. As the Mr Bigs were toppled the industry fell into the hands of the quiet members of the criminal fraternity who had established businesses that had formed a nexus between the criminal economy and the mainstream before the advent of drugs – fencing stolen goods, laundering money, providing getaway cars. It was a grey zone of legality that had evolved from Arthur Daley-style second-hand car lots, scrap metal yards and builders' merchants.

But the end of the underworld didn't just coincide with the introduction of drugs to the menu of British crime, nor with the end of the code of silence.

The communities in which it had been cooped up moved out of their old neighbourhoods, taking their survival skills to fresh pastures. From east London, communities were scattered across Essex, Southend, Chelmsford and Colchester. In south London, crime firms that had been based in Bermondsey, Deptford and Lewisham moved to Kent and the Medway towns. It was a process that was happening to a lesser or greater extent across the country.

Criminals who had once relied on violent reputations soon found that overt displays of thuggery merely drew attention. Servicing the recreational and Class A drug markets meant building contacts in fresh social circles and developing new ways of working. Drugs changed the way in which British crime thought and operated. What had been a closed shop of armed robbers became a near-open network of small-time commodity brokers at a time when Britain was embracing a culture of the entrepreneur.

Networking is still the key to success in the middle market that is the focus of operations at the offices of the Association of Chief Police Officers in London, which since 2006 has housed a 'radar' that is tracking the activities of a new order of British-based criminals.

It holds the details of more than 7,000 organised-crime gangs. Of these, 50 per cent – 3,500 gangs and around 21,000 individuals – are involved in drug crime above street level. Of those, 70 per cent are involved in importation: 45 per cent specialising in cocaine and crack, 22 per cent in heroin, and 22 per cent in cannabis.

The database is not a physical map of crime, as some tabloids have attempted to portray it. It is a 'Linked In' of crime: who knows who, what the connection might be, skills, personal interests, relationships built in school, work or prison, family ties. But as the world has shrunk through globalisation, gangs now have contacts worldwide.

Of foreign OCGs based in the UK and involved in trafficking 8 per cent are from Africa, 20 per cent from the US, 25 per cent are from Asia and the rest are European. It is the global diaspora that has inherited the zones of Britain's cities once known as the homes of the indigenous criminal classes. But while the ability of small organisations to offer door-to-door trafficking services may have fractured the pyramid model, their impact on the UK market is limited, often supplying only very small communities.

Drugs cut across all sectors of violent and economic crime. Risks attributed to OCGs include extreme violence: 6 per cent of those monitored have been involved with kidnapping, 20 per cent use firearms, 20 per cent commit serious violence, 5 per cent are involved in extortion, 33 per cent take part in acquisitive crime, with 10 per cent involved in fraud.

It is a broad church. Some like Marco play their ace card of family ties in a country known for supply, warehousing or trans-shipment but are effectively sole traders. Of the top 10 per cent of organised-crime groups, according to ACPO, around 350 groups hold assets in the millions, while thirty-five of them have more than £10 million in assets such as property across Europe, gold, bonds and businesses.

But the UK market is dominated by Mr Middles, according to the most comprehensive study of high-end trafficking among 222 convicted dealers, conducted on behalf of the Home Office in 2007.

This study sought to define the drug business as a market where dealers were traders – as opposed to crooks – in a bid to discover how they entered the sector, how they perceived and reacted to risk, and what were their modes of operation.

Far from being large family firms, 80 per cent of traffickers operated in small or medium-sized enterprises, using structures found within the legitimate world of business, such as sole traders, partnerships and companies.

While two-thirds of the interviewees entered the drug market for financial reasons the average trafficker made approximately £100,000 a year as opposed to the street myth of 'football money'.

Prison was seen as an 'occupational hazard' rather than as a significant deterrent. It did not appear to be an important point of entry into the drug market, but was an important factor in establishing their credibility and generating trust.

Violence was the final regulator of the industry in the middle market. But without the need for a public intimidatory reputation, and with the need to avoid police scrutiny, any such activity, although extreme, will be a private matter. And, to a large extent, maintaining supply will take priority over settling disputes.

Without the code of silence that the family firms once fostered, enterprises of all sizes firewall themselves by employing runners, couriers, security and sales people with information restricted on a need-to-know basis.

Some crime gangs now specialise in logistics and HGV work, others in supplying security or muscle or guns, while others act within their workplaces overseeing the passage of 'product' through Customs, making suitcases, containers and other shipments – and profits – disappear.

Finding influence within a legitimate company or profession was seen as the fastest way to grow a business – influence in a haulage company, courier service or taxi rank can ease distribution, while secure warehousing, factory space or offices offer room to store and process drugs.

'Contagious' was the only word authors could find to describe the ability of drug dealing to spread in a review of drug research for the Beckley Foundation in 2007. Three-quarters of people entering the drug trade did so through their knowledge of the industry or their contacts within it, while less than 10 per cent entered the trade through their experience of drug use.

But the industry applies a two-tier recruitment policy. Among the seasoned traders, such as Marco, there is still an emphasis on building long-term relationships, getting to know their colleagues, but about those people it invites to join, such as Duncan, they appear to know very little. And the skills required are few: some sort of business sense and no qualms in breaking the law.

With the changing nature of drug crime and the introduction of cutting agents, the sector has been searching ever further afield for connections outside its traditional recruiting ground.

In 2010, for example, the slight and somewhat eerie-looking David Wain was jailed for twelve years for importing and selling seventeen tons of cutting agents in nine months – matching the established legal UK sales of the substances to authorised buyers. He operated his quasi-legal company Sourceachem from his mother's house. He had no previous connection with the cocaine trade, nor apparently had he been near the drug in his life. But he was a major supplier to gangs across the UK.

It is a fluid world where networks intertwine, upsetting perceived linear hierarchies while drawing in individuals, businesses or professions to cloak activities and launder profits. Hobbs describes the market as a mishmash of players who operate in the world around us. 'Among this fragmented middle market you have another life as well, where your master identity is not that of a dealer,' explains Hobbs.

For Hobbs the real machinery of the UK drug trade is operated by white indigenous players who after three decades in the trade have learnt to camouflage their activities and have become well situated in the UK economic landscape with assets in property, transport and security firms that form the fabric and infrastructure required to make the wheels of the vast industry turn. But such businesses also provide a veneer of respectability.

'If you're a courier-company director and your firm gets done it's difficult for that person to be tainted because their master identity is of a company director who has taken a few risks, and in the law's eyes that is completely different to the full-time dealer who is clearly an evil person who lives in the underworld.'

Court cases used to offer a window on the kingpin lifestyles of the criminal elite. They now offer a window on the new face of British drug crime that is concealed in the mainstream.

In 2012, Philip Baron was dubbed Britain's 'last remaining kingpin' as he and his cohorts were handed sentences totalling 200 years for importing £300m worth of narcotics into the UK over a 15-year period. Baron hid his activities from the authorities in Ireland, where he lived, by using a deckchair-rental company in Spain and disguising 55 tonnes of consignments by using the logos of well-known firms – such as the construction company Taylor Woodrow. The gang then used the details of legitimate companies and stolen identities to rent virtual offices in the UK.

Other court cases offer examples of entrepreneurs with feet in both the illicit and legal economies. Planning chiefs at Dundee City Council were outraged but powerless to act in 2010 when the identity of the man behind plans to replace a city-centre landmark cinema with a block of twelve flats came to light.

Stephen Donald had just started a five-year jail sentence for heroin dealing when council planning chiefs rubber-stamped his planning permission for a £1.2 million property development deal. At his trial the court had heard how Donald had been caught in a 2009 police operation that had seized heroin with a street value of £118,490, along with £19,000 in cash, from a Tayside drugs gang. Donald hadn't handled the drugs, but evidence revealed that he had been involved in brokering the deal.

The court heard how Donald's public identity had been that of a respectable businessman who had made his fortune through gas-maintenance, property, publishing and childcare businesses. But despite Donald being behind bars the development was given the go-ahead. When asked about his client being a drug dealer, one of Donald's advisers said: 'I have no comment to make.'

The 'underworld' that Hobbs once knew has been blown away by the drugs trade and the lines between criminality and mainstream society have been blurred. The sheer number of people criminalised countrywide in an increasing number of business interests and professions belies any notion that there is now a criminal underworld.

Crime is no longer restricted to an underworld of specialists such as safe-breakers or getaway drivers. The drug trade is a one-stop employment shop that has made the criminal world accessible to all – your middle-market player could be a local businessman, white-van man, haulier, caterer or electrician.

But it could also be your next-door neighbour. It is a trade that is just as at home in suburbia as in the inner cities and it could be operating in a home, office or industrial estate near you.

*

It wasn't the first time that estate agent Andrew had tried to get in to see the house in a leafy suburb of north London – known as a haven for champagne socialists and for its chocolate-box pubs, close to the home of Labour leader Ed Miliband. He needed access to the property to undertake an annual estate-agent inspection, but repeated telephone calls and warning letters had elicited no response.

On his first visit he had peered through the bay windows at a perfectly normal-looking living room. Everything had seemed in order. He'd spoken to the neighbours, but they hadn't noticed anything untoward. To all intents and purposes the tenants had appeared to be model clients: punctual with rent payments, and quiet for the rest of the month. But the lack of response was becoming an irritation; something wasn't right. This time Andrew came with a key.

When he opened the door he was hit by a pungent smell that he couldn't quite place. But as he made his way around the house it all made sense. A forest of green greeted him in every room. The family home had been converted into a commercial cannabis factory. On the ground floor, hundreds of mature plants were being drip-fed nutrients and water through a series of pipes from the ceiling; an extractor hummed, and the air was thick with the sweet smell of skunk. On the walls were posters with what appeared to be instructions written in Chinese characters; a laptop, a small Buddhist shrine and £4,000 in cash were on display in the kitchen, and a few belongings strewn on two old mattresses made the £1,500-a-month house look as if it had been inhabited by rough sleepers.

Every inch of space had been utilised. On the upper floors cupboards had been converted into drying rooms and in a bathroom Andrew found a mulch of plant cuttings being processed into hash.

Andrew called the police, who confiscated the crop, but no one was ever apprehended. The 'gardeners', those employed to water and look after the plants, had been out at the time of the discovery and had obviously spotted the raid. Going through his paperwork Andrew found that every check had been undertaken prior to the tenants moving in, but the passport details they supplied were fake, the mobile phone numbers dead, and the paper trail they left led nowhere.

Not only estate agents, but police, firemen, neighbours and landlords of both residential and commercial property all over the country have been uncovering secret cannabis farms increasingly over the past decade. If it were not illegal, the

British cannabis-cultivation sector could be declared one of the few growth sectors of the economy.

It is an industry that has exploded with the cross-pollination of crime through global networks and the development of new growing technologies, and it has harnessed the World Wide Web in a fashion only dreamt of by more traditional sectors to create a new commercial cash crop for the criminal gangs – and a hidden cottage industry for the squeezed middle of Middle England.

*

When Jamie first arrived at Heathrow Airport in the spring of 2002 and walked through the 'Nothing to declare' corridor he could not have imagined what was to come. Born into a reasonably wealthy middle-class family in the scenic Canadian city of Vancouver, he left school with few qualifications, a taste for weed and an eye for making money. He had a likeable air and trustworthy manner and most of all he enjoyed his work – people were always happy to see him and he always left a little better off.

In his late teens his home town had become dubbed 'Vansterdam' in recognition of an emerging cannabis trade in potent bioengineered strains of marijuana such as BC Bud that became international marques. He grew a few plants himself, though only for personal use and for sharing with a few close friends. But he also found himself a natural broker for those who didn't have access to the commercial growing community – biker gangs and Vietnamese immigrant gangs. By good fortune Jamie's half-brother did, and at one step removed Jamie saw the risks and reward of the trade as it became an international concern.

But in London, Jamie the gardener would become Jamie the gangster: the accidental middleman in a drug coup that would confound police, politicians and the London crime bosses who had controlled much of the traffic in cannabis since the 1980s. It was a transition that was sharp and sudden, and almost led to, Jamie concedes with a smile, the 'naive young Canadian getting skinned alive'.

Within hours of landing Jamie was settling into a friend's flat in Hackney, east London. Hackney is an area alive with counterculture, steeped in a rich history of criminality, with more street gangs per square foot than any other London borough. Jamie 'worked the circuit of faces' and soon found that his knowledge of the cannabis market, his casual attitude towards criminality and his willingness as an immigrant himself to move between communities opened doors. He started a number of drug ventures. One was an ill-fated bid to export ecstasy to Australia that would have delivered huge profits but which ended with one partner behind bars. Still, despite its failure it established his credentials as someone who was serious. 'Golden opportunities' arise every day for the entrepreneurial broker in Britain's inner cities, says Jamie, but few flourish as the complex, risky and unruly nature of the criminal fraternity means that conflict, deception and violence more often than not undermine potentially profitable ventures. But in Hackney Jamie was a man in the right place at the right time.

It was there that, through one of his Hackney contacts, he would meet a small group of middle-aged, unremarkable Vietnamese gentlemen who had been planning a criminal enterprise never before attempted in Britain. Their plan was audacious yet simple. They wanted to flood east London with cheap, high-strength cannabis. But unlike the established drug barons of the time, they had no intention of importing it from North Africa or Amsterdam. Instead they would rent hundreds of homes and offices, grow it under hi-tech lights, and offer a consistency of quality and supply at a price with which their competitors could not compete. If successful, they would become the Mr Bigs of the supply chain and reap the rewards.

The caper had many factors in its favour. A steady flow of illegal newcomers within the Vietnamese community meant they had the manpower for such heavy work; properties were easy to rent because the buy-to-let market was opening up; and, most importantly, they had the element of surprise. The Vietnamese existed under the police radar and had had no previous involvement in the UK drug market. A decade earlier they had successfully pulled off the same trick in Vancouver. Jamie had seen them do it.

Jamie saw pound signs when he got wind of what was to happen. 'One firm completely consolidated the industry,' says the mild-mannered Canadian. 'They took a thriving cottage industry and turned it into a conglomerate. It was micromanaged so that quality was maintained and the strains were consistent, and the growing cycles synchronised so there was a constant supply. The firm coordinated an army of workers, who in turn ran a vast chain of dispersed farms and created a single chain of supply.'

Jamie sought out an introduction to the Vietnamese. He had already got used to meeting and greeting faces in the underworld from his time back home and while working the Hackney circuit of pubs and clubs, where he quickly made friends with the area's local dealers. His first meetings were held over long meals in the back of dimly lit restaurants where Jamie honed his ability to communicate with actions rather than words – essential, as few of the Vietnamese spoke English. He developed a love of the Vietnamese food that came in course after course from the kitchens and, according to custom, had to be consumed before business could be conducted. The meetings built the foundations for trust. At first he bankrolled his own deals, proving that he could 'move' kilos swiftly and without incident while also bringing in new business.

In Jamie the masterminds found the link between grow house and the suppliers who stocked the street dealers. But he also acted as a firewall between the growers, who drove a hard bargain, and their clients. As the demand for their product increased, the Vietnamese became the sole suppliers to the area, and could, with their influence, demand a higher percentage than traditional importers.

As if starring in a gangster flick Jamie spent his days brokering deals with established East End gangs and overseeing delivery teams. As Jamie puts it, the Vietnamese and local gangsters lacked 'connectivity' – he bridged this gap of trust, bringing together the supply and retail capabilities. The people he was dealing with were neither the celebrity 'Mr Bigs' with villas in Spain, nor the low-level dealers selling to students and professionals in pubs and clubs: they were the back-room entrepreneurs of the middle market, working in the shadowlands of the UK drug world.

His was not a job without risks. The importance of having middlemen like Jamie was underlined to the Vietnamese when a deal between a Lewisham-based grower, Hai Son Nguyen, and a South London drug gang known as the Alligator Crew, didn't go to plan for either party. The Alligator Crew never intended to pay for the cannabis and gunned Hai Son Nguyen down at a 'meet-house' in Dalston. Hai Son Nguyen's partner and friend, Van Phu, heard the shot and witnessed the gunmen fleeing the house with the cannabis. He knew nothing of London's criminal etiquette – that it was better to die than to grass – and was happy to turn to the law to revenge his part-ner's death. He later testified against all three in court and the Alligator gang were sentenced to long stretches.

And the money started rolling in. 'I would make £3,000 on

each 10 kg moved, and drop off the odd kilo here and there on top. It was easy,' says Jamie. The more he sold, the greater his reputation became. 'I had the Vietnamese laying 30 kg on me daily and I would move it within hours. I was moving maybe 10 to 20 kg a week of skunk to Oxford, another 10 kg to Bristol – simultaneously setting up a club that became the centre for my operations. It was like I was winning on the horses. Sometimes I was clearing £12,000 a day. For a short period of time I ran a small part of London – clubs, bars, strip joints. Everything was possible. It was a rush.'

But the rush wasn't just related to the money. It also came from staying one step ahead of the police, who appeared confounded by the sudden flood of skunk on the streets. 'I left the offices one day with a Vietnamese friend and two huge Chinese laundry bags full of weed and walked straight into two police officers. They completely ignored us. I don't think they were looking for a white Canadian or an old Vietnamese guy. It was like the penny hadn't quite dropped. We were new on the block.'

Eventually the penny did drop. The Metropolitan Police closed down 208 cannabis factories in and around the East End between April 2004 and April 2005, then 648 factories in the following twelve months. 'Cannabis cultivation is an increasing problem which must be nipped in the bud,' Alan Gibson, the newly appointed cannabis farm czar told reporters seeking a pun for a headline, before delivering the serious message that those running cannabis-farms, which were starting to spread across the UK, would be brought to justice.

While the courts were becoming increasingly clogged with cannabis growers, police officers openly conceded that they had no idea how the Vietnamese gangs shifted their produce.

They were certainly not dealing it themselves. Police described the unknown connection between the Vietnamese and the distributors as 'the missing link', but they admitted that they rarely had the resources to set up surveillance operations in order to look further up the chain.

'The growing was just one aspect of it – the other players were very well hidden,' said one off-duty drug squad officer at the time. 'We had no idea how the cannabis was getting from the grow rooms to the streets.'

But Jamie did. The key players within the Vietnamese coup acted purely as consultants and providers of equipment who recruited growers from within their own highly contained community – with many of them trafficked. They would develop cells of growers from whom the product would be dispatched to a main distribution hub. The product was then distributed through a series of middlemen to established dealers. As such, no one part of the operation was connected to another, nor had an overview of the operation.

The Vietnamese didn't seek to fight turf wars or undermine the pecking order of established drug groups as they moved around the country. They provided the product and the manpower, but they would often have to negotiate with local gangs to operate, paying a protection tax to ensure their farms were left alone.

With cannabis farms being busted at a rate of more than three a day, some police forces started to follow the trail of illicit profits and discovered that the Vietnamese had not been shy in opening legitimate businesses through which to funnel their new-found wealth – Vietnamese nail and noodle shops flourished countrywide, and many were found to have links to the criminal gangs whose tentacles were entwined with people-trafficking and prostitution. But the kingpins remained elusive.

The nation was on red alert. As cases proceeded to court it became clear that most of the Vietnamese arrested were illegal immigrants. The media wildly exaggerated the potency of the cannabis, declaring skunk to be 'thirty times stronger' than usual strains, and made dramatic claims about its links to schizophrenia. A ripple of fear passed through middle England.

As they shook the Vietnamese hold on Hackney, police forces countrywide were beginning to realise the huge implications of Britain becoming a drug-producing nation. Now the drug trade did not have to span borders in order to operate. The vast profits that once went to foreign producers were now swelling the pockets of British-based drug gangs.

But the greater the disruption caused by the police, the higher the wholesale prices. The potential rewards for cultivators, middlemen and dealers increased. In cities across the country, cannabis-growing operations were dubbed the new ATMs for criminal organisations that sought to use the revenues to fund a portfolio of other crimes from funding Class A drug transactions to mortgage fraud and robberies. And while some gangs moved in on cultivation, others just sought to swoop on grow houses, snatching the plants as if they were gold to be stolen from bank vaults. And, despite the national alert, the more police looked, the more growing operations they discovered.

'DO YOU LIVE NEXT TO A SUBURBAN SKUNK FACTORY?' the *Daily Mail* asked readers in October 2007. According to them no family home was safe from the reach of the cannabis gangs. In 2008 police launched a new national campaign to clamp down on the farms. Forces, at great expense, launched 'spies in the sky': helicopters with infrared cameras to identify the farms that used such high-powered lights that they glowed at night. Routine car stops discovered cells of growers equipped with plants and growing paraphernalia travelling to Yorkshire, Scotland, Wales and Cornwall. Homeowners and landlords were called on to do their civic duties and inform on any suspicious activity. The *Guardian* reported major seizures of the drug in Portsmouth, Lincoln, Doncaster, Reading, Peterborough, Swansea, Norwich, Swindon, Hertford, Hetton-le-Hole near Sunderland, Littleport in Cambridgeshire, Blackpool, Stewarton in Ayrshire and in dozens of other towns and cities.

'All of a sudden you didn't have to be a gangster to make gangster money,' says Allen Morgan, a former undercover drug squad officer who now works as an expert witness providing information to courts on leading drug-trafficking and cannabis-production cases.

'Traditionally a supply chain for cannabis stretched from the growing fields of Africa, Morocco and Amsterdam to the streets of Bristol, Birmingham or Manchester. Getting cannabis into the country has always been where the real profits are made. Few people could say they knew a cannabis grower a decade ago. Today we will all know someone, whether we are aware of it or not, who is involved with the trade.

'The profits once made by importers can be made by anyone. You now have a booming industry that has just spread, not just geographically but to bring in people who would never have considered it before. The cultivation boom has changed the way people look at cannabis and criminality.'

But while becoming public enemy number one, the Vietnamese were not the first to try their hand. Nor were they the first to see that cultivation could revolutionise the UK cannabis market. 'In the 1970s,' says Morgan, 'you had a few people growing in their back gardens. In the 1980s you had allotments and greenhouses, but in the 1990s people started looking at it as a business, as new technology made growing easy.

'By 2005 skunk cultivation was the norm,' says Morgan, 'everybody was at it. Not just the Vietnamese. Fast-forward to 2010 and the amateur cultivator was being drawn into the criminal supply network. Now if I walk ten minutes down the road I can be certain there will be at least one house with a growing crop. It's a layer of criminality that never existed a decade ago. As new and more powerful strains were developed the price of skunk on the street rocketed.'

Where Morgan once spent his days kicking down doors, many dealers and cultivators now seek his services to balance what they claim are inflated estimates provided by police in their bid to secure a conviction. It's not a role that has won him friends among his former colleagues but he believes it is an essential one, as lines between entrepreneurial vigour and criminality become increasingly blurred.

His clients include professional criminals for whom 'getting a crop on' has become a lucrative sideline. But increasingly, in the wake of the global banking crisis and recession, he handles cases for bricklayers, electricians, carpenters and factory workers who've invested their savings in setting up a farm to pay the mortgage, as well as for young bucks lured by the glamour and the money but without a criminal bone in their bodies.

'The men behind the Vietnamese operation never got directly involved, they were master criminals. The people I see are often not. Where the Vietnamese minimised the risk, many of the people I see will have the whole operation – from growing to dealing in one house, often their home, and have people banging on their door to buy weed – in their home. They make an easy target for the police and often face the maximum penalties. Others may just store or transport the plants, put up lights and help with harvests,' says Morgan. 'Many are very naive about what they are doing in terms of the detection and legal risks.'

And while growing remained illegal, it was an industry that achieved quasi-legal status. Growing may be illegal, but the sale and distribution of seeds, nutrients and equipment used to grow them is legal. As such, by the late 2000s it appeared to straddle both the illicit and legal economies, drawing global interest from players in the legitimate cannabis industry.

In 2005 *Bizarre* magazine offered cut-price tickets to its readers for the industry's UK Hemp Expo, which was held in Wembley Arena, a showcase event for the producers of legal hemp products and associated industries, such as hydroponics, lighting, nutrients, seeds and head shops. New Zealand's Kiwiseeds, Germany's Dampkring Growshop, the UK's WeedWorld, and perhaps Britain's most famous drug trafficker, the bestselling author Howard Marks, promoted their ranges of seeds.

Countrywide, head shops selling growing equipment and a range of smoking paraphernalia were operating in the similar grey zone of regulation exploited by the legal-high industry. If wholesaler, middleman and consumer in the distribution chain all denied the intended use of the seeds, equipment or paraphernalia, the police could do nothing.

But in 2008, Tom Brake MP sought to introduce Bill 136, the Prohibition of Cannabis Seeds Bill in a bid to stop the illicit industry gaining a foothold in the high street. But MPs paradoxically voted against it. Opponents claimed it would merely drive currently law-abiding citizens into the clutches of criminal gangs, and impose sanctions on cultivating cannabis that far exceeded those handed down for the use of heroin or cocaine.

As long as there were legitimate reasons for buying and

selling hydroponics equipment, a legal loophole existed. Three Derbyshire hydroponics sellers, for example, were arrested on suspicion of conspiracy to aid and abet the production of cannabis. Prosecutors claimed the defendants supplied equipment specifically to cannabis growers, reasonably foreseeing that the items would be used illegally. But this could not be proven.

Lord Phillips, the lord chief justice, ruled that the offences of conspiracy to aid and abet and counsel the production of cannabis were 'unknown to law' and had to be quashed. 'There can be no conviction for aiding and abetting, counselling or procuring, unless the offence is shown to have occurred,' he said. 'It is not an offence to attempt to aid and abet, counsel or procure the commission of an offence.'

While criminal gangs and the down-at-heel are perhaps easy marks for the police, the more expert farmers make up a core of production that remains largely beneath the purview of the police. 'The police are really only scratching the surface,' says Britain's foremost cannabis-farm expert, Gary Potter, a senior lecturer in criminology at London South Bank University. He has spent the past decade interviewing growers, visiting 'grow ops' and watching the industry evolve and embed itself countrywide. 'The Vietnamese and local UK gangs have become the big players in the cannabis industry, but over half of the grow operations are small operators.'

Some cultivators are activists who believe cannabis to be a natural plant that should be enjoyed by all, others are medical growers who use the weed to control pain and some are ethical growers whose main aim is to cut off their contact with the criminal gangs. But in past years he has witnessed a decline in the numbers of truly ethical dealers. He puts this down to a cultural shift.

Potter's research has revealed a generation of growers for whom social supply comes with added economic benefits that offer the squeezed middle classes a taste of the good life.

'The difference now is that cultivation has become almost a national hobby. We've become a nation of entrepreneurs,' says Potter, talking of his experiences. 'Most start to grow small amounts for personal use, but soon realise that after each harvest they have a surplus – with ten ounces left over you may as well sell some. You realise you can make money. And local growers and smokers are often very well connected. If organised cultivators enter a market suddenly, many of these small operations may downsize or temporarily shut up shop and just wait for the police raids to be over to start again. People work out the risks. These online communities include lawyers, police, court officials. People will be aware when the police start operations in their area and people will simply adapt what they are doing to minimise the risk.'

To avoid dealing individually with crime gangs many growers band together in co-ops that can consist of up to thirty members growing a dozen plants at a time. Others join franchises where a mentor will provide the kit and the know-how if you agree to house and care for the plants, and split the profits fifty-fifty. While a franchise may only produce 5 kg per harvest, many mentors will have up to fifty franchisees.

'I sat down with a major grower,' says Potter, 'and worked out that he'd made around £1 million. He'd bought a couple of cars, a few holidays, the "good life" – it doesn't go through accounts, it's spent as you get it, if it's a lump sum you find a legitimate cover. That's probably doubled by now.'

Grow kits are sold online to suit every need – from equipment for small residences whose owners are looking to make a little extra on the side, to installations for commercial crops in warehouses, derelict pubs and abandoned factories. Where once cultivators would obtain information from US magazines such as *High Times*, gazing in awe at the pictures of California's 'bud' of the month, aspiring growers now have access to all the information they need online – at the UK420 community, for example, a buzzing hub of information with over 40,000 members.'

The police mapping of cannabis cultivation in Britain reveals how the sector now runs up the spine of the country, says Potter, splitting the British market in two: with growers holding supply within cities, and the ports of Liverpool, Humberside and Harwich as hubs of importation.

There is now no part of the British Isles where cultivation hasn't taken hold. On publishing the first report charting the growth and influence of the new industry – *UK National Problem Profile: Commercial Cultivation of Cannabis* – police revealed statistics about a rapidly emerging industry that had colonised the Midlands and the North, opening vast cultivations. 'It's like someone has breathed new life into our deserted factories and mills,' joked one press officer in West Yorkshire after it was named the regional capital of cultivation in 2010.

In 2012, police revealed that over the previous year they had busted nearly 8,000 cannabis farms at a rate of twenty-one a day, double the number in 2008. A report by the Association of Chief Police Officers (ACPO) estimated that in the previous two years they had recovered 1.1 million plants with a total street value of £207 million.

But law enforcers are facing a further conundrum. Such is the scale of the cultivation that police chiefs assume Britain has become a cannabis exporter. But data from the UK Border Agency shows only low levels of cannabis exports. Instead there is a continuing flood of imports, 'indicating that the current demand for the drug is so great that domestic production cannot satisfy it'.

As it has done in more isolated parts of the world where drug supply routes are thin on the ground, DIY drug production has taken the country by storm.

It is a phenomenon that has already seen a rising interest in the home-grown peyote cactus, which contains the hallucinogenic drug mescaline, and could rouse Britain's relatively dormant trade in crystal meth, the DIY drug most feared by police.

While the impact of Britain's role as a drug-producing nation has set law enforcement a fresh set of problems, the World Wide Web and the rise of legal highs have opened up a new front in the war on drugs that could prove a game changer.

*

It's a rainy morning in the scruffy, bohemian, student quarter of Brighton. A young man in his twenties steps into a web café, nods to the assistant and settles down at a chipboard desk, firing up the computer. A website quickly flickers up:

> . . . Tor helps you defend against network surveillance that threatens personal freedom, privacy and confidential business activities

He downloads the software. A green onion icon appears at the bottom right of the screen, indicating his movements and location online are now hidden.

The next page to appear is Hushmail, an ultra-secure webmail site. He taps in his twenty-four-digit password and logs in as 'Recman'. He has fourteen new messages in his inbox. The first says:

Recman,
Welcome to Mail Order Marijuana.

It's an invitation to join an online forum discussing the best places to buy cannabis over the Internet. His encryption serves as a passport to sites like these, which recognise that his actions are cloaked to the government agencies and online trackers who record our forays into cyberspace.

A few mouse clicks later and he's ordered 7 g of a highly aromatic strain of cannabis called Juicy Fruit from a Canadian website through a prepaid credit card. Another click or two and he's bought a month's supply of magic mushrooms from Amsterdam, vacuum-packed, and guaranteed to arrive at his door within three days.

On one side of Recman a Polish girl chats to a relative on Skype, on the other a teenage boy sits immersed in a shoot 'em up game. Another customer is prodded awake after falling asleep in his booth. Meanwhile, Recman continues his journey through a virtual drug shopping centre. A 'Mr Paul' of the Indian Chemical Company in Delhi, India, has confirmed receipt of an order of the illegal anaesthetic GHB, also known as liquid ecstasy. It will be delivered by Royal Mail to a name and address of Recman's choosing in eight separate vials labelled 'Pharmaceutical Sample Insulin'.

Next, he purchases 10 g of 2C-B* from a back-room chemist in the US. The crystal will be rolled paper thin to the dimensions of a folded A4 letter and sent in an envelope. He visits

---

* A synthetic drug that mimics the effect of mescaline.

an eBay-style site for international wholesalers: *Alibaba.com**. More than 7 million wholesalers use the site to showcase their products, from vacuum cleaners to bananas, and invite you to buy in bulk. Searching for the banned drug mephedrone brings up a listing of 3,158 products and 374 suppliers across the globe. In Africa, Mr Labforce Pharmacutical (*sic*) in Malabo, Equatorial Guinea, offers both 'white' and 'black' heroin. The Labforce website advertises thirty-four 'alternative' products, including GBH, opium-soaked hashish, and mephedrone. Minimum orders are 100 g, the prices negotiable, discreet delivery is assured.

Recman started purchasing analogues of drugs such as mescaline and LSD online in 2000. 'I joined community groups, started chatting with people, exchanging information and building contacts,' he says. He regularly visited sites such as the Hive and the Shroomery, which offered a service similar to many legitimate comparison websites, providing a portal to worlds beyond those offered by Google, AOL or Bing – a link first to 'deep web', a virtual dumping ground where dealers can find privacy among redundant web clutter; and then further down into uncharted territories of the 'dark web'.

'When you know where to look, the Internet becomes a far better, more interesting place to buy drugs than from your local dealer,' he says. 'There's more choice, ready availability, and it's reliable.'

He closes the browser and deletes his search history and sign-in details – effectively wiping his virtual fingerprints from

---

* All searches on Alibaba.com made prior to the UK mephedrone ban in 2010. The site has since launched an effective clean-up campaign, but web searches in 2012 revealed many mephedrone vendors still present across the Internet.

the old computer. He pays £1 at the counter and strolls out of the door into the lunch-hour bustle.

As with a growing number of players in Britain's evolving drug market, where the traditional roles are becoming increasingly blurred, Recman is hard to pigeonhole. He is a self-professed psychonaut, an amateur chemist and a small-time importer. Because of his knowledge of the online drug market – his ability to source rare chemicals and high-purity illicit drugs that are unavailable on the streets – he also acts as a regular dealer to his circle of friends.

Recman fits Interpol's loose-fit profile of the average online drug buyer – 'under thirty, open to new experiences and technologically proficient'. He's certainly savvy enough to visit Internet cafés instead of using his laptop, and possesses the knowledge to cloak his activities as best he can. In many respects, he embodies the future of the British drug trade.

The Internet is transforming the drug industry. The unprecedented rise of mephedrone in the second half of 2009 unlocked an online world that had predominantly remained the preserve of a small clique of drug connoisseurs like Recman. Free from the threat of violence that pervades street markets, buyers and sellers feel safe cloaked by anonymous usernames, protected from the authorities by readily available encryption software. Where once established lines of supply could be plotted around the world from global producers to local drug markets, the Internet has decoupled the drug markets from real world trade routes. A new generation of importers are today able to short-cut traditional methods of drug trafficking with a few clicks.

The online drug market accounts for only a fraction of drug sales worldwide. It is a trade in its infancy. But it has opened a door to a completely new way of buying and selling drugs that renders existing enforcement efforts, designed to combat the traditional drug smuggling and distribution system, irrelevant. Already under immense strain in the battle to stem the supply of more widespread drugs such as heroin and cocaine, the Association of Chief Police Officers has told the Home Office that chasing down the use of the new generation of chemical highs will be 'a waste of time'. The fluidity of the Internet, and the privacy it provides, makes policing the online drug trade even more of a 'needle in a haystack' exercise than searching freight. In the new paradigm the producer can deal directly with a large-scale trafficker, a middleman and a consumer alike, dispatching drugs in bulk or gram measures by international delivery services that due to the very volume of world trade allow consignments to pass across sovereign borders with ease. And where supply lines might follow predictable fixed patterns in the real world, online, they become global networks that are rarely what they seem: a pharmacy claiming to be located in India might market a product on a website domiciled in Belgium, dispatch it to a customer in Latvia, who then sells it online in the UK.

The Internet has opened a new market in which anyone can participate, away from the hierarchical controls of criminal gangs. The rising popularity of trading sites is further fracturing the already disappearing pyramid of supply that has tradition-ally defined the UK drug market. 'There's this feeling of anonymity . . . It doesn't always feel illegal; it is seen as a white-collar crime,' said Interpol's Daniel Altmeyer, at the World Forum Against Drugs in Stockholm in 2008. 'There's no more Pablo Escobar with handcuffs behind his back.'

But how does the online trade work, who makes the drugs and who sells them? One man who's likely to know is Eric Chang, a Shanghai-based businessman who was at the forefront of the mephedrone boom, and was widely known on alibaba.

com. He is part of a generation of narco-entrepren[...]
ating in emerging economies in Eastern Europe, Asia, the Far
East and Africa, men who develop new twists on old highs in
advance of government legislation, and who monitor designer-
drug trends carefully.

Prior to the mephedrone ban, Chang sent hundreds, if not
thousands of kilo-weight packages from China via Paris to the
UK, finally clearing Customs at Stansted Airport in the UK for
eventual delivery all over Britain. He charged between £2,500
and £4,000 per kilogram – a fraction of the £50,000 price of
a kilogram of cocaine after it has passed through UK Customs
– and provided customers with FedEx tracking numbers so
they could follow their individual orders. The drug was then
sold via websites at £10–15 a gram, with reductions for bulk
purchases. The typical profit margin on a kilo was approximately £7,500.

In April 2010, after the pre-election mephedrone ban came
into force, a number of other legal-high brands such as NRG-1,
Benzo Fury and Ivory Wave – which contained a varied mixture
of legal and illegal stimulants – took up the baton. But Chang's
success was about to come to an end. Showing undercover
reporters around his laboratory in Shanghai, he told them he
could supply limitless quantities of MDVP – another drug
released following the mephedrone ban. The *Mail on Sunday*
unveiled Chang as the purveyor of this new wave of legal highs
under the headline 'The Chinese laboratories whose scientists
are already at work on the new meow meow.' He was presented
as a hard-nosed businessman of China's new class of wealthy
entrepreneurs, a profiteer with little interest in the end user of
his products, nor the harm they could cause.

While Chang and his gang offered a unique insight into the
behind-the-scenes activity of the mephedrone explosion in

Britain, his small, scruffy laboratory in Shanghai could only hint at the grand bazaar of covert chemists, chemical wholesalers and online communities that make up the global online trade in illicit drugs.

The grey zone of legal highs is expanding despite the ban, claiming to produce an ever larger number of new drugs. A snapshot of the market in 2010 revealed that forty new drugs became available in a twelve-month period, a number that has left law enforcement agencies unable to keep pace. But the trade doesn't just stay ahead of the law by extending its range of products; it has created a loophole within a ring of complicity. If a wholesaler, retailer and consumer all deny knowledge of the true nature of the product or its intended use, the police have no evidence to convict someone of criminal behaviour. If a bath salt is distributed, marketed and purchased as a bath salt, but is later found to be an illegal substance, who is culpable?

Hitching a ride on the Internet using global trading portals, online communities and individual sites, most firms selling 'research chemicals' present themselves as legitimate businesses with online assistants, often pictured wearing lab coats, willing to discuss your needs. Inadvertently, sites across the Internet have become the nexus of the grey economy in psychoactive substances.

Some are 'off-licence' pharmacies that will effectively supply to order. Some are covert chemists moonlighting while working for mainstream brand name corporations. Others are established middlemen buying in bulk and then supplying the retail markets in countries where the chemicals remain legal. Others are hustlers and counterfeiters. But in cyberspace where all sit behind a thin veneer of a company name and a slick website, it is almost impossible to distinguish between them.

Despite increasing vigilance, a cornucopia of legal and illegal highs – from counterfeit valium and cocaine-cutting agents to mephedrone, ecstasy, cannabis and heroin – still changes hands over the Internet. While sophisticated monitoring systems are constantly on the lookout for individuals or firms selling illegal drugs, the sheer volume of trade means that they can only shut down a very small percentage of those that openly flaunt the law.

And while purveyors of both legal and illegal highs dance across both international drug definitions and legal jurisdictions, the evolution in online drug markets has been revitalising sites in the connoisseur market. For many drug enthusiasts the 'legal high' market has damaged their cause, exposing their hidden world to scrutiny of legislators and media, while seeking profits over promoting enlightenment. But the dark web has also come up from the depths. Some dealers are now convinced that the combinations of encryption are so strong that they can defend their position from global law enforcement agencies. Grouping together, they now form mini markets in cyberspace, open to all.

The Silk Road traditionally refers to the interlinking trade routes that helped lay the foundations for modern world trade. But the new Silk Road is a website, a virtual mall of traditional drugs and synthetic derivatives. Customers must download Tor to access the site, and can only pay using Bitcoin – the ecommerce currency that operates outside the mainstream financial service industry and the latest electronic money transfer system to be co-opted to mask activity and transactions.

The Silk Road homepage looks like any other online community trading site, advertising everything from home tuition, jewellery, weaponry and pornography, but also cannabis, ecstasy, psychedelics, opiates, benzos and stimulants, with products pictured and priced and sellers grouped.

In 2011, news of 'Silk Road – the hidden marketplace' was spreading on forums associated with the Bitcoin currency, within weeks it hit the online US news service Gawker and the service went viral – according to one user in a matter of days the number of users on the site spiralled from a few hundred to over 10,000.

One Silk Road administrator set out the mission statement of the website to ABC News: 'Because of the war on drugs, there is a huge gap between what people desire and what they can get. Every transaction on Silk Road reduces that gap, satisfying people and enriching their lives.'

Hanging above the fireplace in Recman's home is a large print of the highly respected and psychedelic Californian chemist Alexander 'Sasha' Shulgin – best known for synthesising ecstasy in the late 1970s and embarking on a prolonged tour of chemistry labs across Europe, giving demonstrations in how to make it.

Shulgin, a World War Two US Navy veteran, was able to carry out his maverick work with the use of a government-approved licence to produce outlawed substances for the DEA. But in his spare time he used the laboratory in his garden shed to create more than 200 new drugs. He espoused the use of these 'analogues' to unlock hidden energies, creativity and understanding.

Shulgin's experiences imbibing different molecular cocktails and his own easy-to-follow recipes were published in two books in the 1990s which became psychonaut bibles – *PiHKAL: A Chemical Love Story* and *TiHKAL: A Continuation*. Until 2003 the work of US-licensed chemists such as Shulgin was strictly classified information, and reports on the production of new chemicals and drug research were confined to a monthly newsletter, *Microgram*, published by the DEA. Its circulation was restricted to law enforcement officials, government investigators, or forensic scientists.

But through community websites the underground bloggers spread Shulgin's message, offering links to a previously hidden world of new highs, suppliers and experiences. Realising they were haemorrhaging information, the DEA made the contents of *Microgram* available online. To onlookers it was a tacit admission that the information genie had been uncorked.

The Internet has created a 'glocal' drug market, where globalisation and localisation meet. The neologism was first coined by British sociologist Roland Robertson, and describes online classified board Craigslist, for example, where local services can be found on a global service, and the social network Facebook where local interest groups develop online photo albums and make contacts across the world.

Where Shulgin's how-to recipes released the chemical equations to devoted followers, just two decades later the web would magnify his message for the masses – bringing together local drug markets and global markets, creating a window through which a local drug trend becomes a global epidemic.

Whereas traditional drug dealers market their wares through word of mouth, the online sellers have the entire Internet network to market their products, to create a viral buzz rivalling anything achieved by corporate brands. Sites such as Facebook and bulletin boards such as Gumtree were used to advertise; YouTube offered the opportunity for viral marketing by self-styled drug testers; while online media coverage only appeared to drive the market, with news stories generating sponsored links and adverts from online dealers, promising twenty-four-hour, within the hour, delivery services.

'They don't just spam like the firms selling Viagra,' says

Mike Slocombe, founding editor of the Brixton-based underground bulletin board and e-zine Urban75, one of the first online communities to start receiving posts about mephedrone. 'They are more subtle than that. They employ people to become members of sites like Urban75, get chatting to people on the drugs forums, and make friends with as many people as possible. Then they will send private messages to around 300 people with links of where to buy this "great new drug" from. Drug sellers are using every trick in the book. If you enter "mephedrone" into a Twitter search engine it produces endless posts with links to sites selling it. Online dealers have learnt the art of attracting as much web traffic as possible from the porn industry, with gateway pages, algorithms and invisible wording,' says Slocombe. 'If you are in a crowded room and you want to draw attention to yourself, you have to shout.

'It's easy to set up a site, start trading and shut it down before you are caught. It's a bit like Del Boy and Rodney on *Only Fools and Horses* selling hooky goods from a suitcase and running off when the cops see them. Sites pop up and disappear before the police get wind.'

As the trade has spread visibly across cyberspace the Internet is becoming a haven not only for chemical adventurers like Recman, or hard-nosed chemical entrepreneurs like Mr Chang, but increasingly for criminal gangs.

The web has also provided the traditional drug industry with an alternative business model in an environment that offers an open-door policy. Some street dealers have bypassed buying drugs from dealers further up the chain and instead buy supplies over the Internet. And where legal-high dealers once colonised websites to market products, now dealers in illicit drugs have started congregating in discussion forums, seeking to escape the violence of traditional drug markets. But these sites are relative free-for-alls compared to the encrypted sites, with a higher risk of detection.

On one site, a 'Charlie White' of London offers 'premium powdered cocaine' and is inundated with responses. As is Leeds' 'Chenman' who offers bulk order Roche valium, while 'Joy Division' of Manchester receives 238 enquiries about his offer of the Class-C 'date rape' drug GBH, for sale in either powered or liquid form. The bulletin board is alive with an endless wave of posts. 'Mephedrone; pure samples available', posts 'Drugfriend', who receives twenty-five responses in half an hour.

On threads scammers and chancers are outed, vendors post pictures of their products against dated newspapers to prove authenticity and law enforcers are nowhere to be seen. A banner warning is highlighted at the top of the message board:

WARNING: Any unlawful distribution of controlled substances via the Internet is in violation of the Controlled Substances Act, Title 21 United States Code (USC). Violations are punishable under 21 USC Section 841, and may include imprisonment and substantial fines. Please think before you post.

The site is hosted by a US community website, but the majority of trade is conducted within the UK among vendors and buyers, in the full knowledge that by operating across jurisdictions the police can look on but face a long and frustrating trail to unearth their identities.

Judith Aldridge, a lecturer in criminology at Manchester University has carried out research among mephedrone traders and gangs moving into cyberspace. It offers a unique insight into the legal market that developed overnight, and found that the internet was attracting a whole new breed of dealer as well as those already involved in the trade of illicit drugs.

Some of her research was sparked by the discovery of students setting up as mephedrone dealers in university halls to meet demand for the new legal high. 'We noticed that student parties started going on for four days, from Friday to Tuesday. What people were doing was taking mephedrone,' says Aldridge. 'Some of the students focused on these kind of parties and set themselves up as dealers in tag-teams to provide a constant supply. The competition was such that they knew if they couldn't deliver within fifteen minutes the customer would go elsewhere.'

Mephedrone sales teams would text customers dozens of times a day, teams of dealers who were no longer attached to turf nor hampered by regulation or police interference moved invisibly around the city by pedal bike, private cars and taxi. Aldridge interviewed twenty-seven sellers, the top tier of which imported and sold 160 kg consignments, with the smallest operations selling 2 g bags. All imported their product over the Internet. Four of the dealers already had established, successful businesses selling cocaine, MDMA, cannabis and ketamine. They responded to a demand for mephedrone from their customers, but also realised they could double or triple their original customer base of illegal drug users if they sold mephedrone.

Aldridge said the new drug trade offered a drastic alternative to the traditional street trade. 'You don't even know who your competition is, you don't see them. It's safer for dealers. You don't have to meet people to do deals in a car park or the pub, you can advertise online and just pop down to the post office every day.' For Aldridge, the Internet has brought the trade full circle: from a market run by drug enthusiasts, to one being adopted by criminal gangs.

Yet even as we come to terms with the shifting market, it moves again. The capabilities of modern smartphones is enabling a blurring of the boundaries between the old and new drug-trade territories. As technology created the Internet drug market, it is also defining the future on the street. 'Foursquare', for example, one of a new generation of location-based social networking applications, allows users to immediately identify where their contacts are at any one time. It is an Internet technology that is allowing friends and families to keep in touch, but is also changing the way people sell drugs face to face.

From basic text messaging, to picture phones and Skype, encryption allows drug gangs to communicate in confidence at any time wherever they are in the world.

But new technology has other features that can also be exploited. Suppliers are able to use smartphone tracking technology to follow bulk shipments, monitoring the movements of drivers to ensure safe passage – an unplanned stop off in a lay-by might indicate that the driver was either being busted, robbed or interfering with the product. And as the convergence of technology and the smartphone continue, the ability to monitor the movement of a consignment, co-ordinate a transaction, or transfer money worldwide will continue to make the drug trade an ever flexible and adaptable business.

While the majority of drug users – most notably crack and heroin users – do not buy their drugs online, it is a marketplace that is turning Britain's drug trade inside out. Not only does the Internet create a bridge to an easily accessible but unpredictable cornucopia of psychoactive chemicals, it turns what previously had been a risky transaction into something only slightly more subversive than buying a mop from Amazon.

The drug market hasn't been globalised as such, but 'glocal-ised', supply lines shortening and the number of links reducing; the local market now has a global element and the drug industry is no longer foreign but embedded.

While the potential of the Internet has been unleashed, and like its bedfellows in 'soft' vice, gambling and adult entertainment, the drug trade has been able to monetise the power of the web far beyond other social networks or high-street stores, and what comes next is anyone's guess.

In the real world, the most visible example of how local and global drug markets have merged is the flow of information, releasing a new generation of DIY drug producers, for whom borders, supply routes and smuggling belong to the last millennium. The potential for a rising DIY drug culture challenging the supply of cheap, good quality smuggled drugs has never been more real.

But perhaps the biggest change is going on beneath the radar. Having links to supply is now less important, as representatives of global drug cartels operate in markets across the UK, correcting the notion of a strict pyramid of supply controlled by the Mr Bigs of yesteryear. The UK's Mr Middles are now part of a global network of criminals, entrepreneurs and adventurers that has become a self-preservation society thriving not in an underworld but in the communities where we live and the businesses in which we work, adopting the infrastructure and technology on which we all rely.

4

Pursuit

A Game of Cat and Mouse

It was approaching midnight on a near-freezing December evening in 2004 in east London's New Spitalfields Market, the daily destination for hundreds of tons of exotic fruit and vegetables from around the globe. Andrew Pritchard pulled his Audi up to a large white delivery van, turned off the engine and waited for the van's back doors to open.

The son of a Jamaican mother and white cockney father, Pritchard was brought up in 1970s Stoke Newington, at the time a tough east London neighbourhood. A self-made millionaire by the age of twenty-two, he had forged his reputation as a party promoter in the 1990s, setting up illegal acid-house raves in derelict sites across London. But after a disastrous involvement in concert promotion, Pritchard turned his entrepreneurial flair to drug smuggling.

Driving to the rendezvous, Pritchard had a feeling that something was not quite right, but dismissed it as paranoia. He should have trusted his senses, because he and his tight-knit gang were about to walk into a carefully laid trap. The smugglers they were meeting had been under police surveillance for some months, initially targeted after an undercover unit linked one member to a Greek cocaine dealer who had just been handed a six-year sentence. By listening in to their conversations, Customs and Excise investigators had learned of a suspect shipment of 300 sacks of coconuts, travelling from Guyana in South America via the Caribbean to Pritchard.

The shipment was intercepted inside a refrigerated container along its route and searched. Customs investigators started smashing coconuts, but all they contained was milk. So they took apart the refrigeration system itself. Hidden inside was their prize: a massive 500 kg of high-purity cocaine packed into blocks and sewn into sacks.

The investigators weighed and fingerprinted the cocaine packages, replaced them with similar-sized blocks of wood, sewed the sacks back up and set the container on its way, seemingly untouched, to New Spitalfields Market. Now all they needed to do was lay in wait for the buyers to show themselves.

Pritchard was checking his watch, waiting for the others to arrive, when the sound of screeching brakes and blinding headlights froze his blood. The next instant a masked man was staving in his front windscreen with a baton, covering Pritchard with shards of broken glass. His first thought as he opened his eyes was that he was about to be shot by a rival gang. Instead he was pulled out of his car, forced to the ground and arrested on suspicion of conspiracy to supply Class A drugs.

By the next morning the drug-bust had hit the national media. With a street-value of £50 million, it was up until that point the largest ever seizure of cocaine on mainland Britain. Customs investigators revealed to a waiting press that the dramatic arrest of Pritchard and six others was the climax of a lengthy, multimillion pound investigation.

'This was an extremely successful operation, and an excellent example of the way Customs is working to prevent the smuggling of Class A drugs,' said Duncan Stewart, assistant chief investigation officer for Customs and Excise. Operation Cyprus was proudly declared a rare victory in the ongoing battle to make a dent in the relentless tide of drugs entering Britain.

But seventeen months later, the showcase cocaine haul had come to nothing. Not one of the gang, many of whom had faced a maximum thirty-five-year sentence, was convicted of cocaine trafficking. The buyers' line of defence was that they were indeed importers of contraband goods, but that they had no idea that drugs were involved. They maintained instead that they were expecting to unwrap a shipment of 'moody' cigars hidden among the coconuts. Someone unknown, they said, had swapped the cigars for cocaine. The defendants even pointed the finger at Customs, who they accused of institutional corruption.

Prosecutors failed to convince any members of the jury that the gang was, without doubt, directly linked to the cocaine, and Pritchard and his fellow smugglers walked free. Charged with the impossible task of stemming the flow of illegal drugs across Britain's 12,000 miles of coastline, the 'cocaine and coconuts' case was a disaster for Customs investigators who saw the bust of a lifetime turn to dust.

While Customs staff were still picking themselves up off the floor, Pritchard's entrepreneurial mind was working overtime. He didn't want to see the inside of a remand cell again.

Chatting in a bar in east London's Hoxton Square, the venue of one of his biggest raves in the 1990s, Pritchard rattles through a colourful backlog of tales. The stories form the narrative of his book *Urban Smuggler*, which was published in 2008 and billed as 'the rollicking life story of one of the most prolific smugglers of our time'.

High-profile cases such as Pritchard's are an embarrassment for the police, exposing their failures in the nationwide 'war on drugs'. The statistics reveal the truth: less than 1 per cent of drug shipments are stopped at British borders, and only 10 per cent of organised gangs supplying drugs to the streets of Britain are under investigation at any one time.

Because of its close association with organised crime, the trafficking and distribution of drugs is viewed as one of the most serious threats that Britain's law-enforcement agencies must deal with, second only to terrorism. It is a mandate that places the police firmly at the front line in the defence of social order and the battle against what is seen by many as the 'chaotic forces' of drug use and drug selling.

Police and drug criminals have been playing out what both sides often refer to as 'the game' in earnest since the spread of illegal drug use in the 1960s. From the bobby on the beat to the drug squad officer, Customs officials to serious organised crime detectives, Britain's law enforcers are charged with stemming the supply of drugs from the borders down to the streets. They have formidable powers to tackle the trade: stop-and-search tactics, undercover drug purchases and the use of sniffer dogs to hi-tech drug detectors outside bars, raids on people's homes and businesses and the power to close down venues where drugs are sold.

In order to target higher-level organisations, these powers can, if sanctioned by the courts, extend to surveillance such as bugging, the use of informants, deep undercover agents, the ability to seek out and seize assets and the control by the Home Office of some drug-selling outfits in order to catch others.

But cases such as Pritchard's only serve to highlight that not only are the dice loaded in favour of the criminal fraternity, but the game leaves the police facing an ever-expanding workload.

The police in Britain deal with an average of 5,000 drug cases a week. Over half of all prisoners in Britain reported committing offences connected to their drug taking. It is estimated that between a third and a half of all acquisitive crime, such as shoplifting, is related to illegal drug use.

Research suggests that most addicted heroin or crack users need to earn between £15,000–30,000 a year to sustain their habit, and while some do so from dealing drugs themselves, many accumulate cash by selling on goods they have stolen. Because stolen goods fetch around a third of their normal value, it is thought that around £2.5 billion worth of goods are taken each year to pay for drugs.

At every stage of that journey, the trafficking, selling and use of drugs is connected to a host of ancillary crimes, from illegal immigration, the payment and exploitation of drug couriers, money laundering, gun-running, violence and corruption to prostitution, pimping, shoplifting, theft, burglary and mugging.

Add to this the antisocial impact that the street drug trade can have on communities, such as drug dealing or injecting in public areas, and the daunting task of policing the trade becomes apparent.

It is a war that was launched a century ago at an international drug conference in The Hague in 1912, where, with war looming on the horizon, it was agreed that opium, morphine and cocaine must be restricted to medical use.

In *Dope Girls*, a book about Britain's early twentieth-century drug scene, writer Marek Kohn describes 'London's first drug-bust' in 1916. Two officers, police sergeants Hedges and Venner, arrested Willy Johnson after seeing him hawking bags of cocaine. But Johnson was acquitted because the officers had not witnessed an actual drug deal. This and similar cases led to the possession of cocaine or opium becoming a criminal offence in 1916, introduced as an amendment to the Defence of the Realm Act.

In the late 1950s, British police began to detect the re-emergence of a drug scene, in the clubland of London's West End. By the 1960s, the street trade in cannabis, cocaine and heroin had begun to proliferate, as had the moral panic surrounding the rise of recreational drug use and bohemian counter-culture. In a decade that witnessed the relaxation of controls on gambling, homosexuality, censorship and abortion, the laws against drugs were tightened.

And they were draconian. Up until the Misuse of Drugs Act 1971, there was little distinction between types of drug and drug-related offences. Those caught possessing or taking small quantities of cannabis and opium received similar sentences to those convicted for manufacturing or dealing. The Act, the basis of which remains the central plank of today's drug laws despite being more than forty years old, divided drugs into three 'classes' based on a falling scale of harm, from A to C.

But what was easy to legislate against has not proved as easy to police. In the space of four decades drug crime has moved from being a neighbourhood concern to winning the status of serious organised crime. It is an arms race in which law enforcers have never had the upper hand.

In the mid-1980s, when criminologist Dick Hobbs began his studies, a maverick era of policing was coming to an end.

'In the days of early drug policing it was all about neighbourhood policing, where local cops would have extensive
knowledge of what was going on in their patch. They would
deal with it or accept bribes to turn a blind eye.'

Despite the huge success in 1977 of Operation Julie, a
well-co-ordinated undercover operation that smashed a prolific
LSD factory in rural Wales, by the end of the 1970s drug squads
had gained a reputation for corruption. On one hand, as an
ex-hippy from Torbay interviewed for a south Devon community website explained, 'The drug squad were known as the
police gardening club because of their fondness for planting
stuff on people.' On the other, the decade saw a series of
corruption cases brought against Met Police drug detectives
accused of bribery, theft and blackmail.

The impact of the corruption cases was far greater than just
being an embarrassment – they signalled the end of the hands-
on community policing of known drug criminals, halting the
natural flow of information that might be exchanged over a
drink or by listening to the chatter on the street. Hobbs says
that from then on, policing and drug crime decoupled, leaving
a black hole in police intelligence.

Throughout the 1970s, individual forces began to establish
specialist drug squads. Most of their work was taken up busting
low-level suppliers of cannabis, speed and LSD, creating further
strains between themselves and local communities, who
accused the police of routinely targeting local black youths on
the premise that they were likely drug users. These heavy-
handed tactics were to become one of the key causes of the
Brixton Riots in 1981, and were cited by rioters as being one
of the main causes of the rioting and looting in London,
Birmingham and Manchester in the summer of 2011.

But regardless of the abilities of police to maintain links

with communities, according to Hobbs, their position has been further compromised as a series of governments have sought to fight the drug war first on a domestic and then on an international platform, turning the focus of policing from Britain's streets to foreign climes and back again, like a searchlight on a watchtower that fails to find its target.

With each new government has come a change in emphasis in policy as it responds to the failures of the last administration. But in doing so the top-down reorganisations have never allowed law enforcers to settle, with changes causing investigations on the ground to lose momentum or be cancelled as resources and staff are redeployed. 'The gangs can react overnight. But governments and police react on a three-to-five-year cycle of policy,' says former Scottish Police Chief Graeme Pearson who believes the constant reorganisation of the police forces since the 1970s has created 'blindspots' for the criminal fraternity in which to work.

'Structural changes create a diversion for staff as they take on new roles, planning structures and new ways of working – and cartels take advantage of this upheaval. SOCA will now merge into the national crime agency, and that doesn't start until 2013, and by that time the drug trade will have shifted considerably.'

The policy changes started in earnest under Margaret Thatcher in the 1980s as cheap, smokable heroin from the Middle East and South East Asia poured into the country. The Tory government acted quickly and drug enforcement was handed substantial amounts of money with which to tackle the new threat. But it was not only front-line police who had a fresh injection of cash. A new era of uber law enforcer was born that would police by intelligence, and drug crime would effectively shape policing.

At first police tried to mimic what they saw as the pyramid-style structure of the drug trade: numerous base-level street sellers, the middle market and a handful of top-end traffickers. At the top sat the National Drugs Intelligence Unit (NDIU), which filtered information down to specialist drug wings of regional crime squads and local drug squads. The NDIU was rebranded as the National Criminal Intelligence Service (NCIS) in 1992, and alongside the National Crime Squad continued to see the drug trade, making up three-quarters of its caseload, as its major quarry.

One of the problems senior organised-crime officers faced was that their foe was highly adaptable, elusive, and very difficult to pin down. Often, by the time investigators were able to gain a composite picture of an organisation, it had mutated. Organised crime was so much easier to tackle if it was, indeed, organised. But police have always been keen to play up the 'highly organised' nature of drug gangs. The more corporate or militaristic organised-crime groups are made to be, according to one senior drug detective, the more money police will be given to fight them.

Three decades ago, John Grieve, head of the Met Police drug squad in the late 1980s and early 1990s, called drug networks 'a threadbare patchwork quilt of alliances and hatreds'. He said that what the police described in the media as a 'drug business' could be, as earlier described, a group of people connected, from a café in Liverpool to a Colombian cocaine producer, by 'four handshakes'.

Yet however streetwise the drug detectives thought they were, or however much the structure at the top was reshuffled, it became increasingly apparent that, with rising levels of drugs use and an increasing number of criminal firms becoming involved in the drug trade, the police's attempts to stem the tide were not enough. And policing powers and responsibilities extended to combat its financial muscle that allowed it to evade detection.

Tony Blair's Labour government came to power in 1997 with a new determination to break the financial backbone of the organisations behind the street drug sellers. 'What we're trying to do is say the issue of drugs and international organised crime is so serious that we have to treat it for what it is, an international business, a cruel business,' Blair told the G8 summit in Japan in 2000.

The upshot was the Proceeds of Crime Act 2002, which consolidated and strengthened the police's ability to investigate and seize the proceeds of crime. It was a legislative sledge-hammer that turned a key principle of British law – of being presumed innocent before proven guilty – on its head. And not just for drug dealers. Anyone with a bank account, mortgage or hidden vaults of cash is now accountable in law to be able to produce a paper trail proving that their financial dealings are legitimate. Any payment of £10,000 or over made in cash is now flagged up as potentially suspicious. For the first time it made British banks, the city, mortgage advisers, car salesmen and shop owners potentially unwitting accomplices where money once passed hands in daily business.

Where once money laundering was considered a crime after the fact, evidence of collusion in trafficking triggers an investigation delving back up to six years into financial accounts. But while the legislation overturned legal principles, it became a PR tool for the government as an ever-growing body of evidence was coming to light that they were losing the war on drugs.

Jumping forward to 2003, an internal 'blue sky' drug-policy document written by Blair's private adviser, former director general of the BBC John Birt, revealed that traditional law enforcement was soaking up large amounts of public cash while doing little to stem the flow of drugs. However, the briefing argued that the present policy should not only be continued, but that it must be 'proclaimed' in the national press as often as possible.

Drug crime took on a fresh international perspective in 2006 as the law-enforcement spotlight was cast on drug criminals, in Spain, West Africa and the Caribbean. It took the fight, and focus, to producing nations. With a £20 million annual budget and 4,000 staff including specialists from MI5 and MI6, SOCA promised to 'make life hell for gangsters and drug barons'.

The agency, dubbed by the media 'Britain's version of the FBI', incorporated the old National Crime Squad and NCIS. Its top priorities were tackling human trafficking and the illegal drugs trade. 'We are not dealing with shambling amateurs. It is a global business, its captains are practical and we have to be equally tough, intelligent, broad-ranging and rigorous in return,' said the prime minister.

But the agency was criticised for failing to fulfil its brief of bringing down Britain's Mr Bigs. The Home Affairs Select Committee described its performance as 'disappointing' in 2009 after it emerged that it was seizing £1 from gangs for every £15 in its budget. And in 2011, when David Cameron laid out his plans to relaunch SOCA as the National Crime Agency in 2014, under the banner Global to Local, and on the back of a consultation exercise called 'Policing in the Twenty-First Century: Reconnecting Police and the People', there were raised eyebrows as observers looked on yet another rebranding of Britain's elite anti-organised crime agency with cynicism. Home Secretary Theresa May declared the new agency would be vital in thwarting the criminal gangs bringing drugs on to the streets, 'affecting neighbourhoods across the country'.

But while law-enforcement agencies are tasked with bringing down the chimera-like Mr Bigs, it is at street level where most drug policing is concentrated. In 2010, only 2 per cent of the 212,784 drug seizures were made by the UK Border Agency. Apart from the clampdown on illegal raves in the early 1990s and calls for middle-class cocaine users to be mindful of the law in the 2000s, the focus of day-to-day policing, prioritised by successive Home Office drug strategies, is fixed firmly upon the cyclical buying and selling on the streets of crack cocaine and heroin.

*

An hour out of east London sits the Suffolk market town of Ipswich. With an eye on the capital's crowded housing market, property developers have built a slew of upmarket new homes near the town's revamped docks. The idea was to encourage economic migration and tempt London's office workers into the relatively cheaper, and more rural, Suffolk commuter belt. But the developers were not the only ones to spot a business opportunity. For nearly a decade now, police in Ipswich, like their counterparts in many commuter towns around Britain, have been struggling to cope with the growing influence on their patch of city-based organisations making trips from the capital to sell crack and heroin.

When the dealers first came on to the radar in Ipswich in 2003, those picked up by police were young black men from gangs in Brent, Hackney and Newham, dressed in the London 'gangsta' uniform of chunky chains, designer jeans and expensive trainers. With cheaper drugs, a reliable supply and a feel for violence, the Londoners had decided to flex their muscle away from the crowded scene in their own backyard by grabbing the business from local dealers, and 'serving up' to the town's estimated 1,000 crack and heroin addicts.

Suffolk Police hit back with Operation Wolf, one of the largest anti-drugs actions ever undertaken in the county. Surveillance teams and three undercover officers bought drugs using traceable banknotes and gathered information on the inner workings of the town's number one crack-and-heroin-selling outfit at the time, the London-based T Business. At dawn one morning, police swooped on the key players in the gang at a series of addresses, seizing mobile phones and the all-important stash – a car boot full of crack and heroin fresh from the capital.

While the T Business were in custody awaiting trial, the Londonisation of Ipswich's drug market continued. In December 2006 it made national headlines when twenty-four-year-old south Londoner Jimoh Plunkett was killed after being caught in the crossfire in a shoot-out between rival London gangs at the town's Zest nightclub. But by the time the Operation Wolf arrests came to trial in 2007, the local newspaper gallantly declared success in the battle to rid the town of the gun- and drug-toting invaders.

POLICE DESTROY IPSWICH'S DRUG NETWORK

TODAY, for the first time, the full story of how Ipswich police decimated a London gang who controlled the town's drug-dealing market can be told.

A massive covert operation ended in raids on five properties, seizures of crack, heroin, and cash, thirty-seven arrests and more than two dozen convictions.

After two long years, a series of court cases and more than twenty defendants, the final trial for the police's Operation

> Wolf ended with the conviction of Ipswich drug dealer Johnny Callie. Callie was one of ten main players in the T Business, which was controlled by a gang of London drug dealers who infiltrated and flooded the town's drug market.

But the headline was not nearly so final as it sounded. While it took two years, considerable amounts of public money and untold hours of police and prosecutors' time to nail the organisation, it took just three weeks for Ipswich's drug market to return to business as usual.

T Business associates from London, as well as new dealers sniffing an opportunity, swiftly arrived to fill the gap. A SIM card belonging to the gang and containing the phone numbers of most of the town's crack and heroin addicts was simply reactivated after being sold to new blood, who promptly sent out a text to all contacts with a new number to call. It was a seamless transition more akin to a company takeover than a drug-market free-for-all. Detectives estimate they identified around twenty-four new drug-selling outfits in the two-year period between the arrest and the conviction of the T Business.

In Ipswich, like everywhere in Britain, drug dealers set up shop and are dismantled by the police in conveyor-belt fashion – a cycle that goes on largely unnoticed by the public. As supermarket shoppers do with checkout workers, crack and heroin buyers view the changing faces of their sellers with little attention. As soon as one outfit is shut down, another appears, often with a different modus operandi. It is a cat-and-mouse game that is played out on Britain's streets every day.

For every police success, those managing the dealers merely tweak their tactics, effectively taking their pursuers back to stage one. When runners are picked up on the streets, they start selling from local drug users' flats. When police target black suspects, they send out white dealers, and when that ploy is rumbled, they switch to Asian dealers. When they realise that mobile-phone texts are being used as evidence to convict their foot soldiers, they make sure that their phones are BlackBerrys and that they are using BlackBerry Messenger (BBM) service (Unlike text messaging or Twitter, BBM is a private social network where almost all messages are encrypted when they leave the sender's phone – meaning that many messages are untraceable by the authorities) and that only short phone calls using coded conversations are made.

To reduce risk and baffle the police, runners are sent out in teams: one with a phone, another with the drugs and a third with the money. When convictions on the basis of DNA evidence begin to rocket, dealers order their sellers to wear gloves. Gang members have even been known to attend court hearings for a free briefing on the latest police tactics.

'I've got two wigs in my wardrobe at home, one black and one brown,' says PC Gemma Astley, in a pub around the corner from her police HQ in a northern coastal town. She is one of only a handful of officers in her police force who specialise in drug enforcement. 'If I'm carrying out surveillance on drug dealers I need to disguise myself. I'll pop one on, change my clothes, maybe put on some leggings and scrape back my hair. I can fit in anywhere.'

A former part-time actress, PC Astley joined the police fourteen years ago. She applied for the drug unit because of a long-running fascination with gangster flicks and a desire to understand how the big fish operated. She was also painfully aware of the other side of the drug trade – several friends from the market town where she grew up had died from heroin overdoses.

'It's easier for women to do undercover drugs work. I can carry out surveillance on a dealer in a park by reading a book on a bench for hours without arousing suspicion. Young male dealers get nervy if another young guy is hanging around. I can literally bump into the dealers I'm watching and they don't bat an eyelid. But if one of the guys on the squad spends hours hanging around a park they are going to look out of place.'

Although the squad have little in common with those involved in the street drug scene, PC Astley enjoys the fact she is au fait with a world about which most members of the public know very little. 'At the moment we have fifteen businesses working side by side. You will usually get at least four who are operating on any one day,' says PC Astley. 'Firm A has reappeared after a few months out. Firm B has several runners and a manager in charge of their phone. Firm C are always about and then you've got Firm D, a new lot.' Heroin and crack addicts will get text messages from the businesses in town telling them their product is available and, like any consumer, they will migrate towards the best deal. 'We look out for users on "the stomp", the unmistakable, determined way of walking they have when they are on the way to buy drugs.'

While there is pressure from the top brass on the drug squad to generate a steady stream of arrests, there is little pride in collaring a user-dealer with two bags of heroin. The results that matter to drug police, and the most likely route to getting to the stash, usually involve resources, manpower and patience.

PC Harry Copeland, a colleague of PC Astley on the drug

team, is in his thirties. Out of uniform he looks more like a member of an indie band than a drug-squad detective. 'There was one group of young lads who moved between here and their base in a major city, supplying drugs to street dealers and returning to replenish their stash,' says PC Copeland. 'They were making about £1,000 a day, and were very switched on. They knew full well we were on the lookout for out-of-towners, so they "embedded" themselves here. They had each found a local girlfriend to help them blend in. One rented a flat above a shop near a church graveyard. They were enjoying themselves – smoking cannabis in the day while dishing out crack and heroin, and taking cocaine when they went out clubbing with the local lasses.

'We hadn't had much success catching them with the stash, which was what we needed in court, so we decided to set up a covert surveillance operation.'

Using a house opposite the flat, the squad watched the gang for a few hours each day. Transactions, chiefly supplying street dealers, were recorded with a video camera, the quick-click camera often featured in TV shows being useless in capturing lightning-fast drug swaps. After two weeks of pains-taking surveillance, the link between the dealers and the stash was made. 'Early one morning we saw one of the lads pop out the front door into a side passage, move a wheelie bin to one side and lift up one of the paving stones. We were wondering what he was up to and then he pulled out a package.' The next day the flat was raided and the gang arrested. The dealer who rented the flat received a five-year sentence.

It is not just the often cunning tactics of the dealers that drug police are up against. Unlike their quarry, they are hampered by limited resources and the criminal justice system within which they operate. One detective who has worked in his force's drug unit in the north-east of England for over a decade recalls his first bust. He caught six men standing in a room in front of £15,000 worth of heroin. Back at the station, flushed with excitement after what seemed like a fine result for a rookie, he was told that the case would be dropped: there was neither the time nor the money to arrest and prosecute all six men.

Even more surprising – and something that police forces are loath to admit – is that because of financial constraints, drug dealers in many parts of the country are less likely to be arrested by specialist drug officers in the afternoon, on bank holidays and on Sundays.

'We would be discouraged by our bosses from arresting someone towards the end of the day because of the overtime factor. And dealers are often aware of that,' says Glen, a drug detective from the Home Counties, who did not want to be identified. Officers who carry out a drug-dealing arrest must complete the process back at the station themselves, rather than hand it on to a colleague working a later shift. 'We spot a user buying a few bags of heroin from a dealer and we grab them both. That would take five officers – two taking out the dealer, two on the user and one doing the surveillance. We would need the user because he holds the vital evidence of the sale. If you arrest two people at 2 p.m. then most of you would be busy till 10 p.m. It's a lot of overtime.'

Another drug detective, based in Merseyside, described a similar situation. 'When we make an arrest, a suspect is grabbed, taken to the station and strip-searched. Evidence – phones, lists of sales, drugs – all needs to be bagged up and put in the property book. The inspector may authorise a search of properties in order to link anything at home to the transaction. This could involve dog handlers and officers looking for something the size of a peanut. Six officers looking for drugs in a house can take four hours. This all has to be listed and documented. Back at the station the suspects are interviewed, so we have to wait for a solicitor to turn up.

'A straightforward job can take hours for all the officers involved and so arrests late in the day are avoided,' says the officer. 'But, by the end of the financial year in March, it's all about spending money: our bosses are desperate to get rid of any under spend. There is usually a feeding frenzy in March by officers in my force fighting for overtime.'

And, as the recession bites the financial divide between the haves (the drugs gangs) and the have-nots (the police) widens. A survey carried out in 2011 found half of all police forces in England and Wales admitted they would have to scale down their efforts to catch drug dealers because of shrinking budgets. Tactics worst affected will be those seen as having more long-term and deeper benefits, such as intelligence gathering, covert surveillance and forensic analysis.

Back in the northern coastal town, it is not just endless cuts to resources – the drug unit has been cut by a half in under ten years – that handicaps drug officers. In a case that still leaves the town's drug team spinning in amazement, officers were delighted to find a 'copybook' drug den during a raid that ended a ten-month investigation into a professional outfit which had set up shop at a local drug user's flat.

Police burst in and collared one of the main dealers. On a bureau in the front room sat a large mound of heroin, a razor blade, a rail ticket from his base in a nearby city to the town (used to scoop up the heroin), a set of weighing scales, small drug-deal bags, made-up wraps and around £500 in crumpled £10 and £20 notes. The icing on the cake was a notebook detailing all the deals that had been done that day, listing what drugs had been sold to whom and where. Everything was covered in fingerprints. 'The local lad even admitted that he had been putting the dealer up and "serving up" for him,' says PC Copeland. 'It was a hook, line and sinker case, something out of a police training manual at Hendon,' he says. 'Case closed? Not at all.

'The dealer was charged with conspiracy to supply Class A drugs. But the jury finds him not guilty. They believed his story, that he'd come up to our town to buy a car but had ended up being locked in a stranger's house after trying to buy some cannabis,' says PC Copeland, laughing. 'He somehow convinced the jury that the reason his fingerprints were all over the drugs, bags and scales was because he picked them up out of curiosity. We were devastated, you don't get a more cut-and-dried case than that – and yet he walks away. We were left thinking why do we bother?'

Even in inner-city areas, drug enforcement is a low-visibility activity which the average citizen will be unlikely to witness. There is a vague public perception, largely shaped by fictional portrayals and by stories in the media, that drug police are hard-bitten mavericks who ply their trade in the chaotic and violent margins of society, using their cunning to take out low-life pushers and big-time villains. But, although the job is punctuated by a string of disappointments and brick walls, PC Astley does not see her quarry as the modern-day folk devil featured in public discourse.

'There are two things that have surprised me about the people I've been chasing over the years. First, that these people are not idiots; it's a clever business. Secondly, while there are some pretty nasty pieces of work out there, some of them are just ordinary people. Behind every user and runner, there's a story,' she says. 'A lot of people say drug addicts and drug dealers are scum of the earth, but they don't know anything about them.'

Although drug policing is a seemingly glamorous and exciting role for a police officer – with proactive investigations, search-warrant busts, surveillance and a large degree of autonomy – most of the drug squad's time is spent scrolling through intelligence databases and catching up with paperwork. Matthew Bacon, a law lecturer at Sheffield University who embedded himself with drug police units around the country, has written a thesis on police drug law enforcement on the streets. 'While they see more action than most police and get the chance to put together cases from the first raid to the court, the time these officers spent on the street was actually very little. The drug police and the drug dealers and the drug users existed in entirely different worlds – occasionally their paths would cross.'

Peter Gair, a senior CPS advocate who has put together scores of cases against drug dealers around the UK, is philosophical about the endless stream of dealers passing through the system. 'In theory, putting dealers in jail is supposed to deter other dealers. The simple fact is: money can be made by selling drugs. As long as there is demand there will always be a supply. Like working on the production line, the quicker you work, the more you get rid of, but whether our efforts are reducing the amount of work I don't honestly know. If we didn't do our job it would be a lot worse. But are we actually getting anywhere, are we reducing the problem, are we just delaying the inevitable? I try not to think about that – it could be very depressing if you come to a certain conclusion.'

For PC Astley, it's the buzz of getting a result that keeps her motivated. 'It's a game of cat and mouse. That's how I've always looked at it. It's my job to catch them and it's their job to get away. If they do get away I know I'll catch them next time. I don't get upset or angry. It's not personal. It's frustrating, but what keeps me going is the hit of a good result.'

There are darker arts that police must use in order to land a heavy blow on drug organisations. Police know that in the criminal world, loyalty is fickle and everyone has a price, especially if their liberty is at stake. Lowly gang associates and acquaintances have a reputation for 'taking one for the team' and doing time in jail rather than confessing all. But police know that for every ultra-loyal associate, there will be several who can be persuaded to drip-feed inside information. Catching dealers selling drugs and working out where the day's stash is kept are commendable results. But it is only when police are able to penetrate the outer layers of foot soldiers and accomplices that an area's drug trade can be disrupted at any kind of meaningful level. To do this, police must place themselves within the drug underworld and into areas of policing that remain shrouded in secrecy and controversy.

'It is no good knowing that people are drug dealers, you need to know the specifics – what is going to happen at what time, and that's where informants come in,' says Peter, a former drug-squad detective. His first informant offered up the address of a prolific cannabis dealer in exchange for being given bail on a charge of credit-card fraud. Soon, he had a constant drip-feed of information, given to him by around a dozen registered informants, which was crucial to building up a picture of the local scene. When he wanted to befriend someone he knew held valuable information, he would conspire to 'bump' into them in the street, at court or in custody suites. One man Peter had been looking at for some time, a familiar face in a gang which ran the crack trade in a large English market town, was recruited days after his car broke down.

'I was driving around and spotted this guy on the side of his road with his head in his car bonnet. I walked up to him and his face dropped because he thought I was going to hassle him. I offered to give him a push and a lift home and he was gobsmacked. He thanked me and I said no problem. Then a week later I get a phone call, he wants a chat.

'He gives me the low-down on this rival crack-dealing gang. Who does what, the hierarchy, phone numbers, how they are planning to spread the trade into the next town. He opened a window on to a world that we might never have known. He was our eyes and ears on that firm, and we managed to bring it down as a result of his information.'

Each year police forces hand over around £6 million, in amounts between £50 and £100,000, to a network of 5,000 registered informants, known officially as CHISs (Covert Human Information Sources). The vast majority of intelligence gathered from informants, around three-quarters, is about drugs, and police admit they have more intelligence on drug dealers, often provided by addicts, rival dealers and disgruntled partners, than they know what to do with.

But drug officers are now forbidden to handle their own informants, since the introduction in 2004 of an imaginary 'sterile corridor' between specialist informant handlers and the officers who act on the intelligence, enacted after mounting instances of violence against informers whose identities have been leaked. While the new system has tightened security, some long-serving drug squad officers admit that its sanitisation has resulted in less reliable, and less fruitful intelligence.

When all efforts to gather evidence against crucial targets have failed, police will attempt to infiltrate their network using specialist undercover officers, a role made infamous in recent years by former undercover detective Mark Kennedy, whose close relationships with women while infiltrating environmental protest groups caused outrage and the collapse of a trial in 2010. Kennedy cut his teeth as an infiltrator of drug gangs before he targeted protest groups.

Police have had many successes by embedding undercover officers in drug organisations, but nevertheless it is a risky strategy prone to the occasional disaster. Two undercover officers posing as crack-cocaine dealers were shot by Birmingham Yardie gang members during a set up 'drugs deal' in 1994 when the bag they were handing over was opened to reveal bundles of banknotes stamped with the words 'WEST MIDLANDS POLICE'.

It was into this highly dangerous line of work that, in the early 2000s, Peter became submerged, after impressing senior officers with his ability to blend into the drug scene. He spent eight years in deep cover as a drug dealer, moving across various forces and parts of the country, working his way slowly and patiently up the drug chain until he was able to get to those in a position of power. His expertise at keeping his nerve in the face of what were some of the country's most violent drug dealers, earned him the respect of his seniors and the nickname 'Donnie Brasco', the undercover name of an FBI agent who infiltrated the Mafia as jewel thief in the late 1970s and helped put more than a hundred leading Mafiosi behind bars, among his fellow detectives.

One of Peter's most high-profile cases involved the son of a Jamaican gangster who had recently retired after a long and profitable drug career in a major northern city. Tyrell was twenty-one years old. Despite his youth, he controlled most of the area's crack and heroin trade, and was selling approximately £1.8 million of the drugs each year. With a growing reputation for extreme violence and a terrifying arsenal of weapons, he had become number one target for the area's organised-crime unit. But all attempts to generate evidence against Tyrell, including the targeting of informers and use of surveillance, had come to nothing. So Peter was dispatched to gather evidence against him. It was a job that lasted over a year and a half.

'He was paranoid about direct involvement, even his runners wore ski masks,' says Peter. 'His gang bought pay-as-you-go mobile phones and changed the number, the SIM card and the handsets every two weeks. He was a very cautious, street-wise, entrepreneurial young man who controlled people a lot older than him through fear and violence. He was ferocious.'

Peter set himself up in the area as a heroin user and sub-dealer who bought in bulk, claiming he sold the drugs on to dealers in a nearby rural town. It was only after six months and around thirty transactions that his runner took off his ski mask. Meanwhile he heard reports of the violence meted out by Tyrell to those who crossed him. One unfortunate runner was stripped and locked in a room with two baited pit bulls. His badly mauled but still alive body was dumped in full display in the high street as a warning to others thinking of ripping off the gang. At a meeting with a target one night, Peter heard that Tyrell was lying low after shooting a rival dealer while he waited in his car.

Around twelve months into the operation Peter made the

breakthrough he had been seeking – he had heard on the grapevine that Tyrell had a weakness: gold.

Peter started using gold jewellery instead of £700 or £800 lumps of cash in return for his regular packages of heroin. When Tyrell heard about this, as Peter had hoped, he took a personal interest, wanting to inspect the goods and pick out his favourites. Every time they met it was in an alley and Tyrell was never close to any heroin. When Peter failed to turn up with the gold one day, Tyrell's frustration led him to calling Peter on his personal mobile phone. The evidence gathered from the secret footage and recordings made by Peter, and from monitoring Tyrell's phone were used to secure a conviction.

Peter never carried a firearm and he never took drugs, nor did he get close to any of his targets. 'They were people I had no real affinity with, they were people who did not flinch at extreme violence, whose job was to make a living from drug addiction.'

In one northern city suburb he worked his way up the chain and befriended its leader, a Yardie named Tony, who ran a firm from the attic of a heavily guarded café situated in a no-go area for the public or police. The first conversation that started their friendship was about the superior taste of a particular chocolate bar.

As a result of their friendship Peter would always be given the best deals. One time Tony summoned him up to the attic room at the dealer's HQ. Certain he was going to be rumbled, and planning his only route of escape – jumping into thin air through a closed window – he was shocked to see his dread-locked friend holding a baby in his arms. 'He just wanted to show me his baby, because he liked me and trusted me. I almost fainted with relief.' In the end his cover remained intact and the gang was taken out. 'Tony was stunned at the revelation that one of his customers was an undercover cop.'

Peter says his time as an undercover drug detective was a period of 'intense pressure' for which he received little reward, and from which there was little respite. Not only did he narrowly escape being stabbed to death in a back alley by someone who had stolen his 'stash', there were many times when he would be discovered, and possibly killed. On one occasion he was bundled into the boot of a car, driven to waste ground and stripped of his clothes because drug dealers were sure they would find a tape recorder. It was one of the few occasions he was not wired up.

It was not only the criminals that made his life difficult. 'It made me realise how bad cops can be to drug addicts. I was abused, assaulted and threatened with being fitted up by having drugs planted on me on a regular basis,' says Peter. Undercover policing is a risky and expensive strategy. That officers are regularly exposed to high levels of danger by infiltrating drug gangs, by essentially double-crossing people who have track records of violence and homicide, is an indication of the level of threat that police believe the drug trade poses to this country. And while drug organisations may tie up a deal in an evening over a handshake and a few drinks, for the police to catch them in the act, and to relieve them of their profits, can run into months and years.

'It took us two years' work to be able to take those pictures,' says a senior detective in the bowels of Scotland Yard, pointing to a selection of police photographs of a Ferrari, a large bundle of €500 notes, a shipment of cocaine and a revolver. One of the Met's most senior money-laundering intelligence officers, he is talking about Operation Eaglewood, Scotland Yard's largest-ever simultaneous raid in 2008 which led to the final jailing in 2011 of thirty-three gang members – including a firefighter commended for his actions in the 7 July tube bombings – and the closure of the London hub of a money-laundering and drug-dealing network which distributed over £100 million worth of cocaine annually.

Operation Eaglewood was significant because the man at the centre of the drug ring, whose connections stretched to Colombia, Spain, Israel, India, Dubai, Morocco and other North African states, was a forty-seven-year-old Palestinian called Eyad Iktilat. He was not only the money man, but the middleman connecting drug gangs across the UK. 'We were monitoring a meeting between two drug gangs when a man turned up we had not seen before,' says the detective. 'So we started to look at him to work out who he was. We thought we might eliminate him in a week or so if nothing came up.'

But something did come up. A lengthy surveillance operation revealed that Iktilat's business, Royal Oak Taxis, on the face of it a run-down taxi-repair garage with metal shutters and a corrugated iron roof beneath the Westway flyover in Paddington, west London, was in fact a 'one-stop shop' for a vast money-laundering network. Iktilat was also a director of the nearby Euro Foreign Exchange, through which up to £1 million a day in drug money was laundered.

Millions of pounds in cash and drugs flowed through the garage's shuttered doors as the gangs used it as a 'clearing bank'. Teams of runners, or 'money mules', dropped sackfuls of sterling to be exchanged at 5 per cent commission into more easily transportable €500 notes – since banned from circulation in Britain because of their appeal to drug dealers – at the nearby foreign exchange.

'Iktilat was in the middle. Everyone else was on the periphery,' says the detective. 'Like the capital's diverse population, there were so many nationalities involved in Operation Eaglewood: Egyptian, Irish, Scottish and Palestinian. They found each other by word of mouth. Differences in ethnicity or religion don't matter when it comes to making money.

'We had to trace every transaction, join every dot to get the complete picture,' he explains. 'It was an exhaustive investigation, but necessary, and worth it in the end. Not only did his assets include the Ferrari, but also a Bentley, and a £750,000 plot of land in Malaga where he was planning to build a £2 million villa. We could have wrapped up the case a lot quicker, but we wouldn't have taken out the network, from the very bottom to the top. Iktilat was the top guy and he got thirty years.'

The Met's money-laundering unit say their work is the purest form of policing. 'Financial investigation is the last bastion of proper investigation,' comments a detective from that team, 'because you take it from arrest straight through to court. We build up the intelligence picture, we follow the money trail, we deal with every aspect of the court case and conviction and then we carry out the investigation for the confiscation order. When you are doing this there is a pride in it. That's why we come to work. Yesterday I seized a Bentley convertable. £75,000 worth of car, that gave me a buzz. Satisfaction is when you hand back mansions and villas bought by criminal proceeds to the local authorities in Spain or Ghana and know that when that drug dealer comes out of prison he won't be flying out to a swimming pool at his palace, he'll be applying for a council house. That's what gives me the buzz to carry on. They can do their time, but they don't like paying for it. POCA allows us to do this properly.'

As was the case in Operation Eaglewood, detectives are

increasingly finding that those who have the ability to turn tainted cash into usable assets, the money men, are often the spider at the centre of the web. They represent a key service industry for the modern drug trade, which by its very nature relies on cash. The practice of disguising or 'cleaning' illegally obtained money to make it appear legitimate is an essential part of business.

Banks are required to contact the authorities if their customers deposit more than £10,000 in cash. Because drug firms would alert the police to their business by doing so, they must find ways to introduce their money into the legitimate economy by whatever means possible. The more complicated the trail, the less likely money assets can be traced back to the street.

Britain's number two in the fight against organised crime is Andy Sellers, Deputy Director of SOCA. He says the new anti-money-laundering powers have already been used to help convict some of Britain's biggest crime lords.

North London gangster Terry Adams, who built up an estimated fortune of £200 million through a vast racketeering and drug-trafficking empire, was jailed in 2007 because he could not account for his wealth. The prosecution case was that Adams made around £11 million from crime by the age of thirty-five, then retired and began laundering the proceeds. The laundering was mainly conducted through the creation of sham companies that claimed to hire Adams as a consultant, giving him a modest taxable income. The funds were also invested into properties, antiques, offshore bank accounts, a yacht and several cars. Adams was released in 2011 and immediately embarked on a spending spree, for which he almost returned to jail. Under POCA rules Adams must declare everything he buys that is over £500.

Glaswegian gangster James Stevenson, nicknamed 'the Iceman' because of his cold and calculating cruelty, was given a twelve-year sentence for money laundering in 2007. His organisation was linked to the importation of drugs from South America, Africa, Turkey and Europe, and the investigation into his organisation's affairs has led to the seizure of more than twelve tons of drugs and the arrest of seventy-one people. Stevenson had previously been arrested on suspicion of murdering another crime boss. But he was jailed only after police discovered evidence of money laundering over a three-year period, chiefly through the acquisition and re-sale of fifty-five high-value watches, and the purchase of a fleet of cars registered in his wife's name used to run a taxi service.

'Chasing the money has a greater impact on disrupting the cycle of business than chasing the product,' says Sellers over a coffee in SOCA's discreet HQ in Southwark, south London. 'That is where we can hurt and disrupt gangs the most. We can force people into living "pay-as-you-go" lifestyles because they know there is a chance if they don't spend it, it's ours. Lots of criminals live hand to mouth, because of our efforts to locate and seize their assets. We are finding fairly sophisticated criminals who live in very basic houses and drive ordinary cars – all their money is going on holidays and fast-living abroad once they have smuggled the cash out of the country.'

But today, money-laundering scams are as varied as the make-up of the drug firms themselves. Methods include breaking cash up into small amounts and placing it in bank accounts (known as 'smurfing' because the sums are small and easily hidden); buying goods that will not depreciate in value such as special-edition Rolexes and vintage cars; washing it via high-street businesses (most commonly pubs, clubs, nail bars and beauty salons), using the hawala banking system, an informal system of transferring money used for centuries in the Middle East and South Asia. Other organisations gamble online and deliberately lose to an accomplice, or simply stuff a suitcase with cash and take it abroad. Police once found £50,000 in a washing machine in the back of a lorry en route to Europe to be 'cleaned'.

'The easy part of the trade is buying drugs and selling them,' says Detective Sergeant Simon Marsh, of Scotland Yard's Serious Crime Directorate's Payback Unit. 'It's dealing with the cash that's the hard bit. If you want to get large amounts of money to be made to look legitimate then cash businesses are the way forward. And the best cash businesses are high-street stores. The amount of money that's declared to the revenue is significantly more than the actual profit. Overnight that drugs money has become part of the legitimate economy; you've paid your VAT and now you can do what you want with it. The cynical policeman would say most of these businesses in London – nail bars, hairdressers, tanning salons – are laundering money.

'There has been a move away from traditional investment in property; it's less of a good option today. Now it's more common to move money out of the country using places like Western Union. Pre-paid cards are another new trend. Put £5,000 of credit on the card, leave the country and when you're abroad, take out the cash. The company charges you 1.5 per cent, so they make money. These cards, unlike cheques, aren't classed as cash under seizure legislation. We've stopped people with shoulder bags containing 200 of them. The same person can order lots of cards out, or use stolen identities to avoid suspicion. The company gets £5 for each card so they don't care who buys them, no checks are made. It's just like the oyster-card system: charge them up, and away you go.'

In the chase for the money, police have even resorted to putting up posters, featuring a man wearing a suit, dark glasses and decked out in gold jewellery, with the message: 'Too much bling? Give us a ring', asking for the public to be on the lookout for flashy drug dealers. Tellingly for the police's new direction in hunting down the proceeds of crime, British Transport Police has begun training its army of sniffer dogs to detect not only the odour of cocaine, cannabis, heroin and ecstasy, but also large quantities of banknotes.

As with the drug dealers on the street, the higher echelons of the trade are cunning, careful, adept at avoiding detection and always inventing new ways of staying one step ahead of the law. As with policing the trade on the street, and despite POCA and the Crime Mapping Project, it is a battle in which police find it hard to make any headway.

Despite new legislation and increasing powers, the ability of police and intelligence agencies to stem the flow of drugs into the country from abroad is severely limited, not just by the scale of the task, but by the unwillingness of some regimes to play ball. Operation Westbridge, a £1 million British-run mission to stem the flow of drugs from Ghana, which had become a major new drug route for South American cocaine, has been beset with problems such as local drug police actively helping traffickers by sabotaging expensive scanning equipment and tipping them off.

It is a game our senior drug gang-busters admit they are losing. 'There are many things that make this an uneven battle,' says Sellers. 'The big players are cash rich and connected. We can't match them from a resource point of view – they have an unfair advantage. And when we get the key players the peripheral figures will morph themselves into a new gang.

'And just as you think you are beginning to understand the machinations of one trade, something else will come along. We were gaining a foothold in the cocaine trade when the online market emerged. You need a completely different sort of investigator for this – not accountants or undercover officers working the streets. There are fundamental changes occurring not only to the drug trade but also to how we can police it. What are they going to do? These are very interesting times to be writing a book on the drug trade in this country.'

What is being done to police drug trading on the web? In its submission to the Home Affairs Select Committee Inquiry on drug policy in 2012, SOCA said that between 2010 and 2011, 120 websites selling mephedrone and naphyrone had been closed down as a result of SOCA action.

But police admit they are perplexed by the battle ahead. 'Police officers on both sides of the Atlantic say the same thing,' John Carr, an Internet security adviser to the British government and the United Nations, told the BBC. 'We don't have enough courts, we don't have enough judges, and we don't have enough police officers to tackle the real scale of illegal behaviour on the Internet. What that means is increasingly we're going to have to look to technical solutions, we're going to have to look to the Internet industry to help civil society deal with this really enormous problem the dark web has created.'

In truth, most of the illegal activity on the Internet, especially that which is encrypted, remains beyond the reach of the police. The right to private communication is enshrined in US law, while the ability to remain anonymous was a key weapon used by pro-revolution bloggers during the Arab Spring.

Despite the challenges faced by the police and UK Border Agency in stemming the drug trade, they have a considerable list of successes on their CVs. Moreover, chasing drug criminals has dragged policing methods into the twenty-first century, having led to many major innovations across the board. Forces recognise the benefits of harm-reduction policies and that police have a role in helping people addicted to drugs, rather than merely arresting them.

As expert players of the long game, as many locked-up drug dealers know, enforcement agencies will eventually get their man. While it is accepted that senior drug figures see being caught and losing their liberty – and now their riches – as an occupational hazard, the continued efforts of the police ensure that the day-to-day existence of many drug criminals is an uncomfortable one, more so than many would be prepared to admit, dominated by a constant need to watch your back, to guard your conversations and to distance yourself from everyday life.

Yet police know there is only so much they can do, that they cannot win the game and that they have to manage the drug trade, rather than drive it away for good. The modern era of drug policing looks set to be a very different one to the days of the maverick drug squad detective in the 1980s. Now the focus, especially for local and regional forces, will be to operate at the level of a public service duty. If there is a specific problem that the public want to get cleared up, the police will respond.

This new way of doing things was revealed in an event that appeared to turn into Britain's first drug-bust safari, as dawn broke on a dark December morning in 2011.

Around 150 local schoolchildren, community workers and senior business leaders stood bleary-eyed and shivering in a warehouse in Manchester. Sharing the room with 1,000 police officers, many in riot gear, the locals listened to a briefing by a senior officer about what they could expect to see on the trip around some of the less salubrious parts of the city. Operation Audacious was, he said, the biggest ever operation against drug dealers in Manchester, and onlookers would have a ringside seat as officers raided the homes of one hundred suspects.

Then the police's guests piled into a fleet of hired minibuses to begin the slow crawl at Safari park speed behind a procession of police vans and officers on foot, into the habitats of drug sellers in Manchester, Bolton and Stockport. As the journey began, Operation Audacious, or #OpAudacious as it was known on Twitter, was launched in a multimedia publicity whirl worthy of the launch of a new pop band.

A press release, Facebook page, flyers and a YouTube video, as well as the Twitter feed, were launched to promote the tour. Senior Manchester police figures were at pains to stress that this was an action brought about as a direct result of public concerns and the wishes of the community. The biggest ever drug bust in the city's history was prompted by, witnessed by, and for the benefit of the public.

The raids began. Peering through the minibus windows, the passengers looked on as suspected drug dealers were dragged out of their freshly broken front doors in various states of undress, blinking under TV spotlights, and into the back of police vans.

Back at the warehouse HQ, a bank of huge TV screens showed the live action as officers dressed in riot gear entered a drug safe house in the suburb of Cheetham Hill. And, complete with the odd rebellious tweet, #OpAudacious was all over Twitter:

@GMPCityCentre
#OpAudacious taking place today across Manchester. GMP will be executing approximately 100 warrants on suspected drug dealers . . . more to come

@TrendsManc
#opaudacious is now trending in #Manchester

@SuptChrisSykes
Chief Supt Jackson: 'Today's strikes will have caused significant disruption to the users and suppliers of drugs in Manchester.'

@GMPCityCentre
On display in Piccadilly Gardens a BMW M3 that was seized from a Drug Dealer. #OpAudacious http://pic.twitter.com/MZoOYFUB

@simonwebbon
#OpAudacious reminds me of that episode of The Wire where the low rises are raided to please the Major, without actually achieving anything.

@GMPCityCentre
#OpAudacious update 72 arrests. Seized thousands of pounds cash, £2k of class A drugs, 15 blocks of cannabis, 20 bags of cannabis.

@gmpolice
Find out more about today's #opaudacious raids targeting drug dealers with this video: http://youtu.be/IMRgz6V0MY0

@Irsmith88
Very proud to watch Greater Manchester Police in action today.

@Alex Georges
#OpAudacious is exciting, keep the updates coming.

According to the Greater Manchester Police, the raids resulted in seventy-two arrests (with twenty-five being the average age of the suspect), £2,000 of Class A drugs seized, including fifteen blocks of cannabis, twenty bags of cannabis and a cannabis farm, a handful of stolen jewellery and a batch of stolen meat.

It would have taken months of planning and hundreds of hours of police and court time, but to Greater Manchester Police it was job done. The public asked for these dealers to be swept up and so they were, in a very public fashion. But, as Damon Barrett of the Harm Reduction Alliance said: what would a cost-benefit analysis of this operation and the laws and policies that underpin it conclude? 'Operation Audacious is representative of the positive feedback loop we've gotten ourselves into where fighting the drug trade is success enough. It is an expensive and circular dynamic which can lead nowhere in the long term.'

Britain's drug police are unkindly sandwiched between pressure from the public, media and politicians to stamp out the drug trade – or to at least appear as if they are – and the endless chase to catch the fox-like figure of the modern drug dealer. And although police put a brave face on it – whether that is in the hope they can outwit the drug gangs or out-resource them – there is something fateful about their mission.

Enforcement, at a global and national level, has had an impact. It has helped to shape the modern drug trade. Clampdowns have forced criminals to adopt new products, trafficking routes and production methods. But from the 1960s to the present day, as the emphasis has switched from chasing the criminal, to the product and then to the money, the battle against the drug trade has always been about chasing shadows.

The police accept that although they can partially dent and disrupt the drug trade they can only displace it, not defeat it. So the mantra of modern drug policing is damage limitation.

The focus of drug policing appears to have come full circle, back to the day-to-day policing of local communities. In the wake of the appointment of new, locally elected police commissioners, local drug chiefs will have to be seen to act swiftly in the face of public concern – reducing fear of drug crime, protecting communities from drug-related nuisance, minimising threats to public health.

So if police get a call about dealers selling drugs in a park they will act on it. As with a request from a resident for the council to come and pick up dumped rubbish, the police now look set to become a public service to be 'called out' to deal with nuisance drug crimes by the most vocal sections of the community.

But even this moderate aim may prove tough for the police to put into action. Since the 1960s, largely due to stop-and-search tactics, the policing of countless national strikes and protests and the demise of the beat bobby, law enforcement has become an institution that has lost its connection with local working class communities.

To the modern police force, if a crackdown on dealing in a public place leads to a favourable story in the local paper and the dealers switching their business operations to a private house, then that can be seen as a result.

It is perfectly reasonable for communities to want to be able to carry on their lives without bumping into drug dealers at every turn. The police, short on resources and fighting a woefully uneven battle against an array of powerful private businesses, know that they must pick their fights carefully. Focusing on the more visible manifestations of the trade diminishes some of the harm caused by the drug economy. However, as Britain's police chiefs are well aware, in the background the drug businesses are left to flourish unchecked. While the police have been forced into thinking local, the drug trade is becoming increasingly global.

5

Money

The Most Addictive Drug of All

In January 2009, Antonio Maria Costa, then the world's most senior official in the fight against the drug trade, gave a seemingly innocuous interview to an Austrian news magazine, *Profil*, about the size of the global drugs market. But, nearing the end of what would be an eight-year tenure as Executive Director of the United Nations Office on Drugs and Crime, Costa decided to lob a verbal grenade into the conversation. He had intelligence that drug money had kept the global banking system afloat during the 2008 financial crisis.

It was a jaw-dropping statement. Costa told *Profil* that he had seen evidence that the proceeds of organised crime was 'the only liquid investment capital' available to some banks on the brink of collapse. He said that a majority of the $352bn of drugs profits was absorbed into the economic system as a result.

'In the second half of 2008, liquidity was the banking system's main problem and hence liquid capital became an important factor,' said Costa, an Italian-born economics expert who spent three decades as a senior UN economist before becoming chief of the UNODC. 'Interbank loans were funded by money that originated from drug trade and other illegal activities [and that] there were signs that some banks were rescued in that way.' He said it was not his place to prosecute or name and shame the guilty institutions, but said he had received tip-offs from intelligence agencies and prosecutors that the tainted money had subsequently poured into banks in the City of London, Switzerland, Italy and the US.

Costa's growing anger at the inability of the banking system to distance itself from drug money had first surfaced in a speech he made at a conference in Frankfurt the previous year. He hinted that the financial crisis had not been entirely about complex issues such as sub-prime mortgages, but also a drive for wealth creation that had lost its moral compass. 'Many of the banks have engaged in something both stupid and diabolical,' wrote Costa. 'They have allowed the world's criminal economy to become part of the global economy.'

Costa wouldn't let it lie. In 2010, he turned to the right-wing *Executive Intelligence Review* magazine seeking support: 'The penetration of the financial sector by criminal money has been so widespread that it would probably be more correct to say that it was not the Mafia trying to penetrate the banking system, but it was the banking sector which was actively looking for capital – including criminal money – not only as deposits, but also as share acquisitions and in some cases, as a presence on boards of directors.'

Costa said that a key link between the banks and the drug gangs is 'an army of white-collar criminals – lawyers, accountants, realtors and bankers – who cover up for the [drug traffickers] and launder their proceeds' and called on governments, regulators and banks to redraw the distinction between the black economy of drug crime and the mainstream economy on which we all rely. 'In the financial institutions there are people who are involved in laundering not necessarily the money, but the paperwork which is necessary for making blood money licit.'

Like the three wise monkeys, British bankers denied knowledge of any transgression, claiming never to have been party to any 'regulatory dialogue' that would support Costa's theory. Regulators remained silent. Costa had offered no evidence. Without evidence the press had nothing to report.

For some commentators, Costa was a scaremonger, trying to steal the headlines to reinvigorate public and government support for a hard line on the drug industry, or to find a scapegoat for his failures to rid the world of the drug economy as he had promised in 1998.

But for others he was exposing the true financial strength and influence of the drug industry – and the City of London's role in facilitating it – for the first time. And in 2011, when a US court found America's fourth-largest bank-holding company awash with drug money, the relationship between the City of London and the cocaine cartels appeared to be much closer than anyone had previously thought.

'How a Big US Bank Laundered Billions from Mexico's Murderous Drug Gangs', screamed the headline. A special investigation in 2011 by the *Observer* revealed the closeness of organised crime to Wachovia, one of America's biggest banks, now owned by Wells Fargo. It was the first case to provide concrete evidence that by turning a blind eye global banks had struck up more than a passing relationship with criminal gangs seeking to wash their dirty profits.

The smoking gun that landed Wachovia in the headlines was discovered on 10 April 2006 when a DC-9 jet landed in the port city of Ciudad del Carmen on the Gulf of Mexico. The cargo included 5.7 tons of cocaine, valued at $100 million; more importantly, there was also a bundle of documents revealing that the smugglers had bought the plane with money cleaned by Wachovia.

The City of London's role in the Wachovia debacle might never have come to light if it had not been for Martin Woods, a Liverpudlian in his mid-forties who joined the London office of the bank in February 2005.

A former London drug-squad officer with twenty years' experience in the UK, he had specialised in probing money laundering first with the Metropolitan Police and then on secondment in the City of London. At Wachovia's London office he discovered an embarrassing paper trail that led from bureaux de change in the border towns of Mexico to the US bank, which had then passed the compliance papers to London for sign-off.

In his role as a compliance officer Woods was responsible for checking the audit trail of transactions to meet the international compliance regulations ensuring that the bank knew who its customers were and where the money had come from. His job was to flag up where transactions appeared tainted and he understood the patterns of money transfers that should alert suspicion.

It wasn't long before Woods' forensic alarm bells rang. The records of transactions being carried out among money changers and wire services in the border towns of Mexico had all the hallmarks of drug money. Just as drug traffickers send smaller consignments to get lost in the flow of trade, money launderers seek to avoid the financial radar of regulation in a similar fashion.

Woods found himself receiving batches of sequentially numbered travellers' cheques that bore neither signatures nor identity numbers and that totalled sums far in excess of that one might expect from the *casas de cambio* (CDC), bureaux de change-style money changers.

'In some cases they were relatively small sums, $600 in six individual cheques, but then at other times bundles of cheques would arrive covering tens of thousands of dollars.' And it wasn't just travellers' cheques that raised his suspicions: Woods received requests from small Mexican textile businesses to authorise multi-currency wire services. Then there were transfer requests to purveyors of luxury goods, largely high-end Swiss watchmakers. According to Woods almost everyone else at Wachovia was convinced the transactions were clean.

The steady drip-feed of travellers' cheques spurred Woods to alert the bank's officials in the US that drug money appeared to be pouring into its coffers. To Woods it was 'smurfing' on an industrial scale: each month, without any form of paper trail, tens of thousands of dollars were deposited which were then withdrawn from US banks. But whereas his discoveries were celebrated in the police force, at Wachovia his investigations were increasingly blocked and ignored by his bosses.

In September 2008 Woods performed what he describes as career suicide, sending a letter to the Financial Services Authority, the organisation charged with holding the banking community to account in the UK. He also sent copies of the letter to the DEA and the office of the Comptroller of the Currency (the most important banking regulator in the US). Wachovia were quick to respond. They challenged not only his right to probe matters outside of UK regulations – what happened abroad should be left abroad – they told him that he didn't understand how CDCs worked, and questioned his professional ability. 'The pressure to turn a blind eye was immense,' says Woods, who now runs his own forensic-accountancy service. In the end he felt he had no choice. At an international money-laundering conference Woods contacted US law-enforcement agencies.

Sitting down with US law enforcers, Woods helped unravel the financial records that had been discovered on the DC-9 jet in 2006. Once the patterns of transactions were identified the paper trail revealed that drug cartels had purchased the plane from the CIA and had used money laundered by Wachovia.

In 2010 Wachovia settled the biggest action brought under the US Bank Secrecy Act. It was sanctioned for failing to apply the proper anti-laundering strictures to the transfer of $378.4bn to CDCs. Court documents from Wachovia's 2010 settlement statement confirmed Woods's initial concerns: 'The nature of the CDC business allows money launderers the opportunity to move drug dollars that are in Mexico into CDCs and ultimately into the US banking system,' said the court document.

'On numerous occasions monies were deposited into a CDC by a drug-trafficking organisation. Using false identities, the CDC then wired that money through its Wachovia correspondent bank accounts for the purchase of airplanes for drug-trafficking organisations. As early as 2004,' the court document continued, 'Wachovia understood the risk that was associated with doing business with the Mexican CDCs. Wachovia was aware of the general industry warnings. As early as July 2005, Wachovia was aware that other large US banks were exiting the CDC business based on those warnings.'

Wachovia also paid federal authorities $110 million in forfeiture for allowing transactions later proved to be connected to drug smuggling, and incurred a $50 million fine for failing to monitor cash used to ship twenty-two tons of cocaine. 'Wachovia's blatant disregard for banking laws gave international cocaine cartels a virtual carte blanche to finance their operations,' said Jeffrey Sloman, the federal prosecutor.

'When I blew the whistle on Wachovia, I blew it on the UK's Financial Services Authority and the Office of the Comptroller of the Currency,' said Woods. 'Both were involved in what was a catastrophic failure of banking regulations – they gave the bank clean bills of health for five years despite an ever-growing mountain of evidence against it. Putting banking secrecy over the public interest is unforgivable.

'There is a way to tackle the drug economy. The question is, is there the will? As a whistle-blower, having gone through what I've gone through I wonder whether the whole thing is a charade. Some people in the City will hate me for saying this but I want people to think about what is happening all around them.

'The banks and the drug industry have what appears to be a mutually highly beneficial relationship. The global system of prohibition is just incentivising production in the poorest sections of the world and driving consumption in the rich. And it now has global influence – shaping the futures of countries and economies. The one thing that brings this all together is money.'

Woods says that few banks at board level would accept that they laundered money (they 'would be horrified') but, where the bonus culture dominates, some individuals will be blinded to the origins of investments by the potential rewards and, according to Woods, no bank is immune – and there are some places in the City where the doors are wide open to drug money.

The global financial services industry has not always been with us as it is today. Prior to 1979 the City was a closed shop that ran like an old boys' network. But that year Margaret Thatcher entered government and started a programme of reforms that would reshape it. Her plan was known as the 'Big Bang' and it heralded a new era.

Thatcher relaxed regulations that barred foreign investors from buying sterling, while removing the barriers that until then had effectively prevented British citizens from transferring wealth out of the country for investment purposes, or to deposits in foreign or offshore accounts.

Opening the doors of the City to international players, she introduced US working practices that changed the nature of City life: adopting the Wall Street mantra of 'greed is good', a bonus culture that haunts Britain to this day, and creating a generation of traders who would relish their status as Masters of the Universe.

Under the changes, the London Stock Exchange was linked to bourses around the world with funds traded at the click of a mouse and investment decisions made by computer programs. But, most importantly, the reforms would see the interlinking of the global banking system, with British high-street banks striking up alliances with small institutions all around the world.

This eased the flow and flight of money and created a global banking system that linked both local and global economies – so when a bureau de change in Mexico became infected with drug money, the infection spread like a computer virus.

World leaders first publicly recognised the exposure of the global banking system to the drug cartels two decades before the banks fell with the formation in 1989 of the Financial Action Task Force (FATF), set up primarily to target the laundering of drug money.

It was the first admission by the masters of the world economy that laundering had become a stand-alone sector of the drug industry that posed a threat in its own right. Their estimate was that some $120 billion of drug money was washing through the world's financial system each year. It warned that the industry's grip in weaker states had the potential to undermine the values of property, of civil institutions and of democracy itself.

FATF conceded that the financial system had become porous to the tainted money, not just in shady offshore centres or private banks but in the high street, through lawyers, solicitors, savings accounts and bureaux de change. And as the biggest centre of foreign-exchange trading, the City of London was a natural conduit. But money laundering was a new crime to the City, which didn't like the sudden imposition of fresh regulations or the unwelcome attention from police who, bankers claimed, knew nothing of their trade. And while money laundering in the City has never been far from the headlines, closing the door to drug money has been harder than many had first imagined.

In 1998, the UK's National Criminal Intelligence Service reported that it was investigating at least six leading City law firms over allegations that their workers were providing a respectable front for laundering drug money from around the world. 'Where organised crime has a presence there are lawyers who are feeding off money laundering,' said Simon Goddard, a spokesman for the NCIS, adding that the lawyers under investigation knew who their clients were and how they made their money. No charges were ever brought in connection with the NCIS investigation.

In 2000, Tony Blair's 'drugs czar' Keith Hellawell cited the collusion of financial institutions and foreign governments as a major obstacle to tackling the spread of narcotics. 'Rather than just seeing dawn raids on dealers and users of drugs, I would like to see dawn raids on a series of banks, travel agents and bureaux de change that front and launder this drug money,' he told delegates at a conference entitled 'Drugs: An

International Dialogue'. While Hellawell hinted that offshore jurisdictions had become havens for dirty money, NCIS expressed concern that only around half of all suspicious transactions taking place at Britain's big four banks were being reported.

London was a magnet for the capital's cash-rich criminal elite. As one former London drug-squad officer pointed out, Britain's drugs gangs were increasingly wealthy: to 'relationship managers' in the City they looked like all the other entrepreneurs, barrow-boy businessmen and property tycoons who made their fortunes in Thatcher's Britain. 'It was business done on the golf course, a share tip here and a little shady information there, and they could launder their money and make a profit overnight. For them it was all about the rogue player in the City.'

But organised crime gangs from the US, South America, Europe, Russia and China were also drawn to the City. The pound was strong, it was a rich consumer market, but, above all else, what made the City of London attractive was its historic reputation as a safe haven for legitimate money – where a man's word was his bond.

And it wasn't just traditional criminals. Blair's focus on drug money in isolation was short-lived. After the 9/11 attacks, terrorism supplanted the drugs trade as public enemy number one. London's reputation as a global hub for dirty money was sealed when a French parliamentary report revealed Britain's role in financing Osama Bin Laden. The report from independent financial experts – *Economic Environment of Osama Bin Laden* – claimed that up to forty British companies, banks and individuals could be legitimately suspected of maintaining direct or indirect relations with the then leader of Al Qaeda – although there is no suggestion they had any idea what he intended to do – and that the City of London was a haven for billions of pounds of tainted money.

Peter Lilley, author of *Dirty Dealing: The Untold Truth About Global Money Laundering, International Crime and Terrorism*, outlines London's position in his online Country Risk Index: 'Because of its key strategic position as a global financial centre, the United Kingdom is a major laundering centre. The continuing and accelerating trend of globalisation and the ease of funds transfer make the City even more vulnerable to money laundering. If you are a money launderer then you know you have made it safely and successfully if your funds are accepted without question in London.'

While in the past three decades new rules have increased scrutiny across the financial sector, the City of London has struggled embarrassingly to meet its obligations to monitor transactions. And in the wake of the financial crash, as the flow of easy credit and cheap money has dried up, the power of the drug economy has been thrown into sharp relief.

The UNODC says that around $2.1 trillion in dirty money moves around the globe each year and, according to Woods, the City now holds dual status with Wall Street as money-laundering capital of the world. The two financial centres have become the gatekeepers to a global grey economy for which the drug industry has become a key revenue earner, producing vast profits that can be used to bribe on a giant scale or simply to buy into property markets, institutions and the wider economy in vulnerable states.

Philip Parham, UK deputy permanent representative at the UN Security Council, spelled out the financial power and danger posed by drug money in 2011, describing the profits from the drug trade to be a 'staggering' $320 billion, and claiming that the most powerful international organised-crime syndicates could earn $1.5 billion a year. 'In practice,' he told Security Council delegates, 'this means criminal groups have access to resources many times those of the countries in which they operate.' The World Bank echoed the warning, claiming that developing countries faced the threat of 'penetration by organised crime of already vulnerable sociopolitical, judicial, and security structures'.

And the danger is no longer confined to failing states abroad. 'Organised crime costs the UK up to £40 billion a year,' said Home Secretary Theresa May, outlining the new threat posed by organised crime in 2011. 'It impacts on government, businesses, individuals and communities across the country. The economic impacts of fraud and money laundering, while perhaps less obvious, affect us all.'

No British business sector appears to be beyond the reach of the illicit drug industry. The telecoms, insurance and recruitment sectors were given a wake-up call that same year by SOCA and CIFAS, the UK's fraud-prevention service. SOCA warned that the profile of the enemy had changed from the local mobsters of yesteryear: 'Organised criminals have learned to compromise employees and contractors. They are enterprising. They have a wide circle of associates and new structures,' Tony Neate, e-crime liaison officer for SOCA, warned, adding that insider 'plants' – employees placed in organisations by criminal gangs – were causing significant damage to companies.

But in the wake of the financial crash it has been the banks that have faced the closest scrutiny. In 2011, the UK banking regulator the FSA conceded that three-quarters of British banks, including HSBC, Barclays, NatWest, RBS and UBS, were failing in their responsibilities to identify corrupt money; a third of banks dismissed serious allegations about their customers without adequate review; and that many 'relationship managers' are rewarded primarily on the basis of profit and new business, regardless of their performance on anti-money-laundering issues.

One year later, HSBC, known globally as the British Bank, made a full apology after a US report revealed how drug lords had laundered billions of dollars through its US arm, HSBC Bank USA. The president of the US arm, Irene Dorner, told a Senate hearing that HSBC had not lived up to the expectations of its regulators, customers, employees or the general public. It paid US authorities just £1.2 million to settle the case – a fraction of the drug money it had laundered. No one faced prosecution.

'The culture at HSBC was pervasively polluted for a long time,' said Senator Carl Levin, chairman of the US Senate Permanent Subcommittee on Investigations. The probe found that the drug cartels had laundered money through the bank's US division from 2002 to 2009. It found: high-profile clients involved in drug trafficking; millions of dollars' worth of suspicious bulk travellers' cheques; and a resistance to closing accounts linked to suspicious activity. In one year alone, 2007-8, one affiliate of the bank – HBMX – shipped $7 billion to HSBC's US operation. But perhaps the most surprising aspect of the findings was that HSBC US had listed Mexico, which sits at the front line of the global war on drugs, as a low-risk jurisdiction for money laundering.

The story of the first global Arab financial institution, Bank of Credit and Commerce International (BCCI), is the best example of what can happen when a City of London bank becomes beguiled by easy money and organised crime. For critics of the banks, BCCI offers an operational blueprint for banks seeking to open their doors to drugs money. BCCI's meteoric rise over the two decades from 1971 is well docu-mented. It launched with offices in London, Luxembourg and Karachi, and at its peak operated in around eighty countries, owned interests in three US banks, held assets in excess of $20 billion, and was the seventh-largest private bank in the world.

It offered a boutique service to legitimate customers seeking to avoid tax, but it also had a colourful array of shady clients. These weren't by any means just drug cartels. There were also arms dealers, those seeking to deal with sanctioned nations, evaders of Customs duties and tax, pilferers of treasuries and members of the intelligence community. BCCI helped its clients through the simple steps of washing their tainted money clean: 'placing' the money into the financial system; then 'layering', moving the 'placed' money into other institutions and jurisdic-tions to obscure its origins; and the final step of integrating the now-clean money back into the legitimate economy, into business, property and assets that no longer needed to be hidden and could earn legitimately, or into investments that could at any time be reconverted to cash or used as collateral in any financial deal or at any time.

BCCI was a financial institution, like others, that recognised the huge volume of 'flight capital' that they could market around the world, says Bob Mazur, a seasoned US undercover investigator who has spent much of his life posing as a member of the Mob. According to Mazur, it was a strategy that would sink the bank. 'Adopting the goal of marketing flight capital pulled them down the slippery slope to become a fundamen-tally corrupt institution with primarily criminal goals – corrupting country leaders to serve their needs, servicing the intelligence community, functioning as gatekeepers of drug-cartel fortunes,' says Mazur. 'Eventually, their goals were so corrupted that they became the funding arm of black ops for the Pakistani secret service agency, the ISI, which – among other things – facilitated Pakistan's nuclear weapons programme. But, make no mistake, there are many international banks sliding down that same path.'

BCCI operated 'financial mechanisms' that left its clients' banking arrangements opaque and, while causing concern to regulators around the world, the bank's modus operandi meant it was impossible for any one individual financial regulator to collate provable evidence by normal means.

The UK was just one of the jurisdictions abused by BCCI, but it initially embraced business with the bank, says Mazur. 'In the case of BCCI, the UK banking authorities uniquely allowed banks to maintain "manager's ledger accounts". Basically, these accounts serve a similar function as "payable through accounts" used in the US to hold funds for offshore clients who don't maintain accounts in the US,' he explains. 'They enable a manager to pool funds of many clients and privately keep an account of who owns what portion of the funds as they flow in and out of the manager's ledger account.'

Using the pseudonym of 'Bob Musella' and posing as a member of a cocaine cartel, Mazur taped conversations in which the bank's representative admitted to taking the money despite being aware of its origins. 'We secretly moved funds through the UK via a "manager's ledger account" at the BCCI London office. I recorded several conversations about those transactions. That's what brought down BCCI. But the UK still gets its share of the global money-laundering pot because it offers mechanisms that serve this money and the fact that it is a stable banking system.' Mazur believes that financial mechanisms similar to those BCCI used are today being touted by banks in a bid to 'entice' business from their competitors.

But banks are commercial creatures, established to make

profits, and it is the financial regulators worldwide that must revise their approach to money laundering if they are to be effective. Mazur claims that regulators have been too concerned with the health of financial institutions, as distinct from their criminal behaviour, but their biggest defect has been failing to recognise the nature of modern banking – that 'banks have two brains'. Mazur says that there is a 'profit (or sales) brain', which is motivated by earning money, and a 'compliance brain', which identifies and minimises risk. But when the compliance and sales brains meet, upper management sides with the sales brain: their interest is profits. 'Until leaders of the world's governments find the courage to put bankers behind bars when they are found managing this type of money,' says Mazur, 'this will continue, as it has for many decades.'

For Mazur, the HSBC case was the largest known example of the marketing of flight capital to date, and is a case that offers an unprecedented insight into the role of intermediaries who firewall banks from responsibility. The US probe of HSBC found that the bank had to close 20,000 bank accounts in the Cayman Islands and that many of them operated behind a screen of privacy offered by service companies.

Service companies offer nominee accounts where the ownership of investments, assets and cash sits with an intermediary shell firm. Many service companies represent perfectly legitimate enterprises and individuals seeking to minimise international tax obligations, utilise property tax breaks or hoard personal wealth beyond the reach of governments or regulators. But once a nominee account is established, finding out who owns it is impossible.

'They are watertight,' says one managing director of a leading commercial property firm in the City Of London. 'The paperwork coming forward from these firms is often rock solid, all the compliance boxes are ticked, but if you ever want to contact them to redraw a clause of a contract, even if it's in the owners' interests, they are completely impenetrable.'

The City of London is historically well positioned to make the most of the offshore industry. Around 50 per cent of the opaque financial centres are based in former dependencies of the British Empire. The offshore banking industry has flourished over the past three decades in line with the City, creating an alternative system based on privacy as distinct from transparency.

According to tax-haven watchdog the Tax Justice Network, the assets held offshore, beyond the reach of effective taxation, are equal to about a third of total global assets; and over half of all world trade passes through tax havens.

Nicholas Shaxson is a full-time writer and researcher for the Tax Justice Network and author of *Treasure Islands – Tax Havens and the Men Who Stole the World*. His book focuses exclusively on the 'legitimate' use of accounts but describes the City of London as the spider at the centre of a web of tax havens scattered around the world, which act as feeder funds to the City.

Shaxson says that 'shell' companies are merely 'booking centres' for London accountants. On his blog he describes how the system conceals London's involvement: 'A company can pretend that it is located in an overseas territory [i.e. outside the jurisdiction of UK regulators], while the real business – the hammering-together of that banking syndicate, the legal work for that giant property deal – gets sent up to London.'

But not all arrangements are 'legitimate' mechanisms for minimising tax. When the World Bank probed 150 cases of corruption 70 per cent had been facilitated by an anonymous company. And in a mystery-shopping exercise in which researchers tested the willingness of service providers to offer a disguise for dirty money, of 3,000 company service providers approached worldwide 48 per cent were prepared to set up a company without requesting the proper identification documents. But the offshore sector is not the only aspect of the global drug trade that anchors Britain at its heart.

The City's involvement with the drug-money business stretches back to the days of the Empire when the British government was the founding architect of the global drug trade. It was a time when government, as the banks are today, appeared to be in two minds about drug profits. While drug use was not encouraged at home, the sale of drugs abroad was not a moral issue but one of free trade – and it was a time when government and the City of London acted as one.

Former Labour Home Secretary Jack Straw highlighted this slice of history in June 2008 in a column for his local constituency newspaper the *Lancashire Telegraph*. Under the headline 'Once the British were the Biggest Drug Dealers In the World', he sought to quash claims by the BNP that prior to immigration Britain had been a drug-free nation. Britain took a localised and cultural appetite for opium in China and turned it into a globalised business, coordinating cultivation, processing and retailing through a network of independent traders. And the City of London not only financed the venture, it became a clearing house for US traders in opium.

In the early 1830s, the British Empire, by way of the state-backed East India Company, started to flood China with Indian opium against its will. The illegal trade was a vital one for Britain, generating the equivalent of $20 billion a year at its peak. Not only did it balance Britain's trade deficit with China, largely created by the Victorians' insatiable thirst for Chinese tea, but the proceeds were later used to prop up the ailing Raj.

But it became a moral issue for China. The trade sparked a plague of opium addiction among the Chinese population, leaving the nation the 'sick man of Asia'. In 1839, Lin Zexu, the Chinese commissioner in Canton, sent a finely worded letter to Queen Victoria begging for mercy. 'Suppose there were people from another country who carried opium for sale to England and seduced your people into buying and smoking it, certainly your honourable ruler would deeply hate it and be bitterly aroused,' Zexu wrote, imploring her to stop the merchants from shipping opium to the Far East. 'By what right do they then in return use the poisonous drug to injure the Chinese people? Even though the barbarians may not necessarily intend to do us harm, yet in coveting profit to an extreme, they have no regard for injuring others. Let us ask, where is your conscience?'

The letter never reached the queen, but the government responded. It deployed the most powerful naval force in the world to launch a series of devastating attacks on China, known as the Opium Wars, which forced open its borders to the opium trade while crippling China. Britain took Hong Kong into the bargain.

Yet by 1912 Britain had made a dramatic volte-face from poacher to gamekeeper. Along with other international superpowers fearful of the spread of opium, Britain spoke out against the 'evil' trade and helped lay down the first international laws banning drugs.

While they mark an embarrassing episode of colonial excess, some claim that these wars, and the sale of opium, created the foundations of the modern world economy and Britain's place within it. While Britain went on to be the banking capital of the world, an essential link in east–west trade, China withdrew from the global community in part due to a nationalism stirred by the actions of 'white devils' who had forced addiction upon its people.

In 1999, Carl Trocki published his controversial book *Opium, Empire and the Global Political Economy*. In it he explored how Britain's monopoly on trade in the 1800s not only centralised drug traffic but also restructured the social and economic terrain. It created mass markets, unprecedented cash flows and vast pools of wealth, laying the primary foundations of global capitalism, the modern nation state itself and the modern consumer society.

Trocki considers how drugs – tea, tobacco, alcohol and opium – were essential in forming markets of mass consumption, the starter motor for capitalism, thus creating cycles of production and consumption. 'Opium was the catalyst of the consumer market, the money economy. Opium created pools of capital and fed in the institutions that accumulated it: the banking and financial systems, the insurance systems and the transportation and information infrastructures.'

The legacy of the opium wars remains an embarrassment for a slew of well-known banks, merchants and hauliers whose histories are intertwined with the pools of capital created. British Hong Kong-based companies such as Jardine Matheson, now one of the world's biggest multinationals, were authorised to operate in Canton, buying cheaply produced opium in Bengal and Malwa and flooding the market with smokable high-grade heroin. The trade also boosted the coffers of maritime businesses and set up many modern-day giants, such as shippers P&O, which won business by introducing high-speed travel to the heroin industry. Many of the merchants that returned to Britain used their war chests to build the grand civic entrances to merchant spa towns such as Cheltenham. In part it funded the industrialisation of the British cotton industry that was to usher in an age when goods were made in Britain. And, perhaps most importantly, British bankers established the Hong Kong and Shanghai Banking Corporation (today's HSBC) that spawned dozens of financial institutions, legal firms and accountants who today service the financial needs of millions of Britons.

But in the wake of the First International Opium Conference in 1912, the leading industrial nations banned the trade in opium. Until the 1970s the influence of drug money was largely controlled, in part due to the world wars, isolationism and political ideology that redrew the world map, interrupting the evolution of world trade. But in the past decade the UK drug industry has become ever more powerful. Valued at £8bn a year, the British drug market is thriving and increasingly crime has been seeking out the services of the professional classes, not just in the City but countrywide, to help them hide their illicit profits.

SOCA was granted one of its largest-ever confiscation orders for £10.5 million in September 2011 against Khalid Mahmood Malik, who had been convicted in 2005 of running a drug network importing and distributing some 300 kg of heroin. The Bradford-based drug dealer posed as a high-performance-car trader to cover his illicit business, had extensive links across Europe, Pakistan and Turkey and ran a well-established criminal enterprise. His criminal activity had allowed him to acquire properties in the UK and abroad worth £3 million, as well as luxury cars, including a Lamborghini.

Among the twenty-six people imprisoned, Malik's cohorts included his financial adviser, who arranged fraudulent mortgages and held Malik's cash in his own bank account, his solicitor who allowed £593,000 of Malik's drug money to be used to purchase property in the names of others, his mortgage adviser and a property developer.

'Everyone involved in his criminal activities, including his wife, her sister, a solicitor, mortgage adviser, property developer and a financial adviser, are all behind bars,' a SOCA spokesman said. 'They have paid for their greed with their livelihoods and freedom. Our warning to other business people in Bradford is simple – if you offer your services to criminals you can expect SOCA to come after you.'

As with the banks, distinguishing whether businesses are naive or complicit is a difficult and time-consuming operation. The case against Malik took five years of financial monitoring to secure the evidence to proceed with the prosecution. But his case is far from unique.

The assistance offered by financial and law firms and local councillors has seen a rash of embarrassing cases making media headlines. This inspired the formation of a new crime squad north of the border that was charged with combating the financial clout of the drug industry as the recession bore down.

Dubbed 'the Untouchables', the squad was established to tackle a 'recession-free' drug industry that was providing loans to many inner-city residents and businesses, filling the gap left by the now overly cautious high-street banks. The unit identified 360 criminal networks with nearly 4,500 members.

Some 90 per cent were involved in the drug trade, and 27 per cent in money laundering. It also identified 93 organised-crime groups seeking to corrupt public- and private-sector organisations, including financial institutions and legal and accounting firms. Scottish crime gangs are aided by 241 'consultants' and 'facilitators', says the SSOCD. Lindsey Miller, head of the new division at the Scottish Serious and Organised Crime Division, described the new generation of professional conspirators: 'It's the lawyers, the accountants, the estate agents. People tend to forget that a lot of these organised-crime groups could not get off the ground, could not do the work they do, without inside, specialist help.

'It's the partners [of crime bosses] in well-thought-of law firms, living in the suburbs, in houses which on the face of it have been legitimately earned. But when you scratch the surface that is not the case.'

Highlighting how organised-crime groups used local firms to assist their business activities, officials in Scotland have conceded that gangs have moved wholesale into providing childcare services and have won public-sector contracts.

The Care Commission, which oversees Scotland's childcare services, signed an agreement with Strathclyde police force with the aim of keeping the sector out of the clutches of known gangsters, their families and associates. Assistant Chief Constable George Hamilton warned: 'Criminal gangs will try anything to clean up the money. Nurseries are just one of the businesses that organised criminals have attempted to infiltrate.'

'If you look up and down the country there's an increasing number of politicians, councillors, accountants and solicitors who are prepared to buffer organised crime. If you turned the clock back forty years, it would be unheard of,' says Labour MSP Graeme Pearson, a former director of the Scottish Crime and Drug Enforcement Agency.

Pearson says that drug gangs are constantly on the lookout for opportunities to conceal their activities behind the most innocuous activities. Infiltrating the middle classes and the professions is now part of the business plan. A first friendly approach will often be made at a business, community or charitable event, where representatives of organised crime gather with the pillars of communities.

Often relationships appear to spring up as any other might, around common interests. And just as new friends can often surprise one, there may be invitations to a night at a spa, tickets to a West End show, or a late-night drink at a lap-dancing club. 'Once befriended, you find yourself involved in plans that will subvert your ability to say no in the future,' says Pearson. 'You become the conspirator, the middleman between the illicit and licit economies.'

As a conspirator you are responsible for creating the local false economy, says Pearson, the one that corrupts, pays no tax, offers no rights to its employees – but is the key revenue source for funding a wider portfolio of crime and that undermines legitimate business. While creating a fizzle of economic activity in bars, nightclubs, taxi ranks and late-night cafes, the ultimate goal of the industry is to withdraw and camouflage the profits from both the sale of drugs and the money laundered.

The global reach of a financial professional to facilitate the flight of profits was exposed by the case of accountant and former chair of the North-West Chelsea Supporter's Club, Malcolm Carle, who was jailed for six years in 2011. A police raid of his offices revealed that he had laundered more than £1.2 million for a convicted cannabis trafficker, Walter Callinan. Carle's accounts and diaries revealed a complex network of trusts and companies in Azerbaijan, the Seychelles and the British Virgin Islands through which Callinan's illicit earnings were channelled. Messages stated that a hotel purchased with 'dirty money' was a 'long-term investment' and the offshore accounts were used to 'hide the way the funds were raised'.

And comparisons with the impact of the drug trade globally offer a shocking picture of the 'economic black hole' created by it in inner-city Britain. When Professor Hamid Ghodse, president of the UN's International Narcotics Control Board, said in 2012 that Manchester, Birmingham and Liverpool contained 'no-go areas' similar to South America's *favelas*, senior police officers raised their hands in disbelief and dismissed him as a crank. But Professor Ghodse had a point when he said there were areas locked in a 'downward spiral' and 'cut adrift' from mainstream society by growing poverty, crime, alienation and hopelessness. Many people in these communities, he said, were being lured into criminal lifestyles, while organised gangs and drug traffickers were able to gain levels of power that made it impossible for police and other authorities to control them.

An undercover police officer, who worked under the guise of being a mid-level dealer, described how there are parts of the country that, while not impassable, are zones in which outsiders rarely set foot. In Toxteth, Liverpool there is a network of streets that are policed by drug gangs, where local shops and houses are used as places to buy and sell drugs and store stashes.

'Whenever I turned along this one street a group of lads would approach me and ask for a code word. If I knew it, I was "legal" and could pass through without getting harassed or attacked. The shop where all the drugs were bought and sold was blatant. It was rammed with well-known dealers. Police never went there. It was seen as beyond worth bothering with.'

But the drugs industry has many guises in the high street. Some operations hide in the glitz and glamour of busy city centres. He Jia Jin, the leader of a drugs gang from London behind a £350 million money-laundering ring, was jailed in 2012 after setting up a money-transfer service, World Travel Service, in the heart of London's Chinatown. It was used by

Chinese expats to send cash home but its public face was a cover for the money-laundering operation: to funnel profits from cannabis farms and brothels in Gloucester back to the Far East.

Other local high-street businesses get absorbed by the back-room dealing of the drug trade. A walk-in recording studio at the back of a store in Enfield, London, offered apparent privacy. Police placed hidden CCTV cameras in the booths and listened in on dealers who travelled from as far afield as Leeds. Over twelve months, Operation Peyzac identified 37 drug dealers and armed criminals who were jailed for a total of more than 400 years. One man told officers he'd travelled to the shop on a bus to buy records, but was recorded selling four guns wrapped in a plastic bag; another man was filmed handing over cocaine with a street value of £4,000.

Even the sleepiest towns in rural England can find that their businesses are targets: a police raid on the Prince Regent pub in Tiverton, Devon unearthed thirteen kilos of benzocaine and evidence to prove that the friendly local was run by an illegally assigned tenant. Gordon Ogilvy, the landlord, was convicted of laundering £300,000 cash for an international drugs operation and was jailed for five years.

But for Pearson the corruption and erosion of values has spread far wider than individual businesses and has ensnared entire communities. And when crime develops relationships with business, identifying criminal groups from everyday traders is a challenge even for professional law enforcers. In 2008 the Metropolitan Police mobilised 1,000 armed officers in raids on some nineteen businesses and forty residential addresses in and around Blackstock Road, a run-down high street in North London. The businesses harbouring the area's rampant trade in Class A drugs, money laundering, stolen goods and forged documents were the subject of Operation Mista. The swoop netted £4,000 worth of cocaine, stolen goods and counterfeit documents. But working out which firms were fronts for crime and which were legitimate businesses was the biggest problem faced by detectives – an illicit operation in the high street looks like any other to an outsider, and a wayward café owner is as likely to shake your hand as any other.

The raid represented the culmination of an eighteen-month surveillance operation. But in the wake of the raids, Detective Inspector Mike Duncan expressed the difficulties faced by the investigation on a local blog. 'We have done our best to target the premises who gave the criminal gangs refuge to operate within the area … I do not want to upset the decent folk who just want to make an honest living, but in my experience some of the more overtly friendly café owners have turned out to be the worst offenders.'

High-street crime now appears to pervade inner-city London. Four years after Operation Mista, Operation Condor targeted all thirty-two London boroughs and 4,896 supermarkets, shops, pubs, clubs and unlicensed minicab offices. Arresting 420 people in a 48-hour crackdown, the city-wide sweep was a message from the Met for local businesses to get their houses in order. It is now a regular feature on the capital's policing calendar.

With the trained eye of a narco-entrepreneur, Yusuf offers an alternative tour of London's streets that brings to life the influence of the drug economy as it rubs shoulders with legitimate business. At one level, Yusuf explains, illegal drugs sit in a portfolio of commodities that ranges from counterfeit food, drink, clothing and Viagra to prostitution, pilfered goods and stolen credit cards. At another level, they provide a revenue stream that helps businesses and communities that might otherwise be foundering.

Where a high-street shopper sees a colourful array of independent small businesses, Yusuf sees the architecture of a sub-economy within which businesses have learnt to turn a blind eye to the activities of others: a newsagent who sells counterfeit alcohol and cigarettes; an international-money-transfer shop where customers will be advised about how to avoid the radar of financial services regulators; and those favoured homes of crime – betting shops and the local pub.

The problem for business is to either attempt to exclude the trade in and consumption of drugs – hiring security, redesigning venues, installing CCTV and, in pubs and restaurants drug-proofing the surfaces of toilet cubicles with Vaseline and WD40 – or to find a way to live with it. For some businesses this means acting as lookouts, for others it means storing boxes of unidentified contraband, for the more brazen it could be hosting a front for the sale of drugs, or it could be commercial cultivation. But largely it is about laundering money.

Yusuf describes a scenario where landlords who have had high-street businesses fail in the recession have found themselves remaining on the hook for business rates, maintenance and quarterly rent. Locked into contracts that can run for months or years, many landlords see the drug industry as one way of limiting the financial burden of an empty store or ailing business. 'Ask yourself who owns businesses. If they are not naive then they know what's going on. They decide what happens – many see it as an opportunity. Cash has a way of smoothing away scruples when people are struggling.'

For Yusuf, Camden in North London is the best example of a local economy that has evolved over four decades to become an international drug hub, attracting millions of visitors from around the world. Established by the hippy drug pioneers of the UK drug industry, Camden Market was, as Yusuf puts it, a motley crew of traders with a real community feel – some were importers, others wholesalers, while cafes, shops and pubs would become dealing forums during busy weekends. But then North London gangs moved in, taking control of the distribution of drugs at pubs and clubs through teams of doormen. As the traditional drugs market became more violent many of the original players sought out new legal markets, selling first magic mushrooms, herbal highs and cannabis seeds, and then later, as regulations changed, synthetic cannabis – Spice – and party pills, and mephedrone.

Such is Camden's notoriety that it led one local councillor to write a tongue-in-cheek letter to the *Guardian*, outlining how the drug economy appeared to be 'an important part' of the local economy. '[Drugs] are one of Camden's most important sources of export earnings, as people tend to come to Camden Town, visit the market, buy drugs, have a drink in one of our pubs and then go home again, leaving their cash in Camden and taking their social problems to other boroughs.'

Criticising police plans to clamp down on the drug trade, he added: 'This is an economically suicidal policy. Drugs are the mainstay of our tourist industry now that the Britpop years are over. Camden Town having an anti-cannabis policy is like Gretna Green having an anti-shortbread policy.'

'We used to literally stop the traffic in Camden,' says Yusuf, who worked in one of the many mushroom shops that brought international media interest and tourists from far and wide before legislation closed their doors. 'A huge refrigerated lorry from Amsterdam used to deliver thousands and thousands of mushrooms, all different strains,' he explains. 'It was a licence to print money.' But Yusuf's shop wasn't just selling mushrooms: it sold drug paraphernalia, digital scales, smoking pipes, and rolling papers, alongside novelty T-shirts, lollipops and libations carrying the cannabis-leaf logo as their brand. 'We had everything you could want in that shop – you could buy the lifestyle,' he says, laughing.

In the winter of 2010 the Wellcome Trust global charitable foundation, dedicated to the betterment of mankind through medical research, hosted an exhibition called 'High Society', which explored the role of mind-altering drugs in history and culture. It displayed more than 200 exhibits: examples of the work of the Romantic poet Samuel Taylor Coleridge, who wrote his famous poem 'Kubla Khan' in 1797, allegedly after an opium dream; a handwritten account by Captain Thomas Bowrey describing his crew's experiments with a cannabis drink known as 'bhang' in seventeenth-century Bengal; eleventh-century poppy remedies written by monks in Suffolk; and a hallucinogenic snuff set collected in the Amazon by the Victorian explorer Richard Spruce. The exhibition charted the spread of drug culture up to the 1960s and early 1970s.

While drugs have always been at the edges of British culture, criminologist Nicholas Dorn was one of the first observers to spot the close link between drugs and consumerism. Writing in the *British Journal of Addiction* in 1975, he matched two new trends in the 1970s: the growing prevalence of recreational drug use among young people, and the new consumerism.

'This quite recent change of economic priority or emphasis requires a new social character orientated to immediate or repeat gratification through consumption . . . It is hypothesised that the consumer character is a potential candidate for potential drug use. Drugs (legal and illegal) are, in many ways, ideal consumer products. Drugs are non-reusable, unlike consumer durables, and therefore lend themselves to repeat purchase. By their very nature, they are valued for the social and personal attributes (attractive, understanding, compassionate, experienced, exciting, etc) they confer on the user, rather than for any non-social utility value.'

In the past three decades the economic relationship between drug use and free time has stepped out of the shadows. Half of the trade has now attained quasi-legitimacy by the sheer number of 'recreational' drug users in the UK. Today, drugs have become a cultural touchstone with a language and lifestyle that has become intertwined with everyday life. We have become a nation that likes to chill out, 'dope' means good and crack has become a barometer of the more-ish nature of our consumer products, with fanatical young business executives dubbing the BlackBerry the Crackberry due to its addictive nature, while on Mumsnet forums middle-class mothers casually refer to their toddlers' teething powder as 'baby crack'.

And drug culture, like all culture, has become a commodity in itself. Where Glastonbury once amounted to a handful of hippies standing in a field, today the festival is a multimillion-pound business, drawing sponsorship from global brands, from drinks manufacturers to mobile-phone makers, state broadcasters and creative funding agencies. The festival is also now used as a barometer of drug use in Britain. Every year teams of researchers and forensic scientists converge on Glastonbury to interview festivalgoers about their drug use and analyse the type of drugs they are using and get caught with. But its value now is not as a small hippy festival, but as a global brand and platform that is beamed around the world.

If Margaret Thatcher could be criticised for leaving the door ajar for money launderers, Tony Blair displayed his very own form of wilful blindness when it came to drugs. While focusing his sights on the Mr Bigs who controlled supply, his close embrace of the creative industries and the night-time economy lent legitimacy to recreational drug use. In choosing to use D:Ream's 'Things Can Only Get Better' – composed by the former ecstasy user – to replace the Labour Party's traditional anthem 'The Red Flag' on his victory night in 1997, he won the respect of clubbers nationwide. 'Suddenly club culture became part of the new economy – in part the success of Cool Britannia was due to UK club culture,' says Jennifer Ward. 'There was a sense that this scene was a legitimate, saleable, marketable part of British life while fuelled by Class A drugs. Drugs became inextricably linked to the dance-music scene, and the event – the festival, rave party and after party.'

As Home Secretary in Tony Blair's Labour government, David Blunkett announced in 2001 that cannabis would be transferred from Class B of the Misuse of Drugs Act to Class C, removing the threat of arrest for possession. In doing so he stimulated the cannabis market by opening debates over how cannabis might best be regulated – whether it might be sold in pubs or cannabis cafés – and, at the same time, the government granted a licence to GW Pharmaceuticals to explore the medicinal qualities of the drug in pain reduction.

While this was happening, daily life changed in a way that suited the drug industry. In 2005, Blair declared Britain a twenty-four-hour country, opening up the workforce to flexible working, and cities to a froth of nightlife adult entertainment in the form of lap-dancing clubs and gambling, that now plays host to binge Britain, while bringing in revenues for local government.

Blair's chosen think-tank, Demos, outlined a plan in its report *BritainTM: Renewing Our Identity* in which the old

Britain was set adrift, and 'Cool Britannia' would place the creative sector at the heart of the New Labour vision. Blair sought to harness the intellectual property of the creative industries and fund it through the City of London, and in doing so he spawned a collective of cocaine-abusing celebrities in Brit Art, Brit Pop, and Brit Journalism who redefined the image of the Good Ship Britannia. According to one high-ranking police detective, before the financial crash it was as if Westminster 'was living an evergreen existence, partly infested with cocaine, in which the boundaries between politicians and banks, journalists and lobby groups, pop stars and policy makers merged, messages became confused and the lines between the licit and illicit became blurred.'

Blair's bipolar approach to drugs was noted by *The Economist* as he set his course in 1998. Under the headline 'E IS FOR ENGLAND' the magazine explained the dilemma: 'The government is keen to celebrate and encourage Britain's vibrant night-time economy. But it also wants to crack down on drugs. A pity the two are so closely entangled.' *The Economist* also made the connection to the rise in new drink products, noting that a government advisory committee on drugs warned that the young people attracted by the advertising for alcopops were precisely the same group of people who might be tempted to try drugs.

For business, the rise of recreational drugs has redefined the spending habits of consumers and driven the innovation of products. In 1995, the Henley Centre for Forecasting on Leisure Futures revealed that the number of drinkers in the country's pubs had fallen by 11 per cent between 1987 and 1992, and forecast a 20 per cent decrease by 1997. It also charted the rise of an emerging drug economy that was reaching critical mass in terms of spending power. The percentage of sixteen-to-twenty-four-year-olds popping pills and snorting powders doubled to nearly 30 per cent between 1989 and 1992; one million UK ravers were spending £1.8 billion a year on entrance fees to rave nights and clubs, cigarettes and illegal drugs.

The discretionary spending power of cannabis smokers was analysed in Project Edge, a six-month study in 2003 by one of Britain's largest trend analysts at the time, TRBI. It found that cannabis users spent an average of £20 on mainstream products each time they smoked, including cigarettes, rolling papers, snacks and entertainment. The study reported that because smoking cannabis heightens appetite, users were handing over an estimated £120 million a week to pizza take-away outlets such as Domino's and Pizza Hut, and to supermarkets for crisps, sweets and soft drinks.

It said video-game brands benefited from the need of a generation of users to be entertained at home while their drug of choice has remained unlawful. In total the Edge project concluded that cannabis smokers spend around £5 billion a year on products associated with their cosy world of home entertainment, only £1 billion less than they spent on the actual product.

'Cannabis users spend tens of millions of pounds each week on places to meet and eat,' Andy Davidson, who commissioned Project Edge, told the *Observer* in 2003. And they had specific tastes that business could court. 'They don't like bright, noisy environments like McDonald's. On the whole, they prefer somewhere with low-key lighting and a straightforward menu. Businesses targeting the youth market can no longer ignore the fact that almost half of their customer base is getting stoned. They need to make specific projections about how that affects them.

'Some of these brands benefit at the moment,' said Davidson, 'but if people become more willing to smoke in public when the law is relaxed, they may be hit.'

Cocaine, on the other hand, is a global marque. An unpublished piece of strategic research carried out for the government in the run-up to its 2009 anti-cocaine TV campaign, *Pablo the Drug-Mule Dog*, concluded that the drug's positive image was a 'formidable adversary'. The research, gained largely from a series of in-depth interviews with teenagers, revealed several unpalatable truths.

'Cocaine behaves like a youth brand,' the researchers concluded. 'It enhances social experiences. It is seen as a drug of success. It has widely held symbolic associations with wealth and status and a long history of elite customers. Cocaine moves in glamorous circles and it is an integral part of the celebrity world.'

The alcohol industry was in a battle with ecstasy to attract teenagers, and it knew it. 'Youngsters can get ecstasy for £10 or £12 and get a much better buzz than they can from alcohol,' admitted Richard Carr, chairman of the beer and spirits conglomerate Allied-Tetley-Lyons in 1992. 'It is a major threat to alcohol-led business.'

The rebranding of alcohol in an advertisement for Holsten Pils starring the US comedian Denis Leary is often cited as the first of a new generation of TV ads. The advert featured a smiley yellow tablet telling Leary to get 'wired', to which he responds 'Get a life.' It was perhaps one of the few adverts that sought to draw a line between drug culture and traditional forms of intoxication. But just as banks have two brains, so do manufacturers, retailers and advertising agencies.

The drinks industry responded by using the rave phenomenon as a marketing tool, adopting its imagery for pub flyers,

introducing what became known as 'alcopops' and transforming the look and feel of pubs from stuffy hang-outs for
old men to places to which young people, especially women,
would want to come and where they could have fun.

And where alcohol had limitations, other manufacturers and
entrepreneurs exploited energy drinks. Red Bull sold the power
of caffeine in a whole new way with the advertising slogan
'Red Bull gives you wings', leading the way for a new generation of energy drinks.

As the 1990s turned into the 2000s publishers, broadcasters
and retailers explored the new market that appeared to be
opening up under Blair. In 1999 publisher IPC was forced to
pull a poster campaign for its magazine *Later*, although its
publishers denied that the posters were 'glorifying drugs'; radio
station VH1 received a rap on its knuckles for appearing to
condone cocaine in its handling of a documentary; and Golden
Wonder crisps had to pull a poster campaign that trivialised
the trade.

But whether business was driving the demand or meeting
the ever-changing demands of the British consumers is unclear.
In her 'Brain Reserve Forecast' that sought to define the
changing habits of British consumers in 2008, brand guru and
trend strategist Faith Popcorn (whose past and present clients
include McDonald's, Bacardi and American Express) identified
a hunger for hedonism not just among the celebrity classes
but also across the UK consumer base.

Consumers were displaying new types of behaviour: 'pleasure
revenge', forbidden pleasures sought out by people tired of
social constraints. Popcorn cited such examples of the UK's
pleasure revenge as binge drinking; unprotected sex despite
warnings; and drug taking, which was forbidden yet endorsed
by a range of icons, from pot-smoking hippy rock stars to the

Wall Street coke addicts of 1980s films to Amy Winehouse.

Drugs are now part of a portfolio of selling 'hooks' used to attract 'young adopters' who set the trends. Fiona Measham, one of the lead researchers into drug use at Glastonbury, explains the new reality in the wake of the cultural shift: 'You can't draw any boundary lines between drug culture, youth culture, music culture and popular culture. You can see why drugs are used to sell things because it represents deviance, rebellion, it's exciting, it's illicit, being out all night. It taps into all the things that companies will want to tap into.'

But increasingly those who are seen to be brazenly promoting drug use in the media, music and entertainment sectors face a barrage of criticism, revealing a chasm between hard-line prohibitionists and those who see drug use as merely a youthful rite of passage.

In the wake of his son Joe's death after taking MDMA at a nightclub on the edge of St Paul's in Bristol in 2012, deputy headmaster Tom Simons told the press: 'Until society as a whole stands up and says no to the dealers and no to those in the media and entertainments industry who glorify and trivialise the taking of drugs, we will continue to count the cost in lives lost and families left bereft. It is our profound hope that Joe's untimely death will serve as a warning to young people of the dangers of taking drugs like MDMA and the far from benign influence that some would have us believe the "soft" drugs culture has on young people.'

Appearing to cross the line in taste can be an expensive business. In 2011, television advertising for the 'Opium' scent from perfumier Estée Lauder, owned by Yves St Laurent, was banned after the Advertising Standards Authority (ASA) upheld complaints claiming that the advert flirted with heroin chic with its scene of a dancer pointing to her elbow and running a finger along her forearm. The advert used the opening line: 'I am your addiction, I am Belle D'Opium.'

Makers YSL denied any deliberate use of drug imagery in the ad, and stated that its research had not indicated that the public would interpret the advert in that way. It added that the tagline 'the addiction' was a core value of YSL, but in a positive way – 'devoted to life, addicted to love.'

The pragmatic response to critics from many in the marketing profession was best summed up in the wake of an ad campaign run by the global sports giant Nike. 'Dope', 'Get High' and 'Ride Pipe' are just three slogans that Nike have used on their T-shirts, claiming that the language reached their target market of skaters, snowboarders and extreme-sports enthusiasts. In the US the slogans caused a mild rumble of outrage among parents, but for many it is seen as a legitimate attempt to appeal to the youth audience. Paul Swanguard, managing director of the University of Oregon's Warsaw Sports Marketing Centre, said: 'I don't think it's necessarily a bad thing. It's not an overt attempt to offend but it is an overt attempt to connect, which is what Nike has always done well.'

Nike's relationship with drug culture appears to have become increasingly buddy-like. In 2011, MSN heralded the launch of the global sports brand's limited-edition trainers by paying homage to Cheech and Chong – 1970s counter-culture comedians who entered American and global drug culture through a series of films, such as *Up In Smoke*, espousing a cannabis-fuelled slacker lifestyle.

Robert Passikoff, president of Brandkeys, a New York- based brand-loyalty consultancy, told MSN: 'This is a harmless brand promotion. And when you think about it, Cheech and Chong have to a large degree become part and parcel of mainstream American culture. Instead of "Just Do It" maybe they should use "Just Smoke It,"' he joked. The launch of the Cheech and Chong trainers followed a theme. In April 2010, US street artist Todd Bratrud and Nike produced the marijuana leaf-coloured Nike Dunk High Skunk range of sports shoe.

But what if a manufacturer has been adopted by this formerly niche audience-cum-mass market culture, how should it react? For the cigarette rolling-paper brand Rizla, accusations that it courted hidden customer base of cannabis smokers have been upheld, but any requirement to consider the health issues has been dismissed. Guidance on health issues, the company said, was the role of government.

In 2003 an advert for Rizla was criticised for carrying the phrase 'twist and burn'. While raising a wry smile among cannabis smokers, the Advertising Standards Authority banned the advert because it could be seen as condoning cannabis use: 'twist' is slang for a joint.

Four years later Imperial Tobacco threatened to sue the mental-health charity Rethink for suggesting that its king-size cigarette papers were used for rolling joints. The legal case came after the charity had specifically mentioned the Rizla brand, which sells £36.8 million king-size packets a year, in a campaign calling for the makers of cigarette papers to act responsibly and put cannabis health warnings on packets.

Rethink was forced to change its publicity material for the campaign – which ultimately failed – while Imperial Tobacco, who maintain that most king-size rolling-paper sales are to long-distance lorry drivers who smoke tobacco roll-ups rather than to cannabis smokers, pointed out that it was up to the government, not businesses, to provide public health advice. Government stayed silent.

Three decades after the Henley report revealed the challenge that ecstasy posed to the drinks industry, and the potential that drugs have to stimulate discretionary spending on associated products, the blurring of the lines between drugs and legitimate products is tangible.

Criticism is now irrelevant for many companies, particularly when a controversial advertising campaign helps to boost sales. A trip to Amsterdam and a free bag of potent cannabis was the prize for the person who found a Willy Wonka-style golden ticket in the winning DVD of *The Wackness*, a film starring Sir Ben Kingsley, when it was released in 2009. Billed as a film that celebrated 'people coming together through a love of weed', the company defended itself by claiming it was something that would 'brighten up people's lives' during the gloom of the global economic crisis.

Research published in 2011 found that the twenty-four-hour society fuelled the consumption of cocaine, with police reporting that the excuse used most often by drug users was 'to stay awake on a big night out'. And while it was not exploring drug use as such, the *Daily Mail* revealed research defining Generation Z as being hooked on energy drinks.

Jonny Forsyth, senior drinks analyst at Mintel, said: 'It highlights a generational difference, specifically the younger generation's use of everyday "uppers" and "downers" to control their moods or enhance their performance. Therefore, in spite of having less money in their pockets, they are happy to pay for added energy to facilitate their full-on lifestyles.'

And nowhere is the blurring of the lines between legal and illegal more apparent than online, where psychonauts, criminal gangs, legal-high sellers, paraphernalia suppliers and drug-community groups rub shoulders with high-street stores, international wholesalers and mainstream banks. In this way the illicit and the legal have become entangled. During the legal-high media frenzy in 2009 and 2010, mephedrone stories on websites run by national newspapers such as the *Guardian* and the *Daily Telegraph* were accompanied by automated Google adverts that directed surprised readers to sites selling the drug. When this was pointed out to Google's HQ the company removed listings mentioning legal highs.

But today the 'legal-high sellers' are tax-paying members of the business community, contributing around £200m a year to the country's coffers, according to research by the drug charity Release. And for Bitcoin, the new e-currency, the fact that Silk Road accepts Bitcoins 'is a really powerful thing,' Amir Taaki, a developer who works with the virtual currency told the BBC in 2012. 'Bitcoin is pure financial freedom of speech. It really changes the dynamics of how money works.'

In the wake of a decade of decadence, the scale and influence of the drug economy is becoming ever clearer. And as the torrent of easy credit that once washed into businesses, high streets and homes has been turned off, our dependence on the credit culture has been revealed and the reach of the illegal economy has been shown to stretch closer to us all. Where once the drug industry could be excluded from the mainstream British economy, culture and communities, today it has become embedded, hardwired to the banks, businesses and services on which we all rely.

For government and law enforcers the mushrooming of the drug industry poses a huge problem. In the past, the British government acted in unison with the business and the banks. It now stands isolated, unable to secure the drug-free nation that Antonio Maria Costa pledged in 1998. Far from being a drug-free nation, today its illicit industry is maintained not only by the constant demand of drug users to get high or to kill their pain, or by the financial greed of foreign suppliers and street dealers, but by domestic financial regulators who appear to overlook the activities of banks in favour of the nation's wider economic health; by middle-class professionals who act as gatekeepers for organised crime in exchange for a taste of the high life; and by the merchandisers and retailers who provide a backdrop for the promotion of drug use by selling the lifestyle to a consumer group raised on drug-culture in a society where money appears to be the most addictive drug of all.

6

Omertà

The Haunted House

June, 1981. A whirring siren and haunting Hammond organ mark the menacing start of 'Ghost Town' by ska band the Specials. The single is a bleak, melancholy take on a nation being ravaged by urban decay, social breakdown and rioting. Britain's first female prime minister, Margaret Thatcher, had sparked an economic revolution by rolling back the red carpet of socialism and removing the barriers of government regulation, unionisation and nationalised industries. But Thatcherism came with a bleeding edge. Unemployment, which had been steadily rising for several years, was accelerating and now stood at 2 million. It would reach 3 million within a year. There was a chronic shortage of social housing. Traditional industrial communities, built on coal, shipping and cars, were being decimated by a harsh programme of reform.

By the time 'Ghost Town' topped the charts in July, the simmering civil unrest that had surfaced in the Brixton riots just a few months before in April, had spread to St Paul's in Bristol and Toxteth in Merseyside. In December, a forty-nine-year-old man admitted to Brompton Hospital in London suffering from pneumonia became the first person to die in the UK of what was being referred to in the press as a mysterious 'American gay syndrome disease'.

Up until the 1960s, drugs could be said to be seen by the authorities as a mere nuisance, to be swatted away at will. Even during the 1960s and 1970s, when British governments publicly joined the US in the war on drugs, ministers were happy to take a back seat, letting doctors deal with the addicts and the police deal with the hippies and punks.

In the 1980s the number of people addicted to heroin began to spiral out of control, and enormous quantities of brown, smokable heroin from Iran and Pakistan flooded into Britain. Once restricted largely to London's bohemian set, opium was spreading to working-class communities in Glasgow, Edinburgh, Bradford and Manchester. For an increasing number of the jobless with nothing else to do, heroin became not only a way of achieving a temporary state of oblivion, but gave a structure and purpose to lives cut adrift by unemployment.

The heroin epidemic was most visible in the coal-mining towns where drug use rose to 27 per cent above the national average. In South Wales, anti-drugs campaigners said the valleys were 'awash with heroin'. Many of those who had started smoking heroin off tinfoil, also known as 'chasing the dragon', were now injecting with syringes – a more potent, cost-effective and far more dangerous method of intoxication. By 1983, there had been a threefold rise in the numbers of addicted heroin users countrywide in the space of five years.

As the government released its infamous 'Heroin Screws You Up' poster and TV campaign, the 'gay syndrome' disease from across the Atlantic was becoming headline news. Now identified as a blood-borne virus, HIV/AIDS had claimed forty-six lives in the UK by 1985. Disturbingly for ministers already left reeling by the surge in heroin addiction, health officials revealed that HIV was not only being transmitted by sexual intercourse and blood transfusions, but by Britain's rapidly expanding army of drug users.

Many heroin injectors shared bloody 'works' with their friends. Chemists often refused to sell syringes to people who looked like drug addicts. By the end of 1985 there were fifty-five confirmed HIV cases among injecting drug users in England and Wales, with reports from Scottish drug agencies that more than two-thirds of drug injectors were sharing their needles. The news from the US was not encouraging. By 1985, there were 20,470 cases of AIDS, and 8,161 deaths from AIDS-related illnesses in America. The pressure for the government to act was further intensified by a report published by the Royal College of Nursing, which predicted that if the current trend continued, the number of HIV infections in the UK would rise to 1 million by 1991.

The government launched a hard-hitting public information campaign on AIDS, 'Don't Die of Ignorance', and anti-drug storylines featured in the popular children's TV show *Grange Hill*, with the show's cast reaching number five in the British pop charts with an upbeat track: 'Just Say No'.

Established under the Misuse of Drugs Act 1971, the government's own drug experts, the Advisory Council on the Misuse of Drugs (ACMD), a group of around twenty-five drug specialists, including scientists, addiction experts and police officers, gave ministers a stark warning that 'the spread of HIV is a greater danger to individual and public health than drug misuse', and that 'all available means' must be used to minimise high-risk injecting behaviour among drug users to stem blood-borne HIV infections.

As a result, in 1988, despite a wail of protest from the tabloid press railing against taxpayers funding 'junkies" needles, the Thatcher administration took the advice of its drug experts and did the unthinkable for a government so opposed to heroin use – it sanctioned the handing out of free syringes to heroin addicts. The illegal practice was already being carried out by groups of gung-ho drug-treatment workers in Dundee, London, Liverpool and Swindon who were determined to provide injecting addicts with a potential lifeline in the form of a sterile syringe, but the government's rubber stamp gave it credibility and, crucially, funding from the taxpayer.

The government released £17 million in public funding for drug treatment services, a sum that would have been unim-aginable prior to the HIV epidemic. By 1990 there were 200 needle exchanges in the UK, providing clean needles and advice.

It was a defining moment in British narco-politics. The heroin epidemic and the threat of HIV had woken the government from its torpor on drug policy. Thatcher and her ministers were the first to face up to the fact that enforcement alone was not enough to tackle the threats posed by drugs. 'Through a combination of this fear of the unknown, and the vision and understanding of key ministers at the time, the UK became one of the first countries in the world to embrace what we now refer to as "harm reduction" approaches to drug use,' says Mike Trace, chairman of the International Drug Policy Consortium and former deputy drug czar under Labour. 'The result stands as one of the most significant public-health successes of our time, with levels of HIV transmission through drug injecting a fraction of those that were being realistically projected.' Thatcher's drug policy in the 1980s was a pivotal moment in the relationship between the government and drugs. Not only did it ensure drugs were pushed up the political agenda, but it was to be the last time ministers were brave enough to defy a group of self-appointed drug experts whose influence on this sensitive area of public policy was set to grow out of all proportion – Britain's tabloid newspaper editors.

The collateral damage of the drug trade affects everyone. The latest research puts the annual cost to the British taxpayer of the drugs trade at around £16.7 billion – more than the entire budget of the Home Office. Whatever attitudes individual members of the public may have towards 'junkies', we are all paying to clean up the mess. The lion's share of that bill covers the costs of drug-related crime and of arresting, prosecuting and jailing drug offenders. The drug treatment system – which includes methadone, needle exchanges, detox and rehab – makes up £739 million. As pointed out earlier, heroin and crack addiction accounts for the vast majority of the total expenditure.

It is precisely because drug crime is the most costly aspect of the drug trade that drug policy is dictated from within the government's 'crime' department, the Home Office. New laws, policies and strategies are centred around the fact that drug possession, dealing, smuggling and production are illegal acts and that drug addiction and the drug trade generate further crimes, such as shoplifting, mugging, violence and homicide. It follows that those tasked with enforcing the law, such as the police, the UK Border Agency and intelligence services, have a central input into policy. No drug policy is considered without its impact on crime, the criminal justice system and enforcement. On a secondary level, departments covering health, education, social services and foreign affairs have a role in implementing and shaping policy.

Drugs first became a political issue in Britain in the 1960s in response to increasing addiction rates, and it was at this point that American and British drug policy began to align. In 1971, US president Richard Nixon described drug abuse as 'public enemy number one' and America became the driving force in global drug control. The United Nations passed a new convention which widened international controls to all known psychoactive drugs. The same year, the British Parliament passed the Misuse of Drugs Act, which introduced a classification system for illegal drugs based on harm, and enshrined the criminal justice system as the key plank in dealing with drug misuse. The Act also marked a clear distinction between the supply and the possession of drugs – until then the penalty for possessing heroin, cocaine, morphine or cannabis had been the same as trafficking.

But apart from enacting the new laws, there was little co-ordinated effort by the government to develop any kind of overarching strategy towards the growing drug problem. Once Thatcher's government decided to take centre stage on drug policy during the 1980s heroin epidemic, the drug remit expanded out from the Home Office to other departments such as health, education and social services. This led to the first government drug strategy, Tackling Drugs Together, launched in 1995 under John Major, which ensured drugs became a cross-departmental issue. The government's mission, outlined in successive strategies, revolved around two key aims: tackling supply through enforcement, and reducing demand through education, such as its current information vehicle 'Talk to Frank' and through drug treatment services.

Despite the increasingly pragmatic and co-ordinated nature of drug policymaking, the debate remains heated. The question of policy is steeped in morality: drug users, dealers and traffickers are not just breaking the law, but also transgressing other boundaries.

Drug policy has always been a moral issue. The first binding treaty on global drug control was signed one hundred years ago, largely at the behest of the United States, by the world's nations at the International Opium Convention in 1912. Under increasing pressure from the United States to toughen up its drug laws after World War One, the UK government called on the advice of its top medical experts and in 1924 set up an inquiry chaired by the respected physician Sir Humphry Rolleston. Two years later the Rolleston Committee concluded that while penal elements of policy were important, drug addiction should be treated as a disease rather than how it was treated in the US, as a vice. Britain's small number of heroin addicts were not chased down by police, instead they were put on withdrawal programmes or prescribed heroin by doctors.

The British approach was based on morality, but of an entirely different character to that of the Americans. In the UK drug policy was based on the moral imperative to offer welfare to the sick, whereas in the US it was a tool with which to defend society from the devilish sin of drug abuse. And also from foreign invaders. Many of America's early drug laws were specifically aimed at recent immigrants, such as 'Hispanics, Negroes and Chinamen', a class of people, it was alleged by those in charge of the fledgling war on drugs, more prone to drug abuse than white people.

Harry J. Anslinger, head of the US Narcotics Bureau, which recruited thousands of agents from the Alcohol Bureau when Prohibition was lifted in 1933, was a fan of scare tactics to ward people off drugs. 'If the hideous monster Frankenstein came face to face with the monster marijuana,' Anslinger pointed out in 1938, 'he would drop dead of fright.' Since then, it has been America that has been the driving force behind international drug law.

Today, the government sees it as its duty to send out the right 'message' to the public, to take a tough stance against all drug use and its negative associations. Intoxication from alcohol is acceptable, but pleasure-seeking from illicit substances is somehow debauched, inauthentic and lazy. In short, highly immoral.

In 2007, a major report by the RSA Drugs Commission, entitled 'Drugs: Facing Facts', described how drug policy is rarely produced from cold, hard analysis. 'There is no escaping the fact that the formulation and implementation of drugs policy takes place in a peculiar atmosphere, one that differentiates drugs policy from most other fields. The field of drugs policy is not "ordinary", "matter of fact", or "routine". It is highly charged, sometimes even hysterical, with people, including the media and politicians, emotionally involved in quite an usual way. The emotional climate in some policy fields is relatively cool. The emotional climate of drugs policy is almost always exceedingly hot.'

The report said that, over and beyond concerns about health and crime, the emotional climate is generated by drugs being seen as 'a peculiarly moral issue'. 'This conviction may be rooted in fundamental values, it may be unreasoned and emotional, and it may be, and often is, both at the same time. We do not presume in this report to lay down what we believe people's moral stance on this overarching issue should be. That is not our business.'

But it is politicians who have to tread the line between science and morality on the drug issue. Drug policy has to take into account how drugs are seen culturally and morally. In Britain, beer is socially acceptable and in some parts of South East Asia, opium smoking is socially acceptable. As Dr Marcus Roberts, head of policy at drug charity DrugScope says: 'Having a pint and smoking heroin have very different meanings for our community and those meanings are as important in shaping attitudes as the science.'

The moral ingredient often creates an overheated brew of truth and fiction. The picture painted by the government is discovered to be well meaning, but misleading. In the day-to-day experiences of the people to whom the government is directing its messages, the moral spin is interpreted as codswallop. There is the very real danger that if the government's messages are deemed by young people and the general public as 'crying wolf', then when a health crisis or a new and highly dangerous drug appears, ministers may not be believed.

As the Runciman Report warned in 2000: 'The most dangerous message of all is the message that all drugs are equally dangerous. When young people know from their own experience that part of the message is either exaggerated or untrue, there is a serious risk that they will discount all of the rest.'

The government's ability to get its message across is today being challenged by an online world that has set the pace on myth-busting and providing unbiased information – the basis for most drug forums' existence. Where five years ago young people may have got the low-down on drugs from the government's own online information service, now they are increasingly likely to get advice, some good some bad, on dosing, brands, effects and price from independent drug forums such as Erowid, Bluelight, Urban75 and Drugs-Forum.

Policymakers in the government are stuck between a rock

and a hard place. They are confronting a problem that is vast, diverse and unpredictable. The end result is pragmatism, but pragmatism that is ultimately mired in inertia. But it is not out of want for the facts. The Home Secretary, supported by the ministers and civil servants that form the Drugs Strategy Directorate within the Home Office, is ultimately responsible for creating drug policy. The minister and the directorate have at their disposal a wide range of statistics and research reports on anything from drug-use trends and treatment outcomes, to prison drug-test results and information on the latest Afghan opium crops.

Major changes in drug law do not happen quickly. As we saw earlier, the Misuse of Drugs Act 1971 still remains the key legislation governing the possession and supply of drugs put into the three classes of risk – A, B and C. The government is assisted in its policymaking by the ACMD, the 'independent expert body that advises government on drug-related issues in the UK', the group whose advice was taken on board by the Tory government during the joint heroin–HIV crisis in the 1980s. It continues to provide in-depth analysis and advice on drugs and their risks. Ministers are legally obliged to seek the ACMD's recommendations before making changes in the law. But more often than not, its advice falls on deaf ears.

Despite three decades of government action, Britain's drug market appears to be as healthy, robust and resilient as ever. There can be few issues that are as pernicious and costly as drugs, and few that are as poorly and hastily considered. In the last general election, drugs only received a passing mention in both the Labour and Conservative manifestos. Labour dedicated fifty words on the subject, or two and a half tweets' worth, boasting about the banning of mephedrone and the reclassification of cannabis. The Tories included a few hundred, promising to crack down on 'drug driving' and trafficking, and dedicating resources to helping methadone users wean themselves off the drug. The statement was clear. For political parties, the drugs issue is not considered a vote winner.

Britain is still one of the largest drug consumers. Subject to the odd drought as experienced with heroin over several months in 2010, most drugs are readily available at low prices. As Tony Blair's leaked Strategy Unit report concluded in 2003: 'Drug seizures in themselves are having little or no impact on reducing harms.'

Against global shifts in patterns of drug use, the stances taken by national governments are akin to boats bobbing up and down on a stormy sea. This powerlessness was clearly described in *An Analysis of Drug Policy*, published in 2007 by the UK Drug Policy Commission: 'The most fundamental point to understand about drug policy is that there is little evidence that it can influence the number of drug users or the share of users who are dependent. There are numerous other cultural and social factors that appear to be more important.' The report said that it was instead globalised popular culture, a 'confluence of broad demographic, social and economic changes', that defined drug use among the young, and that this superseded attempts to stem use by government policy in any one single nation.

However, the report concluded that 'the arena where government drug policy needs to focus further effort and where it can make an impact is in reducing the levels of drug-related harms through the expansion of and innovation in treatment and harm-reduction services.' It called for urgent action on behalf of the government to tackle UK problems, claiming that the shortage in research meant policymakers had to 'operate partially blind when choosing effective measures'.

The reality is that government research, like police intelligence, follows in the wake of a fast-moving, consumer-driven industry that has fickle tastes. Virtually every year for the last decade a new substance is added to the list of banned drugs, or an already banned drug's status is amended. Since 2003, GHB and GBL, raw magic mushrooms, ketamine, Spice, mephedrone and naphyrone have been banned. Mexxy, the ketamine copycat drug, became the first substance to be the subject of a temporary ban in 2012. Cannabis was dropped from Class B to Class C in 2004, only to return to Class B five years later. Methamphetamine, commonly known as crystal meth, was reclassified from Class B to Class A amid fears of a growth in its use.

Outlawing drugs has incurred unexpected consequences for governments in the past decade. Banning ketamine in 2006 failed to halt the drug's rise in popularity. It is now a fixture on the UK drug menu. Its illegality failed to dent either its availability or its price. Dealers merely changed their method of obtaining it, from carrying it in liquid form in rose-water bottles to the UK direct from Indian chemists, to buying powder direct over the Internet and making it up in bulk using raw ingredients in the UK.

Banning drugs, even if it does little to reduce their use, does at least send a message to potential users that a substance poses a substantial risk to their health. But all the evidence from studies among young people shows that unless changes in the law are accompanied by health information about drugs, they will not be deterred from using substances. The government's policy of using the classification system to send out messages about the harms of drugs has been ridiculed by the experts. Even the House of Commons Science and Technology Committee in 2006 strongly criticised this practice. Certainly the shift of cannabis from Class B to Class C and back again during the 2000s had very little effect on patterns of use.

Not only is the government's chosen method of sending out messages about the dangers of drugs ineffective, but any action taken by politicians appears to be influenced more by political expediency than an urgency to respond to incoming evidence. There is a major dislocation between the information that is fed into the government's policymaking machine and the policies that spring forth. Evidence has regularly been pre-empted, buried, twisted or ignored, with policies sometimes flying in the face of scientific reason.

The power of the press plays a critical role in the government's decision-making. Because the drugs issue is seen as such a risky policy area for politicians to tread, it is always safer to be reactive than proactive. And often those setting the agenda are newspaper editors, rather than the government's own experts and researchers. Over the last decade the Home Office has established a strong track record in agreeing more with the tabloids on what drug laws should be, than with their own independent advisers.

When the Police Foundation's independent inquiry into the Misuse of Drugs Act was published in 2000, calling for wholesale changes such as the reclassifying down of ecstasy and cannabis, Tony Blair's spin doctor Alastair Campbell feared the worst. He asked Home Secretary Jack Straw (whose teenage son William was famously, and cruelly, set up as a drug dealer by tabloid journalists) to head the tabloids off at the pass, and write an article for the *News of the World* warning that Britain would become 'the new Amsterdam' if it followed the Inquiry's recommendations.

When Dame Ruth Runciman, the highly respected chair of the Police Foundation's independent inquiry, went to the Home Office for a face-to-face meeting to discuss her report with Straw, he questioned every point. Straw's Cabinet colleague Mo Mowlam cut in, arguing that he should read the report before dismissing its recommendations.

To the surprise of the PR-obsessed government, Runciman's sensibly argued recommendations met with support from across the political spectrum. Even the *Mail on Sunday* welcomed the report and called for a mature debate on the subject. The government changed its views on Runciman's recommendations overnight, and it was the media's initial warmth to the report that set in motion the announcement in 2002 by Home Secretary David Blunkett to downgrade cannabis to Class C.

The media's reaction to the Runciman Report caught the Labour government off guard, but it was a one-off. Since then, government spin doctors and the media have found it mutually beneficial to join forces when faced with individuals who choose to speak 'off message'.

In January 2009, Professor David Nutt, the chairman of the ACMD, wrote an article in the *Journal of Psychopharmacology* titled 'Equasy: An overlooked addiction with implications for the current debate on drug harms', discussing how risks involved in taking ecstasy could be comparable to the risks we take in other parts of life, such as horse riding. A month later, as the ACMD was due to give its advice to the Home Office on whether ecstasy should remain a Class A drug, a copy of the article was sent to a journalist at the *Daily Telegraph* and the professor's musings became headline news.

Within days, Professor Nutt was being publically chastised in the House of Commons by Home Secretary Jacqui Smith for 'trivialising' the dangers of drugs. Like a head teacher admonishing a naughty school child, she demanded Nutt make a formal public apology to the parents of every person who had died after taking ecstasy. 'I've spoken to him this morning about his comments. I've told him that I was surprised and profoundly disappointed by the article reported. I'm sure most people would simply not accept the link that he makes up in his article between horse riding and illegal drug taking,' an angry Smith told MPs. 'For me that makes light of a serious problem, trivialises the dangers of drugs, shows insensitivity to the families of victims of ecstasy and sends the wrong message to young people.'

When a week later the ACMD handed the government its year-long study of 4,000 academic papers, concluding that ecstasy was not as dangerous as other Class A drugs such as heroin and crack and so should be made Class B, the government barely acknowledged it. They didn't need to – its head author had been discredited and Home Office officials had already briefed the media months beforehand that the ACMD study was 'unwelcome'. Whatever its conclusions, ecstasy would remain a Class A drug.

Undeterred by the government's hyper-prickly, yet sometimes dismissive, attitude to his work, Professor Nutt gave a lecture that July repeating his claims that alcohol and tobacco were more harmful than cannabis and ecstasy, accusing ministers of 'devaluing and distorting' the scientific evidence over illicit drugs. The lecture found its way into the public domain when it was published in a pamphlet in October. The new Home Secretary Alan Johnson sacked Professor Nutt for what was seen in Whitehall as a second yellow-card offence. A Home Office spokesman said: 'The Home Secretary expressed surprise and disappointment over Professor Nutt's comments which damage efforts to give the public clear messages about the dangers of drugs.'

The government was supported by much of the tabloid press, which dubbed the respected pharmacologist the 'Nutty professor'. Journalists from the *Sun* befriended his teenage children on Facebook and accused them of being drunks and drug addicts, an accusation for which the paper had to issue an apology after a probe by the Press Complaints Commission. The *Daily Mail*'s Melanie Phillips decided that Professor Nutt was in fact a 'drone' controlled by back-room legalisers in an article titled: 'Fatuous, dangerous, utterly irresponsible – the Nutty professor who's distorting the truth about drugs'.

But the only people distorting the truth about drugs were the media and politicians. The *Daily Mail* repeatedly puts respectable statistics and research through the mangle as part of its mission to exaggerate the harms of drugs, breathe life into the universally discredited 'gateway theory' (that the use of one drug invariably leads to the use of another), and scold anyone who fails to match its bottomless horror at the continued existence of drugs. In a letter to the *Guardian* in defence of his decision to sack Professor Nutt, Johnson wrote, in reference to ecstasy: 'In my constituency . . . there are thousands at risk of being sucked into a world of hopeless despair through drug addiction.' It was an assertion that thousands of his ecstasy-using constituents in Kingston upon Hull would have blinked at in wonderment.

The move caused outrage among Nutt's ACMD colleagues, prompting seven to resign in protest at the government's treatment of the advisory body's advice and the humiliating sacking of its chairman. One of those to resign, Dr Simon Campbell, a synthetic organic chemist, said the government's decision to reclassify cannabis, announced before the ACMD gave its advice, was purely 'a vote-catching exercise'.

But the members of the ACMD were used to senior politicians' cavalier attitude to the evidence. Gordon Brown had declared shortly after becoming prime minister in 2007 his intention, whatever his drug experts recommended, to make cannabis Class B. Brown and his supporters were in agreement with the *Daily Mail* that not only did the new super-strength skunk make you mad and kill people, but that it was a 'gateway' drug to heroin and cocaine.

A year later the ACMD handed the government its detailed analysis of cannabis harms, which disagreed with the wildly exaggerated tales being propagated by the media and Downing Street. Its nine-month review concluded that while more potent, home-grown strains of herbal cannabis, such as skunk, now dominate the British market, the evidence of a substantial link with mental illness remains inconclusive. Rubbishing the commonly held 'gateway theory', it warned that moving cannabis up a class would result in the criminalisation of more young people. The government quickly discarded the findings.

DrugScope, a leading drugs information charity, said in a statement that it was disappointed the government had ignored the ACMD's advice: 'Unfortunately, the message given by this decision is that drugs policy can be driven as much by political considerations, media headlines and scare stories as by the evidence.'

This widening chasm between advice and policy is not just the result of deliberate ignorance or prevailing popular opinion. During Labour's second term in government, instead of policy being based on evidence, the evidence was made to fit the policy.

In October 2004, seven months before the 2005 general election, Tony Blair invited a handpicked group of senior police officers and Home Office officials to 10 Downing Street. According to Jeremy Sare, a Home Office drugs official at the time, the prime minister's agenda was: 'There will be a new Drugs Act next year. What should be in it?' The result was the biggest change to drug law for more than thirty years – the Drugs Act 2005 – described by Sare as 'a low point in drug-policy formation – the most dysfunctional Act of recent times'.

A decade earlier, in 1994, Tony Blair had identified crime as an important policy area in which to square up to the Tories. He became convinced that drugs were one of the key drivers of crime, stating that 'half of all property crime is caused by drug addicts'. But according to Alex Stevens, a senior lecturer in criminology at the University of Kent and an international expert on the links between drugs and crime, the statistic repeated in the government's 2002 drug strategy is a 'mythical figure that has been repeated so often that it has become an unchallenged assumption. When looked at more closely, it crumbles to dust.' Nevertheless, it was a soundbite that launched a series of increasingly coercive initiatives from 1998 to the present day.

Initially, the policy of singling out persistent offenders, through voluntary drug testing of them in police stations after being arrested for drug addict 'trigger' crimes such as shoplifting, mugging and burglary, had the broad support of police, probation officers and the drug treatment sector. All the evidence pointed to the fact that a large proportion of the collateral damage of the drug trade was caused by what the Home Office had identified as a core group of around 330,000 'Problem Drug Users' (PDUs), chiefly high-offending, heavily addicted crack and heroin users. It was an opportunity to catch offenders addicted to drugs and offer them a route out of the revolving door of addiction and crime and into treatment. The initiative to stem the high cost of drug criminals was supported by £600 million a year of Home Office cash, diverted to the Department of Health, in support of a National Treatment Agency, whose aim was to get as many problem drug users into treatment as possible. But the 'test on arrest' strategy's success was proving hard to quantify, and so in the run-up to the 2005 general election, it was given an extra, coercive edge.

Within six months of Tony Blair's Downing Street meeting in 2004, the new Drugs Act 2005 was on the statute books. The key plank of the new law was the expansion of test on arrest, called the Drugs Intervention Programme (DIP) for people suspected of committing drug-related crime. The Act introduced compulsory drug testing of arrestees whom police suspected of taking drugs and of people served with ASBOs. Also stapled on to the Act was the introduction of tougher penalties for drug dealers caught selling near school gates – a law based on zero evidence – and the classification of magic mushrooms as Class A, a decision that the ACMD was not consulted on.

As the Tories had done before them, the New Labour government began to pump money into drug treatment, but this time it was in order to cut crime. Offenders who tested positive for drugs were to be offered a choice of treatment or jail. The logic was that if these prolific offenders were offered the chance of treatment instead of prison, then crime and addiction would fall dramatically, and the revolving door of prison, drug abuse and offending could at last be wedged shut. Treatment agencies, who were happy to play up the drugs-causes-crime link, saw a Home Office windfall of half a billion pounds a year. Under US-style Drug Treatment and Testing Orders (DTTOs) issued by the courts, people whose offences were related to drug misuse avoided jail and were instead treated for their addiction if they submitted to regular drug tests.

Over the years, the government poured money (and still does) into getting the most desperate of drug-addicted offenders into treatment and away from a criminal life. The people whose addictions were costing society the most in terms of health and crime found themselves the target of unprecedented levels of attention: from police clampdowns on buyers and sellers in the crack and heroin market, to a network of probation officers and drug support workers.

However, a study published by the National Audit Office in 2004 concluded that despite the issuing of more than 18,400 DTTOs, imposed at a cost of more than £50 million a year, there was little impact. Some 80 per cent of drug-using offenders entering the programme were reconvicted within two years, and nearly three-quarters dropped out of treatment.

Professor Mike Hough, a senior academic who carried out evaluations for the Home Office during the Labour administration, said that his team was put under considerable pressure by civil servants while assessing the work of the teams that implemented the test-on-arrest programme, in order to make the scheme appear a runaway success. It was a time when Labour was obsessed with meeting targets. 'The Home Office became preoccupied with demonstrating its success. They were making really quite exaggerated claims about the effectiveness of their drug strategy to ministers which were just not sustainable.'

The government is so confused by what statistics show or do not show that it will massage them for the sake of it. A Home Office press release in 2011 initially showed border officials had seized more cocaine and almost double the amount of heroin in the previous six months than in the whole of 2010. But days later the official statistics showed the amount of cocaine seized by border officials in England and Wales had actually fallen by a quarter, and the amount of heroin seized had halved. The Home Office minister subsequently accused by statistics watchdogs of manipulating drug-seizure figures to show the UK Border Agency in a 'good light'.

Not only will the evidence be massaged if it is unsuitable for the government's needs, but it will be buried if it is not palatable. In June 2003 Tony Blair was presented with a report into government drug policy carried out by his own Strategy Unit. It concluded that the enforcement of drug supply laws was ineffective and counterproductive. Nothing greater than a 20 per cent seizure rate had been achieved in recent years, when a rate of 60–80 per cent was needed to have any serious impact on the flow of drugs into Britain.

The report was only made public after repeated requests by the drug-reform charity Transform for it to be published under Freedom of Information laws. The only policy changes made as a result were the more coercive test-on-arrest measures in the Drugs Act 2005.

The lack of information on the progress and success of government policies has been frequently criticised. A report by the National Audit Office on the Drug Strategy concluded: 'Without an evaluative framework for the Strategy as a whole, the NAO is not able to conclude positively on value for money . . . So overall performance measurement across the range of programmes needs to be put in place.' A previous Drugs Value for Money Review, an analysis carried out in 2007 into the effectiveness of government spending on combating drug use, was suppressed by the government, until it was released under FOI laws because it admitted that it was difficult to work out whether the strategy was cost-effective.

A House of Commons Committee of Public Accounts investigation into 'HM Customs and Excise: The Prevention of Drug Smuggling', found that policymakers were pursuing costly policies with no clarity as to their effect. As the chairman of Customs and Excise stated in evidence to the committee: 'I cannot be sure whether we are holding the line.'

In 2002 a fresh-faced Tory MP backed the radical conclusions of a Home Affairs Select Committee inquiry into the effectiveness of Britain's drug policy. As a member of the inquiry, he gave his full support to recommendations to the reclassification of cannabis from Class B to Class C, and ecstasy from Class A to Class B. The report also called for a discussion with the UN about alternative ways of tackling drugs globally, including the possibility of legalisation. The inquiry accepted that 'with a few brave exceptions, drugs policy is an area where politicians have feared to tread'.

In a debate on drug policy later that year, after most of the committee's recommendations had been brushed aside by the Home Office, the MP spoke out in support of prescribing heroin and providing 'shooting galleries' – government-sanctioned injecting rooms for heroin users. 'If one takes a slightly progressive – or, as I like to think of it, thoughtful – view, one can sometimes be accused of being soft. I reject that utterly.' The name of the MP? David Cameron.

Three years later he was of the same mind, telling the *Independent* newspaper in 2005, under the headline 'Tory contender calls for liberal drug laws': 'Politicians attempt to appeal to the lowest common denominator by posturing with tough policies and calling for crackdown after crackdown. Drugs policy has been failing for decades.' Yet since becoming leader of the Tory Party and subsequently prime minister, Cameron has remained remarkably tight-lipped on the subject of drugs, save for making relatively safe comments about how drug education and treatment must be improved. Lord Mancroft, a Tory peer, former heroin user and drug legaliser, told us in the House of Lords bar: 'Cameron still thinks drugs ought to be legalised, but if he's questioned about it he runs sideways like a startled crab.'

Remarkably, once a politician drifts away from the seat of power towards the back benches, the symptoms of this strange form of *omertà* appear to dissipate. A former sheet-metal worker and union leader at Coventry's Jaguar plant, the Labour MP Bob Ainsworth is an unlikely drug-policy maverick. With a sergeant-major moustache, the fifty-eight-year-old former Home Office drugs minister and Secretary of State for Defence strode into political no-man's-land in December 2010 and became one of the most senior British politicians to call for a serious debate about the decriminalisation and legal regulation of all drugs.

'The war on drugs does not work. We spend billions of pounds without preventing the wide availability of drugs', he told a Westminster Hall debate in the House of Commons. 'We need to be bold. It is time to replace our failed war with a strict system of legal regulation to make the world a safer, healthier place, especially for our children.

'It is about time we had a debate in this country, and provoked one internationally, about whether the war on drugs can succeed, or whether we ought to be prepared, in a rational way, to examine the alternatives.'

Despite spending three years as Britain's senior minister in charge of drug policy between 2001 and 2003, his reflections were quickly dismissed by the main political parties. Labour officials moved swiftly to distance the party leadership from the backbencher's 'awkward' outburst. Whispering in the ears of political hacks, Labour spin doctors firmly slapped down Ainsworth's comments as 'extremely irresponsible'.

Meanwhile the government dismissed such a radical notion out of hand. Asked whether Prime Minister David Cameron thought Ainsworth's ideas merited consideration, his spokesman said simply: 'No.' The government's drugs minister, James Brokenshire, responded in time-honoured fashion and told reporters that changing the drug laws was not a subject fit for debate.

The most predictable thing about Ainsworth's self-outing was that he was talking from a position of limited power. He was a *former* Cabinet minister, a backbencher from a party in opposition. His gag, firmly in place when he was in charge, had effectively been removed.

'Many people ask why on earth I did not do or say the things that I am advocating now when I was in government,' said Ainsworth, pre-empting the question on everyone's lips in the hall. 'As you can see from the reaction this morning, if I was now a shadow minister, Ed Miliband would be asking me to resign. If one of David Cameron's ministers – despite the fact [the prime minister] probably agrees with me – agreed publicly with me, he would have to resign. I had a choice to make. So my choice, had I wanted to go further than what I was allowed to do, would have been to resign and make a small splash, which might have dampened my shoes but would not have moved drugs policy far at all, or to stick with it and make some small improvements. I chose to stick with it.'

In an article for a Labour Party website, Labourlist, Ainsworth added: 'Our political culture doesn't allow for an honest and open discussion about drugs policy. As soon as a politician mentions the words decriminalisation or legalisation, the press scream blue murder, colleagues move to distance themselves from you and your political opponents sharpen the knife.' However keen a drug minister might be, says Ainsworth, they are bound by a collective responsibility and confined by wider government policy – and today's government, despite protestations of breaking the mould, is no different.

Caroline Chatwin, a drug policy expert from the University of Kent, commented: 'While this suppression of the opinion of those in power continues to be the case, Britain will not be able to participate in an open and honest debate on this subject.'

'Doing an Ainsworth' is not uncommon in British politics. The list of senior politicians who have called for the reform of drug policy *after* leaving positions where they had privileged access to the facts includes former Labour Cabinet ministers Clare Short, Tony Banks, Mo Mowlam, Lord (Roy) Jenkins and former Tory Cabinet ministers Peter Lilley, Alan Duncan, Michael Portillo, Lord (Ken) Baker and Lord (Nigel) Lawson.

So what of David Cameron? Since arriving in government the coalition has rushed out a drug strategy that was noticeable only for the fact that, apart from an emphasis on putting more people in rehab, it was virtually identical to the strategies set out by Labour in 1998 and 2008: a determination to tackle the demand and supply of drugs, to limit the trade's impact on families and communities, and to reduce addiction and crime. Former Tory deputy leader, the MP Peter Lilley, says the practicalities of calling for radical drug policy changes make it a risky strategy for a senior politician, even if they have been voiced before. 'When David became leader of the party he had to drop the thoughts he had on changing drug policy. Let's suppose he's still in favour of legalisation, he thinks, "Do I say what I really think or not? If I say what I really think I'm going to have to invest a huge amount of political capital to carry it off, convincing my party why we need to change its policy." All politicians are slightly in that position. You've either got to rate the issue as very, very important, or you've got to have nothing much to lose.'

The fallout for those who have opted to dip their feet in the piranha-filled waters of drug policy reform is there to see, although the stakes have got higher and higher. The more the government is cowed by narcomania, the longer it waits to clean out the dark cluttered attic, the more vulnerable Britain becomes.

While the status quo on the drugs problem, perpetuated by inert drug policies, is damaging, this is nothing compared to the kind of predictions made by the government's three-year *Brain Science, Addiction and Drugs* project, set up by Foresight, the government's advisers in 2002 to peer into the drug world in 2025.

In concluding its Drug Futures 2025 report published in 2005, the team of respected experts in the field said a tipping point for the UK drug problem would be reached if one of three things happened in the next twenty years: a rise in female drug use (at the moment three times as many men use drugs as women), a rise in rural drug use or a rise in young people's drug use. This kind of shift would be devastating.

It would result in the number of problem drug users rising from 400,000 to 800,000, 4,000 drug deaths, 300,000 injecting users with hepatitis C, 700,000 children with drug-addict parents and the social and economic costs could be £30 billion a year. With the police and NHS already at breaking point dealing with today's collateral drug damage, it is a future that no one is prepared for. These changes could be triggered by cultural and social shifts at a global level, but also by the increasingly likely emergence of a new drug that, for whatever reason, captures the public's imagination. And the Internet has made the invention, marketing and mass distribution of this kind of drug all the more feasible.

Yet the government's will to address the deep-rooted problems that cause and are created by an ever shifting, and ever more resilient drug trade, appears to be on the wane. It has not been for want of trying. Frustratingly for the architects of the last decade of drug policies, set in motion by Tony Blair's mission to tackle the root causes of drug crime, progress has been slow and hard to quantify. Patience with Britain's hard-core addicts has worn thin. Despite the half a billion pounds a year pumped into drug treatment by Labour, only a small proportion of addicts, less than 4 per cent, were leaving drug-free. Policymakers were discovering what drug workers had known all along: that getting people off drugs is not easy. The average heroin addict goes through multiple phases of rehab and relapse before successful treatment, and effective treatment is pointless unless it is accompanied by decent aftercare, such as housing and training. Now, in an increasingly coercive approach set in motion by Labour and continued by the Conservatives, where once addicts caught committing crimes were steered towards treatment programmes, now they are pushed. Otherwise law-abiding addicts receiving state assistance, such as benefits and housing, have been given a stark choice: either get off drugs and undergo intensive treatment, or the safety net will be removed.

Drug policy is now one of the smaller beasts stalking the political landscape. It is a largely symbolic issue, a political football, and offers a chance to appeal to the lowest common denominator, rather than driving the search for practical responses to wider health, social and crime problems.

'Governments do not give any thought at all to the detail of drug policy,' says Mike Trace. 'The default position is to treat the issue as a no-win situation politically. There is no clear course of action that can be trumpeted as an unqualified success, so the media and political opponents can easily characterise your position as either weak or unrealistic.

'The best a politician can hope for is an association with a minor success such as a big seizure or the backing of a broadly sensible strategy that people will see as a nice try. The option of least risk is to declare one's deep concern about the problem, one's commitment to fight until it is eradicated and to keep your head down when progress is reviewed.'

Trace says that the war-on-drugs rhetoric has always been the easiest path for governments to go down. 'This has a seductive political message – that the government and law enforcement authorities are protecting society from social and moral break-down. It is also a contention that cannot be disproved until alternative models are implemented, and the impact on levels of use and problems fully tested.

'The political alternative – that of questioning the "tough on drugs" orthodoxy, of promoting policies that are more tolerant of drug use, or that reduce enforcement or punishment – represents a high-risk strategy for any politician. As the former prime minister of Luxembourg, Jean-Claude Juncker, has succinctly put it: "We know what to do, but we don't know how to get re-elected once we have done it."'

*

When the damage of the drug trade is set alongside the long-standing inability of the authorities to deal with it, the status quo becomes unacceptable. But what are the alternatives?

Imagine a scenario where the drug trade is entirely legal. Instead of being controlled by gangsters and chancers, it is governed by bean counters and Sir Humphreys in Whitehall. People go to registered chemists to buy cocaine, ecstasy and heroin. Drug users go home or to a monitored lounge zone to get high. Organised crime has been shouldered aside by a new, government-controlled system. The money saved from chasing down the criminals is spent on providing gold-standard drug education and treatment. Guns, crack houses and back alleys have been replaced by form filling, drug rationing and ID cards.

Drug 'legalisation' is an expression that sounds straight out of the 1960 hippy scene, yet it is far less colourful. It is about taking control of the drug market away from criminal organisations and handing it to government to regulate, so drugs would effectively become 'over the counter' medicines. It may sound ideal to the drug legalisers, and it's the default conclusion for most journalists who investigate the illegal drug trade at length. According to the legalisers, it's the very act of prohibition, as with alcohol in America in the 1930s, that has fuelled organised crime, corrupted legitimate society and created dangerous, unregulated drug products. The ills of prohibition are there to be seen: the increasingly hefty bill for the taxpayer and the health risks posed to users buying in an illicit market. Corralled intelligently by pressure groups such as Transform, the modern-day legalisers must be admired for their pragmatic, sensible approach to finding the country an escape route.

Conversely, the champions of prohibition, such as the former cop and now Scottish MSP Graeme Pearson, firmly believe that drugs must not be countenanced; they have a blurring impact on our moral code and a corrosive influence across society. Holding the line is paramount, no matter what comes. Pearson describes the drug cartels as 'corporations without corporate responsibility' who since the onset of cannabis, speed, LSD and heroin have tweaked and repackaged drugs as products to ever younger audiences without regard for the consequences. 'It's like marketing a new game, every four or five years you get a new model, and they're no longer targeting the twenty-two-year-olds who have had a few years' experience of drugs, but the fifteen-year-olds.'

There are also arguments, such as those outlined by the right-wing newspaper commentator Peter Hitchens, that Britain has barely scratched the surface in terms of drug law enforcement and that a more hard-line approach, including zero tolerance towards cannabis and heavier prison sentences for drug possession, would lead to a reduction in crime and addiction.

Despite the collateral damage caused by the status quo, the only message coming from government is that talking tough is more of a priority than seeking any kind of real-world practical solution. Through fear of being seen as unpopular by the electorate or the national press, politicians have decided that it is a subject best left alone to fester in the council estates and run-down high streets of some of Britain's poorest and most socially excluded areas.

The taboo on debate and reform shows no sign of being broken. Although MPs are now more likely than ever to have first-hand experience of drugs, the attitude of government appears to be reversing back into the Victorian era of denial. Ironically, the only hard-hitting debates on drugs in Parliament take place across from the Commons in the House of Lords, where participants, many of them fast approaching old age, feel able to talk openly about the drugs issue because they do not have to fear the reaction of the media attack dogs or an easily scared Middle England electorate.

Whatever the dialogue going on around the Home Office, however many debates in the Commons and the House of Lords, MPs' inquiries, internal documents, heavyweight reports and statements made by powerful individuals and organisations there may be, the response from the heart of government has remained constant: the government is 'opposed to the legalisation of drugs and to decriminalisation for personal use because drugs are harmful and no one should take them.' At every opportunity, Home Office officials have been keen to remind the public, in reassuringly dismissive tones, that the chances of drugs being legalised at the present time are zero. In robotic fashion, successive Home Secretaries have dismissed out of hand the idea that drugs could be decriminalised or legalised in Britain in the foreseeable future.

The manner in which the Home Office dealt with a 2011 report by the Global Commission on Drug Policy, which argued that 'the decades-old global war on drugs has failed with devastating consequences for individuals and societies around the world', was a case in point. The Home Office's response to the report was so quick and dismissive that it gave the impression that even debating the drug issue was off the agenda.

It seems the only options are the status quo under Big Gangster, legalisation under Big Pharma or a hard-line approach under Big Brother. The debate, depressingly in Britain, is highly polarised and therefore set in stone. There are countless intellectual 'battles' between these opposing groups every year, in academic institutions, conferences and in Parliament. But all that happens is that the middle ground shrinks and the argument becomes more about ideology than real-world solutions.

While the UK is one of the world's leading consumers of drugs, it remains one of the most reluctant in trying anything new to reduce the devastating health and crime problems associated with them.

Nestling in the shadows of Frankfurt's thrusting glass towers is one of the most progressive drug harm-reduction strategies in the world. Germany's financial capital is home to several safe-injection areas where heroin users are able to use clean needles, Europe's largest rehab and a crack-smoking room. It is one of about fifty cities in Europe, Canada and Australia where safe-injection sites are part of their urban drug policies. Despite initial fears in all these countries that a change in drug policy could cause chaos, the sky hasn't yet fallen on any of them. There is no evidence showing that measures such as safe-injecting rooms have increased drug use. In fact in most countries which have implemented comprehensive harm-reduction strategies, drug addiction and drug-related crime has fallen.

That doesn't mean to say that experiments have all run smoothly. In an effort to stem the alarming rise in AIDS cases among drug users in Zurich, Switzerland, people were permitted to sell, buy or use drugs in the city's downtown park, the Platzspitz. What became quickly known as 'Needle Park' attracted up to 4,000 drug users a day. Health officials freely distributed clean needles along with advice on social and medical services. While AIDS cases dropped, the park became a magnet for professional dealing gangs, a violent price war erupted, and in 1993 the idea was junked. But at least they gave it a go.

*

Britain lies in a virtual quagmire of drug policy experimentation. Scientists and academics scrabble around for funding to set up small pilot studies to put their theories to the test. But when it comes to actually trying out something for real, nothing ever happens. Even when magical life-saving potions arrive on the scene, Britain stands still. There is a wealth of evidence showing that the heroin antidote naloxone saves the lives of people who have overdosed. A series of small pilot studies in England which handed drug users 'take home' naloxone kits resulted in the saving of sixteen lives. Yet, as with potentially life-saving hepatitis B vaccinations, there is not the will to get it up and running as a bona fide experiment.

Sluggishness also exists in the criminal justice world. The government has little idea which kind of sentences result in a reduction in drug offending, or whether its arrest referral strategy actually works. It seems any research into what works best is carried out purely to give an existing strategy scientific backing, rather than to see if it is actually effective.

While this country sits on its hands, the last two decades has seen a quiet revolution in countries, both rich and poor from around the world, that have set in motion bold criminal justice experiments. Decriminalisation – a broad term which generally refers to more relaxed laws on drug possession – is now being trialled to varying degrees in around thirty countries as disparate as Belgium, the Czech Republic, Estonia, Armenia, Chile, Mexico and, most significantly, Portugal.

In 2001, with the highest rate of HIV among injecting drug users in the European Union, Portugal, a largely conservative country, took radical action – and decided to decriminalise the possession of all drugs. Resources saved on policing and prosecuting people caught in possession of drugs were channelled into getting problem drug users into treatment and re-integrated into mainstream society. Those caught in possession of large amounts of drugs were, as before, to be prosecuted as drug dealers. At the time critics of the scheme predicted a growth in 'drug tourism' – drug users travelling to Portugal because of the new laws and drug use and addiction.

None of this happened. In fact the reverse has been the case. A paper, published by a libertarian think tank, the Cato Institute, in 2009, found that in the five years after personal possession was decriminalised, HIV infection rates and drug use among teenagers had fallen, while the number of people seeking treatment for drug addiction more than doubled.

'Judging by every metric, decriminalisation in Portugal has been a resounding success,' says Glenn Greenwald, an American lawyer and writer who conducted the research. 'It has enabled the Portuguese government to manage and control the drug problem far better than virtually every other Western country does.'

In 2011, a decade after the launch of Portugal's experiment, health experts backed Greenwald's findings. 'There is no doubt that the phenomenon of addiction is in decline in Portugal,' said Joao Goulao, President of the Institute of Drugs and Drugs Addiction, at a press conference to mark the tenth anniversary of the law.

Despite the fact the Home Office has consistently dismissed the policy of decriminalisation out of hand, some commentators say it is already here. Giving evidence to the Home Affairs Select Committee on Drugs in January 2012, Roger Howard, Chief Executive of the UK Drug Policy Commission, told MPs, when asked whether drug policy changes were ever likely: 'If you ask me whether, politically, there can be a shift, I think we have gone part of that way, if we look at cannabis warnings and penalty notices for disorder [warnings issued by police for first and second time cannabis possession offences which do not constitute a criminal record]. If you look at that, I think that we have seen Parliament agree to a gradual, you might call it, decriminalisation.'

Giving evidence to the same Committee, Dame Ruth Runciman, an influential figure in the drug policy world since chairing the 2000 Runciman Report, agreed, adding: 'We think that it is possibly time to be more overt about this, to take a step-by-step approach to decriminalisation, and to evaluate it carefully.'

Runciman and Howard's statements are backed up by evidence. A series of studies carried out by the Institute of

Criminal Policy Research during the 2000s into the policing of cannabis, found that officers often 'turned a blind eye' to possession offences. Police responses to catching people with cannabis, from ignoring it to arrest, also varied widely between different forces and individual officers.

It is not only the possession of 'soft' drugs that police are prone to pass over. We have spoken to several police officers who have told us that small amounts of Class A drugs such as crack and heroin found in people's possession are routinely ignored by officers, chiefly to avoid lengthy paperwork and because an arrest is viewed as a waste of police time. As Britain seems too timid to admit to overseeing a de facto decriminalisation policy that even the police seem comfortable with, other countries continue to explore other options.

In the UK the Foresight team not only sought to identify the potential damage of a new drug epidemic, but also tried to predict the future of drug policy where government, big business and pharmaceutical companies played a variety of roles. They saw that the economic health of the country would to some extent dictate policy, as would the potential convergence of lifestyle and performance drugs; and also how the private sector might enter the fray.

For Antonio Maria Costa, the former chief of the UN Office on Drugs and Crime who we met earlier, the enemy may no longer be just the illicit drug industry: the sinister venture-capitalist funds of the entertainment giants and Big Pharma are among the vultures waiting in the wings to develop any new legalised market.

Costa is not alone in believing profit could hold sway over morality. For many years *The Economist*, *Forbes* and the *Financial Times* have made the economic case in support of legalisation. In 2009 an editorial in *The Economist* repeated the magazine's long-held view on the international drug policy conundrum: 'The war on drugs has been a disaster, creating failed states in the developing world even as addiction has flourished in the rich world. By any sensible measure, this 100-year struggle has been illiberal, murderous and pointless. That is why *The Economist* continues to believe that the least bad policy is to legalise drugs.' These journals of capitalism suggest legalisation makes strong business sense. It can be taxed and it can be lucrative for the corporate world. Governments, they say, should not be constrained by morality when it comes to controlling the drug trade.

History is on the legalisers' side. Prohibition of alcohol was lifted not only due to its various ills, but largely due to the fact that the US was entering the Great Recession and tax revenues, however soiled, were needed to pay the unemployment bills.

For some, the future is already here, and it is not in a mad-cap experiment in a struggling Latin American state, but in the heart of America, where the cannabis lobby in a medicinal guise has won a legitimate platform under local legislation. Medical marijuana is now a formidable investment option there, spawning a sub-industry that has brought an economic glow to the otherwise ailing states like California.

The idea of private companies becoming involved in illegal trade sounds far-fetched in Britain, but in America, the flag-bearer of the war on drugs, it's all the rage. Marijuana is illegal under US federal law, but that has not stopped marijuana farms and dispensaries from setting up business in the fifteen states that allow the drug to be used for medical purposes. While it is a badly kept secret that there are lots of people who are permitted to buy cannabis legally for the most spurious reasons, the state authorities are willing to turn a blind eye because of the huge kickback in taxes they receive.

In Colorado there are more marijuana dispensaries than

Starbucks outlets, and more than 100,000 people in the state are legally registered to use the drug for medicinal purposes. In Sacramento, California, a 10,000-square-foot cannabis gardening emporium, weGrow, opened in 2011, with how-to experts and merchandise to help medical marijuana patients grow pot. The 'Walmart of weed' plans to open stores in Arizona, Colorado, New Jersey and Oregon in 2012. In its State of Medical Marijuana Markets 2011 report, the 'first credible business analysis of medical marijuana', analysis firm See Change Strategy estimated the size of the legal cannabis industry at $1.7 billion, rising to $8.9 billion by 2016 – which would make it one of America's fastest-growing industries.

And the industry now has a lobby group to stand up for the right to make a decent profit out of selling cannabis. Launched in 2010, the National Cannabis Industry Association (NCIA), largely peopled by the people who own America's legal cannabis dispensaries, is dedicated to representing the interests of the medical marijuana industry. In 2011 the NCIA held its first official 'congressional lobbying day', during which representatives met with members of Congress to argue for the protection of medical marijuana interests. They want their industry to be treated like any other.

As the government treads water and seems content with the status quo, the collateral damage of the drug trade continues to be felt within society. Politicians can't solve the social inequality that fuels the most damaging aspects of the drug trade – addiction, crime and lives wasted dealing on street corners – but politicians can be brave and experiment, as other countries have done. Economic interests have in the past and will have a big influence on the future of drug policy. But the institution that perhaps has the greatest influence on government drug policy, because it is an issue it watches over like a hawk, is the press.

7

Warped

Media, Myth and Propaganda

It took only a few days in November 2009 for mephedrone to go from a relatively unknown substance to the UK's public enemy number one.

'The spectre of a Christmas killer is a synthetic substance called mephedrone', warned the *Northern Echo* in true penny-dreadful style, describing how police in County Durham had been dealing with a rash of teenagers being hospitalised after using the new drug.

Over the course of a month, reports of young mephedrone users, from remote Scottish backwaters to the leafy Home Counties, began popping up across Britain. On 24 November, four days after the *Northern Echo* story, the *Daily Mail* revealed that fourteen-year-old Woking schoolgirl Gabrielle Price had died after taking mephedrone at a house party in Brighton. Two days later, a well-respected news agency sent round an eye-watering story about an unnamed teenager from Durham who had been hospitalised after taking mephedrone, headlined 'USER RIPS OFF SCROTUM ON LEGAL DRUG', which was subsequently (and unsurprisingly) picked up by the national press.

Meanwhile, the story of Finn, the Cockfield boy we met in Chapter 1, was repeated in newspapers as far away as South Africa and New Zealand.

A report that appeared in the *Sun*, *Daily Mail*, *Telegraph* and *Metro* revealed that 180 pupils had been off sick from a Leicestershire school after taking mephedrone. Then, eight days later, two Scunthorpe teenagers, Louis Wainwright and Nicholas Smith, were reported to have died after overdosing on the drug. The tragedy appeared all over the press. One of the boy's heartbroken parents called for the drug to be banned, telling the BBC, 'he would be alive if the ban was in place'.

In a story headlined 'KIDS' DEADLY COCKTAIL MIX', the *Sun* highlighted a claim from a drug worker that dealers were mixing mephedrone with crystal meth to get children hooked. The *Daily Star* labelled the drug 'the powder of death', stating that '90 per cent of Liverpool' were taking it, and that South African crime gangs were busy stockpiling the drug to meet demand among fans at the 2010 World Cup.

With the whiff of a fresh drug scare hanging in the air, the tabloid press had cranked its creaking 'drug craze' machinery into action. 'Meow meow' was a nickname unfamiliar to most mephedrone users, but one that newspapers latched on to. By March 2010, the *Sun* was printing an average of two 'meow meow' stories a day, and had kicked off a 'BAN MEOW NOW' campaign. The pressure to prohibit Britain's latest 'killer drug', as the paper called it, was sent into overdrive as the terrifying reports kept flooding in.

Over thirty-nine days, from 8 March, when the '180 school-kids off sick' story broke, the national press printed 210 articles devoted to the drug, a third of which appeared in the *Sun*,

Britain's bestselling newspaper. The tabloid tales were given added gravity when the government's own drug advisory body, the ACMD, reported that the drug could have been linked to twenty-six further deaths in Britain.

On 16 April the Labour government took action, and in a move claimed as a 'major victory' by the *Sun*, banned mephedrone, classifying it as a Class B substance. The decision was undoubtedly a sensible one. Mephedrone was a cheap, potent, unpredictable substance that children and teenagers could buy easily and take anywhere. Job done.

Except that, when the dust had settled, it transpired that most of the big-hitting mephedrone stories reported in the press were not true.

The source for the 'scrotum-ripping' story, for example, was discovered to be a post on a mephedrone chat site. The owner of the website, mephedrone.com, said it was 'a joke'. A spokeswoman for Leicestershire County Council denied reports of the 180 sick pupils, stating: 'those figures don't relate to any school in Leicestershire'. The police and the local newspaper blamed each other for the fake story. Embarrassingly for the Humberside police officer who had briefed the press about the deaths of the two Scunthorpe boys, a coroner's report later revealed they had in fact died after drinking alcohol and taking the similar-sounding heroin substitute methadone. Many other reports, including the fatalities associated with the drug identified by the ACMD, were found to be unsubstantiated. Subsequent toxicology tests showed that most of those deaths were not caused by mephedrone. In fact in 2010, in England and Wales, there were just six deaths where mephedrone was mentioned on the death certificate. Few newspapers bothered correcting their facts.

As the science journalist Nic Fleming argued, the legislation banning 'meow meow' was prompted by a mixture of 'inaccurate and hysterical journalism, the advice of a scientific committee weakened by confrontation with ministers, and a government so desperate to be loved it would have done practically anything the press demanded'.

Three days after the decision was made to ban mephedrone, two members of the ACMD, who had warned against the measure, resigned in protest. In a letter to the Home Secretary, drug treatment expert Eric Carlin said the ACMD's advice to the government to ban mephedrone 'was unduly based on media and political pressure'.

In *Crime, Policy and the Media*, a book by Jon Silverman, professor of media and criminal justice at the University of Bedfordshire, the former Home Secretary Alan Johnson explained: 'The reason we hurried up banning mephedrone was, firstly, a lot of newspaper stories . . . but also an election was coming – we wanted to get it through Parliament.'

Asked by Silverman whether there was a desire to show the media ahead of the election that the government was being 'tough' on drugs, Johnson said: 'Well, you never know whether there are other considerations . . . I like to think it was the importance of getting the ban on the statute book.'

Not only did the 'inaccurate and hysterical' press coverage end with a questionable change to the law, it could be said it prompted exactly the wrong response. Sales of mephedrone actually increased during the media campaign.

During the blaze of publicity in newspapers and on TV between November 2009 and April 2010, analysis of Google statistics showed the number of searches for 'mephedrone' 'drone' and 'meow meow' spiralled, as did queries about the drug in online drug forums. And it was clearly not just worried parents looking for help. According to a survey by music magazine *Mixmag*, in a matter of months mephedrone had been transformed into one of the most popular drugs among young clubbers.

Online mephedrone sellers were so inundated by new custom in March and April that they ran out of stock. One major London-based dealer said: 'Since all the stuff in the papers about meph, it's more of a money-spinner than ever. I've had to order in bulk.'

But just two weeks after the government announced the decision to ban mephedrone, the *Sun* published a story on a new legal high called NRG-1: 'NRG-1 IS 25P A HIT AND WILL KILL MANY MORE THAN MEOW MEOW', adding that the substance would lead to 'enough mass brain damage and death . . . to fill an Olympic stadium'. And so it continued.

Around twelve million newspapers are sold every day. Polling data from Ipsos MORI in 2007 showed that six out of ten people who 'knew something about illegal drugs' cited 'the media' as their primary source of information; three times as many as cited 'government public health campaigns'. But the subject of illegal drugs is vulnerable to sensationalism, scapegoating and misinformation. It is seemingly one of a select group of subjects in which emergency reporting powers are enacted to give journalists, in the face of a common 'evil', a licence to play fast and loose with the facts. The media is a dominant carrier of the contagion we describe in this book as narcomania, a self-perpetuating cycle of confusion, ignorance and misinformation.

When it comes to reporting on drugs, the print media, arguably the most powerful quarter of the Fourth Estate, can be said to be influenced by three interconnected agendas, above and beyond their remit to report the objective truth: a need to sell newspapers, a desire to keep their readers happy, and an incentive to reflect the prevailing political and moral outlook.

The Fourth Estate has historically played the role of a mouthpiece to government when it comes to influencing behaviour. Unlike politicians, newspapers have the ability to reach the common man and Middle England. In the past, broadsheets and tabloids have not only reflected public opinion, but have been used by governments to rally the country to war and bind communities with common narratives, and their role has also been harnessed to define acceptable behaviour.

These loyal, paying readerships, which have been carefully groomed by newspapers over the decades and in some cases centuries, have become hugely powerful weapons for editors. In return for being so charmed, readers buy into the newspaper's ideology – providing newspaper editors with a fully signed up moral army, a guaranteed, voting readership of wealthy, middle-class taxpayers – and the government has to listen. The balance of power between government and newspapers has tipped in favour of the Fourth Estate. It is because of this that, regardless of the reality, newspapers set the parameters for political debate. This relationship between the press, its readers and political elite is one that until recently has rarely been aired.

Facing the Leveson Inquiry in 2012, set up to investigate the culture, practices and ethics of the British press, *Daily Mail* editor Paul Dacre defended his paper's scrutiny of the misdemeanours of public figures by quoting Tim Luckhurst, a journalism professor at Kent University, on privacy and freedom of expression. Luckhurst had outlined the tryst the press has with the status quo of the day to infuse news with a moral tone, to guide British citizens away from temptations of vice:

> In the eighteenth and nineteenth centuries, British philosophers developed a concept called the 'sanction of public opinion'. They concluded that popular morality should not ban infidelity or imprison men for betraying their wives, but it could create an incentive to behave responsibly. People tempted to stray might be persuaded to think again by the certainty that their friends and neighbours would think less of them.

Sanctioned to guide the British public over their sexual mores, appetite for intoxicants and the threat posed by the deviant and foreign to mainstream society, the press has played its part in sparking waves of moral panic with each new drug that has entered mass use within the UK, from opium to cocaine. These messages play to the fears of an island nation, to protect its borders from a foreign threat, but they also seek to underpin British values of hard work, honesty and thrift. And the press's loyalty to the narrative is well rewarded.

Not only do the British public want to know the details of their neighbours' private lives, they are prepared to pay every day for lurid tales of the unwanted and dispossessed, the gruesome and the criminal. Journalists even have a phrase for the kind of stories that middle-class readers love to be shocked by at the breakfast table: 'marmalade droppers'.

Drug stories sell newspapers. To the writer Will Self, the drug story is chiefly an excuse for cheap voyeurism. 'There's an appetite for what I call "drug pornography",' he has said. 'Lots of people who would never dream of taking drugs get a vicarious kick out of the exposure to other people's abandonment. That's why imagery of people using drugs sells papers.' Newspaper editors are well aware of the human drama of a drug story, and its capacity to shock, scare, and provide a window into an unfamiliar yet strangely fascinating world. Newspapers play on the fact that most parents are worried about their children getting into drugs.

After cannabis had been reclassified from a Class B to a Class C drug in 2004, the tabloid press filled hundreds of column inches with exaggerated scare stories about the drug, particularly about its more potent strain, skunk, which was being grown on cannabis farms throughout Britain and had overtaken hashish to dominate the market. At the height of the panic about skunk in 2007, newspapers informed readers of the threats. The *Liverpool Echo* warned of 'Super-strength cannabis so potent that just one puff can cause schizophrenia', while the *Daily Mail* argued that 'smoking just one cannabis joint raises the danger of mental illness by 40 per cent'.

Not only could smoking cannabis jeopardise your mental health, it could also turn you into a killer. In 2002, shortly after David Blunkett had announced his intention to reclassify cannabis to a Class C drug, the national press covered the horrific case of Mathew Hardman, a satanic vampire fantasist who brutally murdered a ninety-year-old woman. The *Daily Mail* published the story under the headline: 'THE VAMPIRE MURDERER WHOSE MIND WAS WARPED BY CANNABIS'. During Hardman's trial it was mentioned by one witness that Hardman had once smoked cannabis, a detail deemed unimportant by every other agency.

To the opponents of drug law reform, cannabis is a key drug. It is seen as the thin end of the wedge: if laws and attitudes become relaxed on cannabis, so too will they become on ecstasy, cocaine and the rest. If teenagers start smoking cannabis, they will progress to using Class A drugs. Cannabis represents a front line in their battle against any kind of liberalisation. As a result, its image as a 'soft' drug no worse than tobacco or alcohol is attacked with vigour. It leads you to hard drugs, it makes you mad, and it makes you kill.

The *Mail* has published a string of stories linking cannabis to acute mental health problems and extreme acts of violence, gleaned largely from cases where defendants plead diminished responsibility on account of smoking the drug.

Despite claims made in papers such as the *Mail* about cannabis's ability to cause mental health problems, the scientific evidence is not so conclusive. The ACMD found a 'probable but weak causal link between psychotic illness and cannabis use', while drug information charity DrugScope has concluded: 'Psychologically, use of cannabis has been reported to cause anxiety and paranoia in some users and may in rarer cases be a trigger for underlying mental health problems. Some research has suggested that cannabis can stimulate mental health disorders such as schizophrenia.'

But there is little evidence to back claims that cannabis, or its long-term effects, can trigger violence. Virtually every piece of research carried out in the last forty-five years debunks the 'cannabis causes violence' myth.

Two of the most quoted studies into the links between cannabis, mental health and violence, carried out among 1,000 young adults in New Zealand and published in 2000 and 2002, have been used as major planks by the *Daily Mail* columnist Melanie Phillips, in the 'cannabis causes aggression' argument.

Dr Louise Arseneault, the lead author on both studies, says her work has been misrepresented: 'We found that people dependent on cannabis were more likely to commit violent crime. But to say our studies showed that cannabis itself caused violence is wrong. We found that it was not the substance that caused the violence, it was more related to the user's past history and circumstance. To say the paranoia created by smoking cannabis makes you more likely to be violent is a bold claim,' she says, 'there is no evidence for this.'

The *Daily Mail*'s claims are not without precedent. *Reefer Madness* is an anti-marijuana propaganda film first broadcast in the US in 1936. It begins with a teacher warning pupils and their parents against the dangers of marijuana, relating the story of a group of students whose lives swiftly descend into mayhem and murder after they smoke 'reefers' and listen to jazz. By the end of the cautionary tale, Jimmy has killed a pedestrian while driving 'high', Jack has shot Mary, Ralph has beaten Jack to death in a fit of insanity, and Blanche has committed suicide.

But it isn't just the tabloids that have issued overblown warnings against the dangers of cannabis. In March 2007 the *Independent on Sunday* published a front page headlined: 'Cannabis: An Apology'. It said: 'In 1997 this newspaper launched a campaign to decriminalise the drug. If only we had known then what we can reveal today.' Unfortunately what the paper revealed were some very shaky facts. By taking the most potent form of cannabis available and comparing it to the weakest a decade ago, the paper declared the drug was 'twenty-five times' stronger than it was in the 1990s. As with many of the scare stories about skunk, the facts were less dramatic. According to forensic analysis, the average cannabis joint is now approximately twice the strength of the average 1970s joint.

It is not just dubious conclusions that are being drawn. The British press are also anxious to warn us of the threat of new drugs – and have done so with considerable success, despite the questionable veracity of the warning. Throughout the 2000s media outlets were desperate to be the first to herald Britain's crystal meth epidemic. As one *Sun* journalist said when quizzed on why the paper was printing another 'false dawn' crystal meth story in 2011: 'I know there hasn't been a significant rise in crystal meth use, but the stories fill column inches. We've been talking about heroin and crack since the 80s, people want to hear about something new – and it's a good opportunity to reprint those "before and after" images of the American crystal meth addicts.'

The idea that what happens in America – crystal meth has had a catastrophic impact in many parts of the country – will also happen here is a scare story that has been gleefully pursued by the supposedly more respectable media as well. An ITV documentary entitled *London's Most Dangerous Drug* in 2005 and a full front-page story in the *Independent*, 'CRYSTAL METH: BRITAIN'S DEADLIEST DRUG PROBLEM', in 2007 both gained much attention, despite the fact that their research showed that the drug was nothing more than a faint blip on police and drug-use statistics. Between 2007 and 2008 Home Office figures show there were less than fifty seizures of crystal meth, compared to over 7,000 seizures of crack cocaine. The British Crime Survey in 2008 revealed 0.1 per cent of people questioned about their drug use in the past month had used crystal meth, with the figure falling to zero in the 2010–11 survey.

What role do journalists themselves play? How much do they know of the drug world? In an interview with *Guardian* journalist Nick Davies, former *Sun* showbiz reporter Sean Hoare said: 'I was paid to go out and take drugs with rock stars – get drunk with them, take pills with them, take cocaine with them.

It was so competitive. You are going to go beyond the call of duty. You are going to do things that no sane man would do. You're in a machine.'

'He made no secret of his massive ingestion of drugs,' wrote Davies. 'He told me how he used to start the day with "a rock star's breakfast" – a line of cocaine and a Jack Daniel's – usually in the company of a journalist who now occupies a senior position at the *Sun*. He reckoned he was using three grams of cocaine a day, spending about £1,000 a week . . . Looking back, he could see it had done him enormous damage. But at the time, as he recalled, most of his colleagues were doing it, too . . . It must have scared the rest of Fleet Street when he started talking – he had bought, sold and snorted cocaine with some of the most powerful names in tabloid journalism. One retains a senior position at the *Daily Mirror*. "I last saw him in Little Havana" [Hoare] recalled, "at three in the morning, on his hands and knees. He had lost his cocaine wrap. I said to him, 'This is not really the behaviour we expect of a senior journalist from a great Labour paper.' He said, 'Have you got any fucking drugs?'"'

Journalists, especially young, up-and-coming reporters, are always looking for a big scoop with which to make their name. Urban decay and a broken society often prove fertile ground for gritty, award-winning investigations. In 1981 a young, tenacious *Washington Post* reporter named Janet Cooke was awarded a Pulitzer Prize for a heart-rending article called 'Jimmy's World', about a black eight-year-old heroin addict who was regularly injected by his parents. Cooke described Jimmy's dad Ron injecting his son: 'He grabs Jimmy's left arm just above the elbow, his massive hand tightly encircling the child's small limb. The needle slides into the boy's soft skin like a straw pushed into the center of a freshly baked cake.'

Cooke reported that Jimmy was not alone, that he was one of many child addicts and kids wrapped up in the drugs world.

The article prompted waves of outrage across America, with the police immediately launching a full-scale search for Jimmy. The *Post*'s famous assistant managing editor, Bob Woodward, submitted the article for the Pulitzer. But Jimmy could not be found. Two days after receiving the award, Cooke admitted her story was a fake and her newspaper had to issue a grovelling front-page apology.

The cause of the *Post* scandal, and the crux of how and why the media continues to get it wrong over drugs was eloquently described by sociologists Craig Reinarman and Ceres Duskin in an article titled: 'Dominant Ideology and Drugs in the Media', published in the *International Journal on Drugs Policy* in 1992.

'These things were possible, we contend, precisely because America's guardians of truth had no touchstone of truth on drug problems apart from their own scare stories. Editors seem to believe that readers don't like to be reminded that there is something fundamentally wrong with the social system from which most of them benefit. Editors and readers alike feel more comfortable believing that the worsening horrors of our inner cities are caused by evil individuals from a different gene pool – addicts.'

They said Cooke's article bypassed the usual filters of the newspaper editors and Pulitzer judges because they were rendered incapable of differentiating the truth from the myths and scare stories that had been built around the drug trade – by the media. That a family would have got the child they bathed, clothed and fed, addicted to drugs, that Jimmy would enjoy having a needle stuck in his arm or that impoverished, heavily addicted heroin users would give their drugs to a child should have raised some eyebrows. But it didn't.

As Reinarman and Duskin pointed out during the intense and extensive seventeen-day search by police and *Post* reporters looking for Jimmy, 'no one found any child addict – not an eight-year-old, not a ten-year-old, not a twelve-year-old. Stories that simply depict addicts as complicated, troubled human beings would be neither comforting enough for readers nor dramatic enough for prizes.

'If the *Post* scandal has value,' Reinarman and Duskin concluded, 'it inheres in the accidental glimpse it affords into the normally hidden process by which media institutions force the untidy facts of social life through the sieve of dominant ideology. We submit that it is this process that allowed Cooke's tale to sail undetected past *Post* editors, Pulitzer jurors, and the hundreds of other journalists who analysed the fraud. And we suggest that this process continues to camouflage the ways our world produces drug problems in the first place, and thereby helps to forge a public prepared to swallow the next junkie stereotype and to enlist in the next drug war.'

Fleet Street Fox, an anonymous journalist blogger and Twitter legend who has worked for the *Sun*, the *Mail*, the *Guardian* and the *Mirror*, says: 'Most tabloids have the same attitude on drugs, "we don't like them, they are bad," otherwise you will lose readers. For newspapers it's simple economics. You have to print what sells. On top of that a paper might have a political line because it is selling to that particular part of society. It's how you sell advertising, how you present stories. That will affect the editor's view, that's why you are the editor, because you know your reader. You do what your readers want you to do. If you have a certain package you deliver, you don't want to change it too much or you could risk it all.'

Whether it is the *Sun* or the *Financial Times*, drug stories are a staple of the British press, yet despite the huge coverage the issue receives, it remains one of the most misrepresented of all.

For most newspapers, the complex dilemmas of the drug trade are boiled down to a black and white realm of heroes and villains, good and evil, ne'er-do-wells and innocent victims. As the *Guardian*'s media commentator Roy Greenslade, a former editor of the *Daily Mirror*, puts it: 'There are many complex dilemmas that are, to a popular newspaper editor, so straightforward that the solutions do not require a second thought. Among the most glaringly obvious is the matter of drugs. All drugs are evil. They threaten the orderliness of society. The people who supply them are scum.' It is a view based on a presumption, of a composite picture of what the average, law-abiding, tabloid reader would probably think. 'Drug culture challenges the status quo that journalists subconsciously seek to maintain,' says Greenslade.

Newspaper editors are aware that to survive, they must give their customers what they want. British society is generally conservative and the outlook and readership of the popular press reflects that. Opinion polls on the public's attitude to drugs show there is not a huge demand for the liberalisation of drug laws and certainly little support for legalisation. An ICM Research poll carried out in 2008 found 18 per cent of people questioned believed drugs laws are 'not liberal enough' compared to 32 per cent who said laws were 'too liberal'. Two-thirds believe addicts arrested in possession of drugs should be sent to jail.

The two biggest selling newspapers in Britain in April 2012, the *Sun* (2.6 million copies a day) and the *Daily Mail* (1.9 million), have readerships dominated by Conservative voters. While the *Sun*'s readers are chiefly working-class people from a broad range of ages and regions, the *Mail* has a high number of middle-class readers living in the south of England. The *Mail* is the only paper read by more than 50 per cent women, and over half (60 per cent) of its readership is over fifty-five. The third biggest selling newspaper, the *Metro* (1.3 million) is owned by Associated Newspapers, also owners of the *Mail*. Because it is free, its readership is generalised, although the content is heavily influenced by its conservative stablemate.

The fourth and fifth biggest selling newspapers, the *Daily Mirror* (1.1 million), and the *Daily Star* (611,000), like the *Sun*, have a broad-ranging working-class readership, although the readers of both papers are chiefly Labour voters. The next four biggest selling papers, the *Daily Telegraph* (576,000), *Daily Express* (568,000), *Times* (393,000) and *Financial Times* (305,000) all have high proportions of Conservative voters. The readership of the three broadsheets are dominated by the ageing middle and upper classes (half the *Telegraph*'s readers are over sixty-five), while the readers of the *Express* (well known for its obsession with front-page stories on immigration and the weather) are from a lower social class.

Newspaper circulation is dwarfed, however, by online traffic and the huge reach of Internet news sites. The dominant force in this arena is the *Daily Mail*, whose Mail Online site had 100 million monthly browsers in January 2012. It is the world's most popular news website. The *Guardian* is the second largest newspaper website in the UK, with 63 million monthly users.

For newspapers whose key agenda is to reflect readers' anxiety over the breakdown of society, drugs are the perfect mechanism. The threat posed by a new drug, that smoking cannabis will lead to heroin addiction or the thought that drug dealers are stalking the streets with impunity, is designed to fill readers, especially the parents of teenagers, with dread.

And the villain of the piece does not always take the form of the evil drug dealer or smuggler: they can be the lax parent, the drug fiend who will do anything for a fix, the pro-legalisation liberal or the feeble government minister failing to act in the face of an impending threat to civil society. Many media outlets are well aware of their audience's fears and are more than willing to turn the scare-factor dial to 10 when it comes to narcotics.

Take the *Daily Mail* for example. It is, as many journalists know, a newspaper which employs some of the best reporters in the business, with a reputation for thoroughness and fact checking. But when it comes to drugs, their high standards seem not to apply.

As the *Mail*'s long-standing editor Paul Dacre repeats whenever he's asked, its success as one of Britain's most popular and influential newspapers is based on understanding the wants and needs of its audience. Dacre logically presumes that many of his readers, as he possibly does himself, see the drug world and its impact not just as an immediate threat to their family, their valuables and their personal safety, but to the very fabric of society. This anxiety is repackaged back to his readers, in articles aimed to engender fear or moral outrage or both, on a near daily basis. Danny Kushlick of the drug-law reform pressure group Transform explains the dynamic through the 'securitisation theory', a term used in foreign-policy discussions to explain how states react with extraordinary measures when they perceive a threat to their existence. 'In a securitised system, normal rules don't apply,' he says. 'You don't check value for money on wars, you don't apply evidence-based templates to assess cost-benefit analysis. What you do is fight, and as in any war you require propaganda to sustain the fight.'

To the *Daily Mail*, stories about drugs not only sell papers, but ensure that policymakers will incur the wrath of nearly 2 million voters if they follow anything other than the newspaper's hard-line stance on illegal drugs. A former *Mail* journalist, who did not want to be named, said drugs are one of a hit list of subjects given what she calls the '*Daily Mail* treatment'. 'Stories are used to panic people. All Dacre knows is the *Daily Mail*, he has no proper perspective on the world.'

The public perception of how drug users and dealers behave has been drilled into Britain's psyche for decades. It is coloured by a media industry which, since the days of American media mogul William Randolph Hearst, has revelled in tales of evil drug peddlers, spineless addicts and strange substances that literally have a life of their own.

'All the lines of attack we still see today in the media were in place before 1914,' says Harry Shapiro in his book on drugs and Hollywood, *Shooting Stars*. 'The public wanted heroes and villains, they wanted scapegoats, people to blame for everything that went wrong in their lives, they wanted sex, depravity, mystery and murder. Hearst quickly realised that drug stories could provide the lot.

'The game plan was to take some kernels of truth around the undeniable dangers of drugs – the addictive potential of morphine or the anxiety and paranoia of chronic cocaine use – and magnify them through a prism of racism, nativism and fear.' One headline, 'Negro cocaine fiends are a new southern menace', based on the fact black slaves had been given cocaine to relieve fatigue while working on Southern plantations, sparked calls by local police for an upgrade in pistol power.

The tightening of alcohol licensing laws and the outlawing of opium and cocaine during World War One created the first underground drugs scene in Britain. It was largely based around the 'theatre set' in London's Soho and featured a mix of famous actors and actresses, opium merchants and prostitutes. For the media, the mix of drugs, foreigners and stage stars was too appetising to ignore.

The deaths from drug overdoses of two famous stage stars, Billie Carleton in 1918 and Freda Kempton in 1922, caused outrage. On both occasions newspapers depicted the innocent damsels seduced to ruin by the evil drug peddlers. 'There was already a moral panic associated with drugs, but Billie Carleton was seen as different, she was portrayed as this waif-like figure when she was nothing of the sort,' says Marek Kohn in his book, *Dope Girls*.

Since then the dominant media message has primarily been that drug users are either mad, bad or sad. Roy Greenslade commented: 'From the middle of the 1960s onwards it has been a roller-coaster ride, with the media "discovering" new evils at regular intervals, starting with cannabis and progressing through heroin, LSD, speed, cocaine, ecstasy and all manner of combinations and spin-offs.'

It is no coincidence that some of the biggest-hitting drug stories of the last two decades have revolved around iconic images of young women and drugs: Leah Betts lying dead in hospital surrounded by tubes as the innocent victim of ecstasy, the well brought-up Rachel Whitear, supplicant on the floor of a dingy flat with a needle in her hand; any model or celebrity corrupted by drugs.

In his book *Drugs and Popular Culture*, Paul Manning compared the reporting of deaths from ecstasy and heroin overdoses in the 2000s. He described the explosion in media coverage of ecstasy as being all about the 'threat to the inno-cent'. While heroin addiction was portrayed as a problem of the underclass, and therefore a less pressing issue for the newspaper-reading public, 'in the minds of journalists might it be that ecstasy is more newsworthy because it is understood as a threat to respectable middle-class families?'

This would explain why the media has paid more attention to deaths linked to ecstasy than other drugs. An analysis by the Information is Beautiful website, which specialises in presenting visualised statistics, found the media reported 100 per cent of deaths relating to ecstasy use, compared to only 9 per cent of heroin deaths and 2 per cent of deaths from alcohol poisoning. Meanwhile a review of ten years of Scottish drug-death reporting carried out by researchers at Glasgow University found that the likelihood of a newspaper reporting a death from paracetamol was only one in 250. For diazepam, it was one in fifty. For amphetamine, it was one in three. For ecstasy, a drug associated with teenagers from Middle England, every associated death was reported.

*

When it comes to drugs, the ideology of a newspaper usurps its basic journalistic remit to convey the facts (objectively) to the public. Richard Peppiatt, the former *Daily Star* reporter who quit in protest at the newspaper's alleged 'anti-Muslim' coverage, told the Leveson Inquiry: 'If a scientist announces their research has found ecstasy to be safer than alcohol, I know my job as a tabloid reporter is to portray this man as a quack. If a judge passes down a community sentence to a controversial offender, I know my job is to make them appear out of touch. Positive peer reviews are ignored; sentencing guidelines are buried. The ideological imperative comes before the journalistic one – drugs are always bad, British justice is always soft.'

For newspapers eager to push forward a strong moral or political agenda, the drug issue provides an ideal grandstanding opportunity. This will influence the spin they put on drugs stories, the kind of stories they will and will not run, and any specific campaigns that are launched. Newspapers will leave room for opposing voices on their pages, and may veer away from their established line on occasions, but generally if an editor wants to get across the message that their publication is vociferously 'anti-drugs', then the readers, and the policy-makers will know about it.

It is no coincidence that since the barrage of stories about the dangers of cannabis published in papers such as the *Daily Mail* throughout the 2000s, the public's perception of the dangers of the drug has shifted. In 2001 nearly half those asked as part of the annual British Social Attitudes Survey carried out by the National Centre for Social Research said cannabis was not 'as damaging as you think'. By 2010 this had fallen to 24 per cent.

There are few areas of public policy where the press has more power than on the issue of drugs. In its 2012 submission to the Leveson Inquiry, the UK Drug Policy Commission concluded that press reporting on drugs issues is 'overwhelming the policy process'. The influence of the press is so great when it comes to drugs that policies have been generated from myths printed in newspapers whose primary concern is generating favourable headlines.

In the run-up to the 2005 general election, Labour floated a series of policies to make it clear that it was as tough as the Tories on drugs and crime. Cleverly, they linked fear of drugs with the need to protect children. Tony Blair wrote an article in the *News of the World* backing the paper's campaign to drug-test schoolchildren and subject them to regular sniffer-dog searches. The paper had even gone so far as to fund a six-month drug-testing trial at a state school in Kent.

Secondly, and with much fanfare, the tastiest bone thrown to the press pack was an idea first mooted by William Hague and the Conservatives in 2000: a new US-style law to stem the 'scourge' of drug dealers preying on vulnerable schoolchildren. Anyone caught selling drugs within 500 metres of a school would be given a lengthier sentence.

The national tabloids promptly heralded a 'PURGE ON PUSHERS AT THE SCHOOL GATE'. One local newspaper editorial grimly warned: 'Catch them young seems to be the motto of drug pushers, and all schools need to be aware that these suppliers of death are hanging around school gates looking for potential new customers.' The campaign provided great publicity for Labour's desperate need to appear tough on crime, but there was only one problem, and Labour knew it: the school-gate dealer is a chimera. While newspapers and politicians are keen to give the phenomenon airtime, drug squad officers will quietly explain that it never actually happens. It's an urban myth inspired by the belief that people who sell drugs are motivated by a desire to corrupt innocent children rather than a need to make money.

Parliament would not be fooled so easily. When the 'school-gate law' was debated in the House of Commons, it was branded a 'media stunt' by the Labour MP for Bassetlaw, John Mann, adding to the scepticism surrounding his own party's proposal. He told MPs that a detailed investigation of 200 complaints from constituents about drug dealing outside school gates found none was based on concrete evidence. When he put the issue to school pupils he said they 'derided' him. 'The idea that dealers would wait at the school gate was laughed out of court. They asked me,

"Why do you think we'd be stupid enough to buy or sell drugs by our school? If we want drugs, we know where to get them.'"

A parliamentary review could find no evidence before or since the law change that police, prosecutors or the courts have found, arrested or prosecuted anyone for selling drugs outside a school.

Amusingly, the only example of an adult dealer caught selling drugs outside school gates was a fake. In 2003 the *People* newspaper ran an article headlined 'On sale at school gates . . . kiddie coke at 50p a go', which described how a dealer was 'cynically targeting youngsters' with pills outside a London school. The story was accompanied by a photograph of 'Rev', the dealer, 'a surly nineteen-year-old dressed in ripped jeans and a leather jacket, with short black spiky hair'. But it turned out 'Rev' was in fact the teenage son of the newspaper's photographer. The scam was spotted by the boy's mother, who promptly called up the *People* to complain. Journalist and photographer were sacked for gross misconduct, despite a defence in court that the paper 'made up stories all the time'.

The media's power to affect drug policy is undoubted, but are the changes good or bad for society? In the case of the school-gate drug-dealers law, which was largely based on newspaper fantasies, the answer is no. Since the law came into effect in January 2006, the courts are yet to convict a single dealer of pushing drugs outside the school gates. Instead the law is being used by West Yorkshire police force to ramp up sentences for dealers caught selling drugs to adults arrested in alleys or pubs that just happen to be up to 500 metres away from the nearest school. Not only has the law got police chasing shadows, it is being used against people it was not meant to target.

*   *   *

There appeared to be a detectable, and somewhat mutually beneficial meeting of minds between prime minister-in-waiting Gordon Brown and *Daily Mail* editor Paul Dacre in the middle of 2007. Brown, gearing up to lead the Labour Party and take over from Tony Blair, was eager to ensure he had continued support from the influential mid-market tabloid. Dacre was eager to see a triumphant end to his personal, three-year mission to return cannabis to being a Class B drug.

David Blunkett had moved it to Class C in 2004 on the grounds that making cannabis possession a non-arrestable offence would reduce the number of otherwise law-abiding people being criminalised, reduce friction between the police and the wider community and allow police more time to spend investigating more serious crimes. But to Dacre and the *Mail*, the move was the thin end of a wedge that would turn Britain into a drug free-for-all.

Unlike in the Blair–Dacre relationship, both men respected each other. Dacre had already gone on the record as saying Brown was 'touched by the mantle of greatness'. They shared the same highly moralistic outlooks and espoused the virtues of traditional family life, hard work and patriotism.

In the run-up to the Labour leadership battle in May 2007 Brown was declared in a *Mail* editorial as being 'head and shoulders' above the other candidates. The paper ran affectionate pieces about Brown's love for his family and his wife's charming fashion sense. And within weeks of becoming prime minister, Brown announced his intention to reclassify cannabis to Class B, despite the fact that the ACMD had concluded only a year before that all the evidence showed the drug should remain at Class C.

Gordon Brown's statement of intent was welcomed by the *Daily Mail* as a major victory for the paper. It quoted Whitehall sources saying the move was inspired by a 'personal instinct of Mr Brown', although many at the paper believed its own editor was the real inspiration. After the reclassification to Class B was announced in May 2008 – against the advice of yet another analysis of the dangers of cannabis by the ACMD – the *Daily Mail* rejoiced and said the PM's 'brave, justified' decision showed 'moral courage'.

What left the experts on the ACMD spinning was that the new prime minister justified his decision to ignore their carefully gathered scientific evidence by pointing out, on the *GMTV* sofa, that skunk was in fact 'lethal' to users. They couldn't believe their ears – and the statistics were there to see – no one had ever died as a direct result of cannabis poisoning.

Few were more surprised than Dr Les King, formerly head of the Forensic Science Service's (FSS) drugs intelligence unit, who had handed Brown a report into cannabis potency only days before the *GMTV* appearance. 'To our surprise, Gordon Brown asked to see a copy of our conclusions,' Dr King later told the media academic, former BBC home affairs correspondent and author Jon Silverman. 'He clearly read it, but not long afterwards came out with the statement that skunk is lethal. We all laughed. It wasn't supported by our research at all. I think the newspaper stories must have had an impact on policy.'

The cannabis reclassification debacle was a classic case of policies being carried out by a political and media elite without due reference to the popular will. A survey of public attitudes to cannabis carried out by Ipsos MORI in 2008 showed that there is little support for Class B level penalties for cannabis possession. Of the survey's 1,003 respondents, 41 per cent believed that two years' imprisonment was an appropriate penalty for cannabis possession (equivalent to Class C), whereas 27 per cent of those polled believed that there should be no legal penalty whatsoever.

It is unlikely that cannabis would now be a Class B drug unless the media had exerted so much pressure on the government to amend its 'mistake', a claim backed by the government's own Science and Technology Committee in its 2006 report, *Drug Classification: Making a Hash of it*. On the decision by Home Secretary Charles Clarke to review the classification of cannabis in 2005, it concluded: 'The timing of the second review against a backdrop of intense media hype and so soon after the change in cannabis classification had come into effect gave the impression that a media outcry was sufficient to trigger a review.'

But it is equally unlikely that it would have become a Class C drug in the first place, had it not been for the media's reasonable reaction to the Runciman Report's recommendation in 2000 to downgrade cannabis. Yet by the time the politicians had come round to the idea and set the wheels in motion for a change in the law, the media had turned. Commander Brian Paddick, who oversaw the Brixton Experiment, whereby police were directed to tackle heroin and crack above cannabis, was hounded out of his job, and the government was pilloried for being soft on drugs. As a result, the law was watered down so much as to become no different from what it had been before, and therefore no one was any the wiser as to whether the initial aims of downgrading cannabis would have been achieved. The experiment was wrecked before it had even begun.

*

In studying the media influence on government drug policy, Jon Silverman discovered that examples of the media's fingerprints were everywhere. He concluded: 'There is no field of public affairs which reflects the media influence more vividly than that of drugs and that, especially over the past decade, a small number of newspaper editors have acted as a policy "satnav", which ministers have followed almost slavishly in their desire to send "messages", with the outcome that drug classification has become ludicrously detached from drug harm.'

In a debate on the phone-hacking scandal in the House of Commons in July 2011, the Liberal Democrat MP Tom Brake used the opportunity to make a point about the media's influence on policies such as drugs: 'Does the prime minister believe that once a healthier relationship is established between politicians and the media, it will be easier for governments to adopt evidence-based policy in relation to, for instance, tackling drugs, community sentences, or immigration and asylum?'

To which David Cameron replied: 'That is a lovely idea. As I say, the inquiry will not mean no contact between politicians and the media. There are difficult issues – the Hon. Gentleman mentioned a couple of them – where we need to try and explain and take people with us when we are making difficult decisions. We cannot do that ourselves through direct communications. We need a lively and questioning media to help us do that, but perhaps a healthy relationship will make what he wants more possible.'

Rather than solving the problems of the drug trade, the media's approach merely locks the debate in the Victorian era, with little acknowledgement of the deep-seated problems behind the drug trade's impact. In simplifying the issues, boiling them down and appealing to the lowest common denominator, newspapers are stalling progress.

As the Royal Society of Arts Commission noted in its well-respected report, *Drugs: Facing the Facts*, in 2007: 'Much of the current debate about illegal drugs, especially in Parliament and the press, strikes us as positively medieval, with drug users demonised as though at the beginning of the twenty-first century we were still in the business of casting out demons and burning witches. As one of this commission's members put it, "it's time to get real".'

The same could be said of the broadcast media. While some intelligent documentaries and TV series have been commissioned, most TV programmes tend to enforce stereotypes and myths rather than address them. In the fly-on-the-wall police show *Coppers*, well-known local drug addicts routinely have their often pitiful-looking existences interrupted by what looks suspiciously like human-rights abuse dressed up as a drug raid. As the cameras follow police officers around decrepit council homes, typically to unearth a few measly rocks of crack gaffer-taped inside a cistern, the addict is treated like a subhuman before the camera crew departs, stepping over the now trashed front door.

In the age of Ofcom, programme makers are under pressure to make sure controversial storylines, such as those about drugs, are as realistic as possible. But sometimes this doesn't quite pan out. In 2008, for example, the soap opera *Hollyoaks* featured a dramatic story charting the descent of a model school pupil, from her first cannabis joint into heroin addiction – all in the space of only four weeks. Conversely, some TV shows seek to soothe their audiences, with footage of the drug war being won by plucky officers cleverly busting the sneaky bad guys, such as *Border Control* and *Police Interceptors*.

Channel 4 announced it had hit 'TV gold' in 2012 with a programme format that was to revitalise their 'mischievous' reputation: *Drugs Live* would feature volunteers who would consume a range of illicit intoxicants and then be filmed in order to show viewers the effects. It would put to the test the claims of the former drugs adviser Professor David Nutt that the effects of ecstasy were less damaging than alcohol. Critics lined up to claim the show was sensationalism wrapped in an educational format, and that it would only further the normalisation of drugs among viewers. Channel 4 hit back saying it was a 'radical' new science series which would add to the 'social policy' debate around the harmful effects of drugs.

As the journalism industry continues to allow reporters less time and space to seek out the truth amid ever increasing demands for content, the standards of reporting can only get worse and the need to pander to the reader and seek out scapegoats heightened. Drug addicts or those who speak out in favour of being 'soft on drugs' have come under a barrage of visceral attacks from columnists. At times it is difficult to spot where opinion slips into incitement.

A 2011 column in the *Irish Independent*, headlined 'STERILISING JUNKIES: MAY SEEM HARSH BUT IT DOES MAKE SENSE', commented favourably on a suggestion that drug users should be offered money to be sterilised. The journalist Ian O'Doherty went on to describe a group of drug users as 'feral, worthless scumbags' and said 'if every junkie in this country were to die tomorrow, I would cheer'.

In a world where the consumer is king, it's too simple just to blame newspapers. The public has a choice, and to a large extent it chooses to buy the *Daily Mail* and the *Sun*. The *Mail* is perhaps the last bastion of Middle England – and it plays a more active role in the debate on drugs than any other paper, with leading columnists drawing a line in the sand over drugs and accusing successive governments of inaction.

Its commitment to maintaining the war on drugs is based on the traditional morality of the middle classes, and the belief that a drug-free Britain is not only preferable but achievable, as if the wheels of demographic change, social mores and the Internet can be reversed. It is a powerful lobby, representing professional classes who work, pay taxes and, most importantly for any politician, vote. In short, once mobilised by stirring headlines, Middle England can still decide elections – something of which Gordon Brown was only too aware.

But the press's grip on government policy, if not loosened by Leveson, is being challenged online where the news is largely free and opinion diverse. The next generation is becoming less reliant on newspapers for information on drugs. Teenagers are increasingly getting information over the Internet on specialist forums and social networking sites. As the writer Nic Fleming points out in an article in which he discusses the findings of the drug researcher Dr Fiona Measham: 'Some of the more ridiculous newspaper stories about mephedrone were being debunked and mocked on Twitter within hours of publication. Whereas once sensationalist and inaccurate reporting in mainstream newspapers and television would have gone largely unchallenged, the Internet is slowly starting to undermine ill-informed, knee-jerk media and policy responses, potentially giving those with alternative and better-informed perspectives a louder voice, if people choose to listen.'

If Twitter were to establish itself by defining the outcome of the next British election, then perhaps the ideology of the press as a tool to be a 'sanction of public opinion' might be jolted into the twenty-first century. Until that point, the debate between the press, the public and politicians over drugs will remain firmly confined within parameters defined in the mists of time.

8

Overworld

Closer Than You Think

The UK drug market is a hybrid beast – shaped by myriad factors, including the availability and popularity of the product, demand and local policing tactics – that now stretches country-wide. While no two local drug markets are the same, they do share characteristics. Drug markets have traditionally evolved where the number of users and lines of supply converge: in the melting pots of Britain's inner cities and in the long-neglected estates of northern cities. Most develop in communities that bear the hallmarks of urban decay, spiralling unemployment and urban deprivation, and where the numbers of users and local dealers dwarf national averages. But there is an average . . .

Whether you like or hate drugs, the industry's culture and cash is now washing through society, a giant but hidden edifice that is all around us.

In a well-heeled county in the cradle of Middle England, a short drive from the Cotswolds and the official prime ministerial country residence, Chequers, lies a sedate market town.

Bordered by picturesque villages, it is a popular destination for professionals and young families who have opted to escape the noise, grime and chaos of London for a more peaceful life. But the veneer of rural harmony is thin. Beneath the top-class grammar school system, the food fairs, festivals and quaint architecture, all is not what it seems.

'If you sit up there by that window,' says Dave, pointing to a coffee shop overlooking the town's historic cobbled square, 'you can spot the deals being done by the clock tower.' An ebullient, bear-like ex-cop, Dave has worked for the town's young person's drug project for the last decade. He's able to see things most local residents would prefer to ignore.

As with much of Middle England, crime has been on the rise in the town for decades. A leaflet published by the town's Residents' Society in the mid-1970s warned of a coming crisis, prompted by rising levels of vandalism, crime and an over-stretched police force. By the mid-1990s the leaflet's warnings had seemingly come to pass, with newspaper reports of a wave of crime hitting Middle England. Guns, gangsters and drugs had proliferated.

The story of this town is the story of drugs in the UK – an example of the growing pervasiveness and proximity of the drug trade, and how drugs have become embedded in Britain's heartlands.

'The big change is that ten years ago, being a drug dealer was a negative thing for the young people in this town – and now it's almost a badge of honour,' says Dave.

While the number of young people using illegal drugs has plateaued, the same cannot be said of their involvement in selling them. For some teenagers living amidst respectable modern Britain, the drug trade is not only part of their local scene, but a viable, and sometimes natural, career option.

Now nineteen, with a world-weary attitude and a three-year-old son, there is nothing average about Amber. She is an intelligent girl whose attractive looks wouldn't be out of place on a dance video for her favourite singer, Beyoncé. At twelve, four years before she was legally allowed to buy cigarettes, she was earning £300 a week selling cocaine and cannabis on the streets of the town.

She started selling, she says, in order to earn enough cash to keep her mother, a severe alcoholic, in drink. Her friends, cousins, aunts and uncles either used drugs or sold them. Her older sister is a long-term heroin addict. Her father, a career criminal and crack addict, spent much of Amber's childhood locked up for armed robbery. By the age of fifteen she had been expelled from school, taken into care and spent three months incarcerated in a children's secure unit.

'Dealing drugs was the only thing that made me happy,' says Amber. 'I wanted to make money and fit in, get high, be a gangster like my dad.'

Amber, described by Dave as 'a lovely girl considering the childhood she had', says she learnt from her father. 'I wanted to be like him – make a little bit of money, play the game.' And she was a success. While many of her deals were done with local addicts, she was able to attract a more lucrative stream of revenue from well-off middle-class professionals who would pay her to deliver deals to their homes in the town and its outlying villages. Unsurprisingly for a teenage dealer in regular contact with large quantities of cash, Amber treated it like Monopoly money. She chose to spend it on instant fun: drugs, alcohol, clothes and partying. But her own dealing almost ended in disaster when she ended up owing one supplier £1,000. It was then that she met Riz, a charming twenty-three-year-old well known in the town's drug scene.

e her around town in his expensive car and agreed
her debt. Flattered by the valiant gesture, and
by his flash lifestyle and his age, Amber was
hen they became girlfriend and boyfriend. When he
asked her to sell crack and heroin for him, she was proud to
step up to the mark.

Amber returned to street hustling, but on a more extreme
scale: selling deals on street corners and from park benches
from 9 a.m. until late in the evening, pulling deals from a
well-stocked mesh-and-string washing-powder bag hooked to
her tracksuit. She made between £700 and £800 a day from
her pool of 120 customers. As she became known to the local
police, she brought in her friends, and local children she knew
to run drugs.

Although she describes herself as 'gobby' and someone who
looked way older than she was, she carried a knife for protection, Amber admits she survived on her wits and was
protected in part by her dad's reputation. Her network of
clients spread, and she occasionally became involved higher
up the chain, shifting drugs from Liverpool and Slough into
the town – but she describes dealing with the northern
suppliers as scary, and said they constantly had to change
supply routes in case police caught on. What was her goal?
'I didn't have one. It was the only thing I had and it was
making me happy.'

When Amber and Riz were stopped by the police in possession of a large quantity of heroin, her valiant boyfriend tried
to pin it on her. Luckily for Amber the courts believed her
story, and it was the 'boyfriend' who had groomed her who
ended up with the prison sentence.

'I was a slow learner at school but I was clever at selling
drugs. But in reality I couldn't handle myself, I was a runner,

I was just a "little girl"." She finds it hard to accept, but for all her street talk and tough exterior, Amber has spent most of her drug-selling career being cultivated or 'groomed' by various older men in the town to sell drugs for them. 'Drug culture is on your doorstep these days. Most of my friends still sell drugs. Communities grow up around drugs. Dealing is always an option.'

Amber, who has retreated from the drug trade since having her child, still gets hassled for heroin and crack from her old regulars when she is pushing her buggy down the high street. A three-month stint as a secretary, where for the first time in her life she 'got dressed up and felt important, like a lady instead of a tramp' before getting fired for unreliability, is the only straight job she has had. Now she would love to be a nurse or a midwife. Yet, reflecting on the path her life has already taken, she says: 'But that's it, I've ruined it, I don't think I will have a job ever again.'

To watch Amber walking off with her young child you would never imagine her other life, nor the spider's web of an economy that has ensnared the community.

Like most towns of its size in Britain, this one has a hard core of around 500 of what are known to the authorities as 'problem drug users'. Most will be heroin or crack addicts, visiting the local drug treatment service, a needle exchange for clean syringes and a network of chemists to pick up their prescription of methadone. Many of them will be living in a mix of sheltered accommodation, hostels and council flats. Some will be user-dealers, some rough sleepers and some sex workers, and around three-quarters will be receiving some sort of welfare benefit. And apart from the occasional story in the local paper about an arrest for possession, to the average resident they will go largely unnoticed. They are certainly less visible than the group of leather-skinned town-centre drunks who congregate on benches with their dogs.

With an adult population of around 80,000, most of the town's 4,500 regular drug users will be taking drugs such as cannabis, cocaine, ecstasy and ketamine, getting high in the privacy of their own home, in the town's pubs and clubs or in the local park. It is the park spaces where much of the crack and heroin drug dealing takes place, with dealers situated at well-sighted vantage points which enable them to keep an eye on any approaching police officers. Cocaine, ecstasy and cannabis secretly change hands in more guarded locations, either within people's homes or in local shops and pubs.

Pizza Express, O2, Clintons, Waterstones, Body Shop, Thorntons and Caffè Nero. The identikit shops found in every market town in Britain. And like in every market town in Middle England, the drug trade is woven into the fabric of everyday life. In the most deprived ward of the town, with high crime, birth rates and unemployment, street drug dealing is noticeable to the trained eye, while in other parts of the town, the drug trade takes cover, in nail bars, pubs, bookmakers', taxi firms, beauty parlours and gyms.

The town's local newspaper archive is peppered with reports of illicit drug activity over the last couple of years. A thirty-eight-year-old owner of the local car wash was jailed for seven years after being caught using his business as a convenient vehicle for a cocaine-dealing enterprise. A teenage boy dealing ecstasy from a town-centre pub was jailed for two years after police sniffer dogs found a bag of pills behind a toilet in the Gents. And police, responding to concerns from residents that a bookmaker's on the high street was being used to deal drugs, arrested three men after finding bags of cannabis and some scales in a backpack dumped in the shop. The owner of a health store in the town's shopping centre was jailed for running an illegal trade in banned steroids and black-market valium.

The local police have their suspicions about three other businesses in the town. There is intelligence that one of the county's cab firms is doubling up as a highly mobile drug dealing operation, in particularly targeting students at the nearby public school, but as yet they have no evidence. Two other businesses have managed to survive the recession with admirable resilience, despite hosting an average of two customers a day between them. They are suspected of being money-laundering centres.

A Vietnamese man from London is caught growing 800 cannabis plants, while sniffer dogs deployed at the local station manage to catch out an unfortunate pair of students with their weekend stash of skunk.

Knocking on the door of a luxury country pile in one of the scenic villages not far from the market town, the police arrest one of the drug trade's elusive money men.

This is a composite picture of how the drug trade exists side by side with everyday public life in an average Middle England market town.

During the writing of this book we have spoken to dozens of players in Britain's drug economy, from clubbers, teenage runners and beat officers to undercover detectives, traffickers and senior organised-crime officers. All the people you have met in this book are real. Some of the drug dealers we spoke to are greedy and violent, some of the drug detectives blinkered, and some of the drug users self-obsessed, yet our journey through the drug trade provided us with a new perspective: that this is an economy entirely different from how it is perceived and presented.

'Narcomania', the defunct Victorian term to which we have

given new meaning – the confused and irrational state of mind affecting individuals and institutions when confronted by the issue of drugs – thrives in modern Britain. It is a disease that means teenagers are thrown in a cell for buying the narcotic equivalent of a round of drinks for their friends; where laws are as likely to be based on urban myths or tabloid hysteria as on evidence. It's a collective state of mind where age-old myths continue to be peddled and where everything that society is railing against is, in reality, of its own creation.

It is a trade that has caught a ride on the coat-tails of enterprise, modern culture and the explosion in global trade. While Britain is not a land overflowing with wide-eyed schoolyard junkies, as some in the media would have it, it *is* a leading global consumer of illegal drugs. Despite recent falls in the use of traditional drugs such as cannabis and heroin, which have been counterbalanced by a rise in poly-drug use and the taking of legal highs, Britain consistently hovers around the top three in the European all-round drug-use leagues. It is one of the biggest per-head cocaine consumers on the planet. In the same way that we can grab a Chilean wine and a Brazilian papaya from the shelves of the local supermarket, so can drug users now pick and choose from a low-cost, expansive and exotic drug menu.

On the street, the stereotype of the evil foreign dealer preying on the weak and vulnerable is no more: the trade is dominated by teenagers seeking a future in inner cities where public- and private-sector institutions have withdrawn. For many, the relatively small sums of money made at the bottom of the drug 'food chain' merely allow runners and low-level dealers to participate in Britain's pay-as-you-go economy – buying the designer clothes, topping up smart phones and covering a weekend's clubbing, which for some has become their only link to mainstream society. As such, they have become '*uber* consumers', willing to break the law to attain the symbols of success and a taste of the good life. Many of them come from socially deprived areas where selling drugs has become one of only a few ways of making your mark.

It is not all about greed. Some see it as a route to becoming popular or as a way of gaining respect, others as a way of impressing the opposite sex or as a route to freedom. In a society which promotes consumerism and instant celebrity culture and where roped-off Ferraris sit gleaming in shopping centres in some of the county's poorest areas, it should come as no shock that people who perceive that they are 'locked out' of the system, for whatever reason, choose to take a short cut. And it should be no surprise either that eventually, as was made plain during the 2010 London riots, they will return to bite the system on the arse.

As it has become elevated from the streets by the vast profits available, like a chameleon crime has sought cover in the licit world. Where once there were easily identifiable criminal profiles, such as the old-school family crime syndicate, the ever-increasing access of UK-based dealers to cheaper and higher-quality bulk consignments of drugs has spawned a new generation of Mr Middles for whom the drug industry has become a cash cow. Today your local drug kingpin is as likely to be a local businessman or entrepreneur as a career criminal flitting from villa to villa in Malaga.

Britain's ability to defend its sovereign borders from unwanted goods disappeared along with the Spitfire. Geopolitical change, the opening of borders between European states to allow the free flow of people, services and products, plus the arrival of mass immigration, tourism and cheap travel, has left Britain porous. Law enforcers have always known, despite the occasional well-trumpeted success, that attempts to stem the steady flow of narcotics by sea, rail, road and air into Britain is a needle-in-haystack exercise.

Moreover, apart from a spate of LSD-making in the 1970s, Britain was never previously a drug-producing nation. The blossoming of the cannabis cultivation industry, at a suburban loft near you, has effectively put paid to that.

And while police struggle to manage the traditional drug markets, the ease with which people can buy a vast array of legal and illegal substances via the expanding online drug trade makes their job virtually impossible. Police have admitted to us that monitoring the postal system and the World Wide Web for small drug packages is perhaps a challenge too far for law enforcement, barring the establishment of serious restrictions on people's civil rights.

Enforcement can only shape the drug trade, not end it. Ultimately, in terms of financial resources and expertise, it is an incredibly uneven battle. As sellers adopt new and varied tactics to deter and avoid detection, with gangs relying on an endless supply of new recruits to sell their product, the police's already Sisyphean task is made harder still by cash-sapping austerity measures. No wonder, then, that many police forces have gone back to basics in their drugs operations, responding to calls from the public about nuisance dealers while leaving those less visible, but more lucrative, enterprises, to get on with business as usual.

And the police look increasingly isolated as businesses small and large have – intentionally or not – disengaged themselves from the national anti-drug drive by pocketing drug money in the wake of the financial crash. This grey economy is buffered by a new generation of middle-class professionals – lawyers, solicitors and financial intermediaries – for whom the promise of easy money appears even more addictive than the drugs themselves.

But at the eye of the storm of Narcomania sit Britain's politicians, scared of talking honestly about drugs for fear of losing the support of the centre ground as defined by Middle England. With little overview of the reality of the drug world, policy is far too easily swayed by colourful and emotive accounts of personal experience and the endless noise of tabloid propaganda. Few areas of government policy are so influenced by the media. This is made possible because of the huge vacuum left in any democratic discussion within Parliament about drugs. As soon as politicians gain a position of power in government, any previously radical views on drugs that they might have held appear to vanish. As if by magic, this *omertà* is lifted when they return to the back benches and are strangely able once again to speak their mind on the issue.

With a ticker tape of conflicting messages about the drug trade from politicians, the police and newspapers running on a loop through our multimedia world, the British public can't be blamed for being a bit confused about the subject. Genuine public warnings over the dangers of drug use are now undermined by drug policies that are kick-started and championed by a braying media and contradicted by a culture of celebrity that appears to condone the substances that others claim are corroding society from within.

But perhaps the greatest misconception is that the laws intended to protect hard-working people and Middle England from the dangers of drugs are fit for purpose.

The original edition of *Narcomania* (published in October 2012) gained the rare accolade of being used as evidence in a House of Commons report in December 2012. *Drugs: Breaking the Cycle*, the result of a year-long inquiry into drug policy conducted by the influential Home Affairs Select Committee, quoted extensively from our book. It used our interviews and research to make key points about the difficulty of monitoring the drug trade on the streets, online and within the banking system.

The influential cross-party group of MPs concluded that, after taking evidence from all sides of the drug debate, 'now, more than ever' there was a case for a fundamental review of all UK drug policy. The report said that the prime minister should urgently set up a royal commission to consider all the alternatives to Britain's current drug laws, including decriminalisation and legalisation. However, David Cameron dismissed this out of hand, on the risible grounds that the government's current approach 'is working'.

Back in the real world, the drug trade thrives on prohibition – the tougher the enforcement, the higher the risk. The higher the risk, the bigger the mark-up. The bigger the mark-up, the more profit that can be made. Indeed, in a report published in *The Wall Street Journal* in January 2013, Nobel prize-winner Gary Becker and Kevin Murphy, professors in economics at the University of Chicago, wrote: 'The paradox of the war on drugs is that the harder governments push the fight, the higher drug prices become to compensate for the greater risks. That leads to larger profits for traffickers who avoid being punished.

'This is why larger drug gangs often benefit from a tougher war on drugs, especially if the war mainly targets small-fry dealers and not the major drug gangs. Moreover, to the extent that a more aggressive war on drugs leads dealers to respond with higher levels of violence and corruption, an increase in enforcement can exacerbate the costs imposed on society.'

And while fuelling crime, the laws have no impact on use. Research shows that people who abstain from using drugs do not make this choice because they are illegal, but because it is a lifestyle-and-health choice. Of those who do use drugs, the classification of a drug is of little relevance: apart from cannabis, two Class A drugs, ecstasy and cocaine, are the most commonly taken substances in Britain.

The allure of the illicit has created mirror economies in the worlds of entertainment and fashion, while entire business sectors, from financial services to hydroponics, have found themselves co-opted by a UK Drug PLC that approaches the world with open arms.

Whether you take or hate drugs the situation is pernicious. The collateral damage of the drug trade comes in many forms: disease, addiction, crime, death – and huge amounts of hard cash. The cost of the drug trade has been estimated as at least £16.7 billion a year in crime and disease, while the cost of chasing down Britain's drug-money-fuelled organised-crime gangs is up to £40 billion a year. Drug users are estimated to commit a third of all acquisitive crime, such as shoplifting, vehicle crime, and commercial and domestic burglary and robbery. It is estimated that addicted heroin and crack users need to raise between £20,000 and £50,000 a year to fund their habits. In Britain six people every day die as a result of drugs, more than those who die on the roads, while injecting drugs spreads hepatitis C and HIV.

Paradoxically, it is a war which is increasingly being fought against our own people. The punitive approach to solving the drug problem is merely creating a pool of criminalised young men and women. But there are other, less obvious ways in which society pays. The routine use of sniffer dogs at transport hubs, the satellite heat-mapping of entire cities to scan for cannabis farms, the use of drug testing and sniffer dogs in schools, drug testing in the workplace and police drug-swab tests on people entering pubs and bars represent high levels of surveillance that sail close to the wind when it comes to human rights.

One of the problems faced by those seeking to regulate drugs, is that the desire to use drugs is part of the human condition. The 'fourth drive' to intoxication identified by Dr Ronald K. Siegel is a powerful force that has been keeping humans searching for new highs since prehistoric times. While there are signs that drug use in Britain is falling slightly after escalating for decades, it appears this is a reflection of a tipping point in the nature of the substances that people are using to get high, a move away from more traditional plant-based drugs such as heroin and cannabis and on to an alphabet soup of chemicals. Much like the sex urge, the 'fourth drive' is too powerful a force to be dealt with by laws alone. So is the temptation of the huge profits that can be made from smuggling and selling drugs.

Just as drug *dealers* are not drug *pushers*, the drug trade is not some sort of spectre descending on society to dispense its wares. It is an economy fuelled by public demand. Our drug trade is a product of modern British society and is therefore a reflection of its problems, passions and peccadillos.

A significant chunk of the population feels the need to buy their thrills off the shelf and by doing so complement their downtime or bury their boredom and frustration. Alcohol has for centuries been the drug of choice for this. Illegal drugs are just a more varied way of doing it. But the drug trade is also a symptom of one of the greatest ills of society: inequality.

For those addicted to drugs, they offer a desperate but alternative existence, and, for however brief a moment, they provide comfort and an escape from past and present horrors and dismal lives. And those living in deprived communities are more likely to become addicted to drugs – whether they be heroin, cocaine, speed, Valium or alcohol – than better-off drug users.

Inequality not only breeds addiction, it breeds drug dealers. Most of the tens of thousands of people employed to sell crack and heroin on the streets come from poverty. The drug trade merely offers a way out. And because they are grafting at the sharp end of the trade, they are more likely to get beaten, convicted and jailed than those operating above them, those who are earning the kind of money that is worth laundering in the financial system or in some local business.

However, the gritty reality of the drug trade at street level is largely ignored. Where society's views on sexuality, alcohol and gambling have been translated into relaxed legislation that chimes with the times, drugs have become a symbolic line in the sand for the moral majority who are also the gatekeepers of change. The overriding political narrative around drugs has become frozen in time, detached from the world around us. There is a black hole in intelligent debate; the complex issues that drugs pose for society are liquidised by politicians and the media and spoon-fed to the public in simple, yet highly misleading, doses.

The drug trade has continued to be one of the great unsolvable moral, social and legal issues of our time because it's a problem with no quick or easy solution. But this is no excuse for resorting to using drug addiction or low-level drug crimes as sticks to beat people with, or devising piecemeal policies and failing to experiment with bolder ones.

The way in which society looks at drugs has changed during the hundred-year drug war: what was originally defined as a moral problem has since been diagnosed as a disease and then reincarnated as a crime. Yet the majority of those participating in the UK drug market are not immoral, sick or criminally minded.

Yet today, politicians and the voting public alike appear to be in a state of narcomania, drunk on the rhetoric of the war on drugs and beguiled by stereotypes of yesteryear, they have become convinced that a drug free world is possible despite irreversible change.

Whether we like it or not, for a short period of time before the banks fell, it is highly possible dirty money propped up Britain's ailing financial institutions. These illicit chemicals grease the wheels of society. The drug trade is the hidden mixer in Britain's booming night-time economy, a major employer of the disenfranchised and a cultural touchstone for an increasing percentage of the population and a 'hook' for advertisers.

And who is the key driver of the new British drug economy? The middle classes, who have become the most vociferous customers of the new drug menu and who are taking advantage of the sanitized ways of buying them. The drug trade has become so embedded, into the very sinews of a nation, it is now impossible to extract without causing irreparable damage. The clock cannot be turned back, but it continues to tick.

The fact is, as we dither, our ability to exercise any significant authority over a business that is weighted to win is disappearing. The parameters of the prohibition debate are changing and fluctuating as never before. Change, whether we like it or not, will be inevitable. Britain is in the midst of a demographic tipping point in drug use – and drug dealing. Rising numbers of drug users in their thirties, forties, fifties and sixties puts paid to the myth that illegal highs are purely a rite of passage or rebellion of youth.

Relying on the status quo means taking a gamble that with heroin and crack, the world has seen the worst of the most troublesome drugs. But there is a very real fear that with falling heroin and crack use, a new substance with ten times their appeal and with the distribution network of mephedrone could be waiting on the sidelines. And in the age of the Internet and legal highs, law enforcers are finding it hard to draft a law that encompasses the sheer variety of drugs available.

So this raises the question: what should we do about all this? It's certainly a classic school or TV debate – 'how do we end the war on drugs?' Most documentary makers, journalists, authors, academics and economists who probe the drug world say that the answer is legalisation. Opposing them are the zero-tolerance brigade. The former group is more often driven by hard science, and the latter by an acute sense of morality. The debate, depressingly in Britain, is highly polarised and therefore set in stone. There are countless intellectual 'battles' between these opposing groups every year, in academic institutions, conferences and in Parliament. But all that happens is that the middle ground shrinks and the argument becomes more about ideology than real-world solutions.

But do these ding-dong, TV-friendly debates between amateur analysts half-blinded by their own agendas ever get us anywhere? As the country continues to exist in a state of narcomania, we think that this kind of polarised, agenda-led debate is a red herring.

Despite a growing global movement for more liberal policies and the increased involvement of Transform in public discourse concerning the matter it would take a monumental shift in political will and public attitudes to take this huge step. Particularly for a government that took nearly a decade of hand-wringing, reports and meetings to decide that tinfoil could be legally handed out to heroin users in a bid to switch them from the risks of injecting. Or whether naloxone, a life-saving antidote to heroin overdoses, should be made widely available to front-line drug services. There is little political gain in reducing the impact of the drug war because most of those adversely affected by it are the poor and relatively disenfranchised.

If a government was brave enough to go for legalisation – and many think that the only party capable of achieving it, on the 'Nixon goes to China' principle, is the Tory Party – there are major doubts about how drugs such as crack would be made available to the public, concerns over the inevitable undercutting of government drug prices by illicit drug sellers, and understandable fears about the inevitable involvement of Big Pharma in running the new regime. And not everyone would want to live in a Brave New World where performance-enhancing drugs would see the British workforce revitalised.

A hard-line approach would have to ensure that the extra resources spent on monitoring, catching and punishing drug offenders – and the impact this would have on civil liberties – would be effective enough to warrant them. Yet this is unlikely. In prisons, where most inmates are locked up for twenty-two hours a day, routinely searched, drug tested and, surrounded by high security, and where visitors are searched by prison guards and sniffer dogs, drugs are rife. In China and Iran, where drug users and traffickers are often executed, drug use is rocketing.

It seems that the only options are the status quo under Big Gangster, legalisation under Big Pharma or a hard-line approach under Big Brother.

Because the drugs problem is such a moral issue, the government is likely to follow the will of the people. And there are no strong signs yet that the public is ready for legalised heroin and crack. However, Britain is in a very different place when it comes to the use and supply of 'softer' recreational drugs.

As traditional social bonds such as religion and lifelong employment have grown weaker, counter-culture has moved centre stage – and in many cases passed into legitimacy. The stamp of approval is less and less in the hands of the traditional Establishment and increasingly in the hands of all of us as consumers. The drug and sex trades are huge economies, with their legitimacy given the nod by consumers, not by moral leaders.

As drug use and drug selling become increasingly normalised, the reactions to it will become less ignorant and confused. In a decade or two, the *Daily Mail* – whose vociferous antipathy has had the clear effect of muzzling any rational debate on drugs – will be required to change its tune and appeal to a new, younger, more drug-savvy audience who are less likely to be hoodwinked and scared on these matters.

Our immediate solution is to take the focus away from the somewhat ivory-tower debate on legalisation, however promising this policy sounds, and to concentrate on the immediate future, on what can be done to help those that suffer the most as a result of the war on drugs. We need to make sure that the symptoms of this problem – drug addiction and criminalisation – are tackled.

People should not go to jail for drug possession. Drugs should not be used as a convenient excuse to lock up people who have been failed and rejected by society. Such individuals are often seen as legitimate casualties in the war on drugs – chavs, scum, junkies. The criminalisation of large numbers of people far outweighs the problems caused by the drugs themselves.

Successive governments have agonised in public about how the main victims of the drug trade are children – the schoolchildren smoking skunk and the children in care lured into prostitution through crack cocaine. But in fact, the government has done very little to educate our kids about the dangers of drugs, let alone the drug trade. The statutory amount of time that the average 16-year-old will have spent on drug education amounts to about one hour for their entire school life. This is a scandal that needs to be addressed. Until it is, expressions of distress by government about teenage drug use just appear hypocritical.

People who have severe drug problems must have access to the best treatment, and those who are the most socially excluded need proper support to get their lives together. On a larger scale, the more resources that are channelled towards decreasing social exclusion, the fewer future problem drug users and street dealers there will be. The same can be said of global drug production.

Ultimately, drug use must be seen by society for what it is: a vice, rather than a crime. As a first step to cutting the Gordian knot woven by successive governments, this simple shift in emphasis would do more to break the link between drugs and crime than any national enforcement initiative.

The British public must rid themselves of their own wilful blindness, look beyond their own personal experience of drugs and ask whether future generations deserve to inherit this moral maze, or can afford to maintain it. The parents of a drug-addicted son cannot expect help for their child while opposing, nimby-style, the setting up of a new drug-rehab unit in their town. If communities have problems with heroin buyers and sellers in their neighbourhood, they should be campaigning for better services, not blaming the symptoms of a neglected society.

The arguments about the future of drugs in Britain no longer sits at the sidelines of public discourse, it should be raging across the dinner tables of Middle England. Driving the market is the middle-class recreational drug user, perhaps the most hidden player in Britain's drugscape because they remain largely unknown to the police and health services, and is paying twice for his or her illicit entertainment. Not only is their £50 for a weekend gram of cocaine driving up the profits of the drug trade, but they are also picking up the bill for enforcement and imprisonment of those people who supply them.

As in all wars, the collateral damage mounts daily. But this war is no longer being fought against an exterior enemy: it is being waged against ourselves.

Notes

Introduction: The Face Behind the Mask

1 'The ketamine hit': Interview with authors
2 'landmark UN declaration': UN General Assembly Special Session 1998 slogan: 'A Drug-Free World: We Can Do It'
2 'UN had changed its tune': World Drug Report 2010, UNODC
3 'a Canadian soldier': *Dope Girls: The Birth of the British Drug Underground*, Marek Kohn, Granta
4 'The term was': 'Inebriety or *Narcomania*: Its Etiology, Pathology, Treatment, and Jurisprudence', Norman Kerr, HK Lewis
5 'twenty tonnes of heroin': 'Tackling Drug Markets and Distribution Networks in the UK: A Review of the Recent Literature', 2008 (UKDPC)

1: Intoxication: Into the Mind of Drug Britain

9 'He saw my car': 'Teenage Kicks', Max Daly, *Druglink*, January 2010
13 'Britain sits alongside': World Drug Report 2011, UNODC
13 'average British citizen': 2010 Annual Report on the State of the Drugs Problem in Europe, EMCDDA
13 'Official figures': Drug Misuse Declared: Findings from the 2010/11 British Crime Survey, England and Wales (Home Office)
13 'half of all the money': The Illicit Drug Trade in the United Kingdom, 2007 (Matrix Knowledge Group/Home Office)

313

13 'a quarter of people': An Analysis of UK Drug Policy, Reuter/Stevens, 2007 (UKDPC)

15 Michael Linnell: Interview with authors

15 'Where you live': Street Drug Trends Survey 2011, Max Daly, *Druglink*, Nov 2011

15 'Nepalese heroin users': 'Hidden Habits', Gibby Zobel, *Druglink*, November 2008

16 'homeless Portuguese': ibid

17 'drug worker based in Penzance': Interview with authors

17 'people seeking treatment': Cornwall and Isles of Scilly DAAT, Adult Drug Treatment Needs Assessment 2009/10 + National Treatment Agency for Substance Abuse

18 Cannabis milkman: 'Pint of Gold Top and an Eighth of Hash – Milkman who also Delivered Drugs', Helen Carter, *Guardian*, 6 February 2009

19 'I was taking it': Nick Cohen, *Observer*, 6 April 1997

19 WPC Susan: Interview with authors

20 WPC Claire: 'Cop on the rocks', Max Daly, *Druglink*, Sept 2004

21 Amy the teacher: Interview with authors

23 *The Social Control of Drugs*, Philip Bean, Wiley Blackwell, 1974

24 Beatlesinterviews.org

24 *The Drugtakers*, Jock Young, Harper Collins, 1971

25 'must-have drug': *Altered State: The Story of Ecstasy Culture and Acid House*, Matthew Collin, Serpent's Tail, 1997

25 'Suburban Londoners': ibid

26 'It is difficult': ibid

27 'around 10 million': Drug Misuse Declared: Findings from the 2010/11 British Crime Survey, England and Wales, Home Office

28 Psychonaut: Interview with authors

30 'After sampling': *Intoxication: Life in Pursuit of Artificial Paradise*, Ronald K. Siegel, EP Dutton, 1989

30 'on bees' backs': 'High flyers: Bees on Cocaine "Behave like Humans"', James Randerson, *Guardian*, 23 December 2008

31 'chillum-style pipes': *High Society*, Mike Jay, Thames & Hudson, 2010

31 'By the 1890s': ibid

32 'number of ladies': *British Medical Journal*, 1902

32 'pleasurable lifestyle choice': *International Journal of Drug Policy, Special Issue: Pleasure and Drugs*, Vol. 19, Issue 5, Elsevier

33 Global Drug Survey: Globaldrugsurvey.com

Notes

33 'If you sent': 'Truth about Young People and Drugs Revealed in *Guardian* Survey', Patrick Butler, Alexandra Topping and Sarah Boseley, *Guardian*, 15 Mar 2012

33 University of Cambridge: 'Drug Survey: The Score', *Varsity* magazine, 24 Feb 2012

33 London-based managers: Survey conducted by OnePoll for London*loves*Business.com, 2011

34 Paul: Interview with authors

34 'Freud ordered': *High Society*, Mike Jay, Thames & Hudson, 2010

36 'television interview recorded': BBC Wales Today, 19 May 2008

37 'hard to explain': 'Born into Addiction', Max Daly, *Druglink*, July 2008 (DrugScope)

37 'children in Britain': 'Hidden Harm', Home Office, 2003

37 'in-depth study': 'Living with an elephant: drug misuse, parenting and child welfare, Kroll and Taylor, 2006–2008 (Department of Health)

38 'Exclusive: Cocaine Kate', Stephen Moyes, *Daily Mirror*, 15 Sept 2005

39 'She was someone': 'Who gets angry over Anne Marie?', Lyn Matthews, *Druglink*, November 2005

39 '140 murders': According to Hilary Kinnell, the former co-ordinator of the UK Network of Sex Work Projects and the author of *Violence and Sex Work in Britain*

39 'sex workers in Tyneside': 'Hidden for Survival', Voices Heard Group

39 'the consistent thread': 'A Safe Exit for Sex Workers', Brian Tobin, *Guardian*, 27 May 2010

40 'There were 2,182': Drug-related deaths in the UK Annual Report 2010, National Programme on Substance Abuse Deaths, St George's, University of London

40 'murders in England': 'Exploring the links between homicide and organised crime', Home Office, 2011

40 'hepatitis C': United Kingdom Drug Situation 2011 Edition (UK Focal Point on Drugs)

40 'level of HIV': ibid

40 'mental illness': ibid

41 'receptions into prison': Bromley Briefings Prison Factfile, 2011, Prison Reform Trust

41 'A quarter of all': Bromley Briefings, ibid

42 *A Land Fit for Heroin?*, Eds Dorn/South [Ch3, Social deprivation, unemployment and patterns of heroin use by G. Pearson], Macmillan, 1983

43 'conclusion of a study': 'Exploring User Perceptions of Occasional and Controlled Heroin Use', McSweeney/Turnbull, JRF, 2007

2: Transaction: The Frontline of the Drug Trade

45 Vernon: Interview with authors

46 'a moral cesspit': 'Junkie Street', Jon Wise and Simon Atkinson, *People*, 16 October 2005

46 'The drug supermarket': ibid

48 Ralph: Interview with authors

49 '$322 billion worldwide': UNDOC World Drugs Report, 2005

49 'turnover of between £7bn': The Illicit Drug Trade in the United Kingdom, 2007 (Matrix Knowledge Group/Home Office)

50 'The farm gate': 'Price Understanding Drug Markets and How to Influence Them', Laura Wilson (Matrix Knowledge Group), Alex Stevens (University of Kent), Beckley Foundation, 2008

50 'It is like': 'Middle Market Drug Distribution', Pearson and Hobbs, 2002 (Home Office)

51 'considerable complexity and diversity': 'The Illicit Drug Trade in the United Kingdom', Home Office, Matrix Knowledge Group, 2007

51 'the lines between': Tackling Drug Markets and Distribution Networks in the UK a review of the recent literature by McSweeney, Turnbull , Hough, Institute for Criminal Policy Research, School of Law, King's College London, 2008

51 'a quarter of': Criminal Justice Statistics, England and Wales, (Ministry of Justice) 2010

52 John Pitts: Interview with authors

52 '£500 a week': Understanding Drug Selling in Local Communities, Joseph Rowntree Foundation, Institute for Criminal Policy Research, King's College London, 2005

53 'local drug markets': 'Drug Markets in the Community: A London Borough Case Study', Gavin Hales and Richard Hobbs, from *Trends in Organised Crime*, LSE, 2010

54 'an analysis': 'Reluctant Gangsters: Youth Gangs in Waltham Forest', John Pitts, University of Bedfordshire, 2007

55 'A twenty-month investigation': 'Understanding Drug Selling in Communities. Insider or Outsider Trading?' Tiggey May, Martin Duffy, Bradley Few and Mike Hough, King's College London, Joseph Rowntree Foundation, 2005

Notes

56 'Britain was first warned': *Crack of Doom: The Extraordinary True Story Behind Crack Cocaine*, Jon Silverman, Headline, 1994

56 'crack babies': ibid

57 'three quarters of': ibid

57 'In his paper': 'The Menace of the War on Crack in Britain', Richard Hammersley, Behavioural Sciences Group, University of Glasgow, 1990

57 'than one kilogram': *Crack of Doom: The Extraordinary True Story Behind Crack Cocaine*, Jon Silverman, Headline, 1994

58 Mark the undercover cop: Interview with authors

58 'Home office research': 'Disrupting Crack Markets: A Practice Guide', Robin Burgess with Naomi Abigail, Michelle Lacriarde and Jacob Hawkins, Home Office, 2003

58 Gary Sutton: Interview with authors

59 'Crack became so': 'Disrupting Crack Markets: A Practice Guide', 2002 (Home Office)

60 'To dealers, crack': *Crack of Doom: The Extraordinary True Story Behind Crack Cocaine*, Jon Silverman, Headline, 1994

61 'They [street dealers] recoup their': ibid

61 'Europe became the': 'Reluctant Gangsters: Youth Gangs in Waltham Forest', John Pitts, University of Bedfordshire, 2007

62 'Yardie gangs were': 'Yardie Terror Grips London', Ed Vulliamy and Tony Thompson, *Observer*, 18 July 1999

62 'Britain's most raided': 'Legendary Jamaican Drugs Cafe is Closed', Jason Bennetto, *Independent*, 26 June, 2004

62 'For thirty years' ibid

63 'Smart cards can': 'Drug Markets and Distribution Systems', May and Hough, Institute for Criminal Policy Research, Birkbeck, University of London, published in *Addiction Research and Theory*, 2004

65 'By the late': DI Willie Findlay, Grampian's drug squad, *Druglink*, (Drugscope)

65 'One such firm': 'Sophisticated Flava Gang Jailed', BBC News, 17 February 2006

66 'In January 2012': 'Aberdeen Drug Syndicate "Main Operator" Daniel Sterling Jailed', BBC News NE Scotland, Orkney & Shetland, 20 January 2012

66 'The word must' ibid

67 Gavin: Interview with authors

68 Documentary makers: Interview with authors

74 'enrol for degrees': 'Police Launch Probe into Drug Dealing Scam in Southampton', Jenny Makin, *This Is Hampshire*, 14 December 2009

74 Kareem: Interview with authors

79 Miles Quest: Interview with authors

79 'A six-month undercover': 'Club where Ronnie Wood met Teen Russian Lover is Shut Down after Vice Raid', Rebecca Camber, *Daily Mail*, 27 November 2009

79 'Bar 9 club': 'Police Arrest Manager and Customers of City Bar "That Sold Cocaine with Cocktails"', Justin Davenport, *Evening Standard*, 16 July 2010

80 'Sir Ian Blair': 'Cocaine, Anyone?', Leo Benedictus , *Guardian*, 3 February 2005

80 'People are having': ibid

80 Alan McGauley: Interview with authors

82 Jennifer Ward: Interview with authors

83 Patrick the librarian: Interview with authors

85 '182 eleven-to-nineteen-year-olds': 'Cannabis Supply and Young People', Martin Duffy, Nadine Schafer, Ross Coomber, Lauren O'Connell and Paul Turnbull, Joseph Rowntree Foundation, 2008

85 '500 adult cannabis users': Unpublished research, Gary Potter and Caroline Chatwin

86 'for profit dealers': Sentencing guideline for drug offences comes into force. Sentencing Council press release, 27 February, 2012

87 'an account manager': 'Cocaine deal at the concierge club', Jonathan Calvert and Claire Newell, *The Sunday Times*, 27 May, 2007

3: Network: From Underworld to Virtual World

89 Marco: Interview with authors

93 Duncan: Interview with authors

98 'But when the UK': 'Tackling Drug Markets and Distribution Networks in the UK: A Review of the Recent Literature', 2008 (UKDPC)

98 'Until 1970 the': 'Organized Crime in London: A Comparative Perspective', Philip Jenkins and Gary Potter, published in *Corruption and Reform*, Vol. 1 No 3, 1986

99 Dick Hobbs: Interview with authors

100 'aspect of Smalls' life': 'Bertie Smalls: Armed Robber Turned Supergrass', Dick Hobbs, *Independent*, 1 March, 2008

101 'Operation Extend': '"UK's richest criminal" brought to justice', BBC Online, April 2007

102 '$900 million': 'Executive Director: West Africa Challenged by Rapidly Evolving Transnational Threats', UNODC, 22 February 2012

Notes

102 'the Balkan Route': UNODC World Drug Report, 2010

102 'more frequent consignments': The United Kingdom Threat Assessment of Organised Crime, SOCA, 2009/10

103 'The shrinking effect': 'Super-Pure Drug Catches Cut Out Middlemen', Gareth Rose, *Scotsman*, 14 October 2011

103 'second-largest drug market': Peter Reuter: Interview with authors

104 'producing a profile': Middle Market Drug Distribution, Hobbs, 2001, (Home Office/Matrix)

104 'In one section': *King Pin? A Case Study of a Middle-Market Drug Broker*, Dick Hobbs, Goldsmiths University of London, 2001

106 'It holds the': ACPO: Interview with authors

106 'Of foreign OCGs': ibid

107 'Risks attributed to': ibid

107 'Of the top 10': ibid

107 '222 convicted dealers': 'The Illicit Drug Trade in the United Kingdom', 2007 (Matrix Knowledge Group/Home Office)

108 'Contagious' was the': 'Understanding Drug Markets and How To Influence Them', Laura Wilson (Matrix Knowledge Group), Alex Stevens (University of Kent)

109 'the slight and': 'Man Jailed for 12 Years for Supplying Cutting Agents', SOCA press office, 10 December 2010

110 'last remaining kingpin': 'Drug lord jailed as police shut down largest smuggling operation in UK', Jim Norton, *Guardian*, March 2013

110 'Planning chiefs at': 'Millionaire Heroin Dealer Runs Property Empire from Jail Cell', Stephen Donald, *Scotsman*, February 2011

111 Andrew the estate agent: Interview with authors

113 Jamie: Interview with authors

116 'The importance of': 'Yardie Informer Freed by Judge', *Surrey Comet*, 22 April 2004

117 '208 cannabis factories': 'Plant warfare', Max Daly and Steve Sampson, *Druglink*, March 2007

117 'Cannabis cultivation is': Alan Gibson, BBC News, 26 September 2006

118 'the missing link': Interview with authors

118 'very well hidden': Interview with authors

118 'more than three a day': 'Plant warfare', Max Daly and Steve Sampson, *Druglink*, March 2007

119 'thirty times stronger': 'Skunk is dangerous. But I still believe in my campaign to decriminalise cannabis', *Independent*, Rosie Boycott, March 2007

119 'links to schizophrenia': 'Just ONE cannabis joint "can cause psychiatric episodes similar to schizophrenia" as well as damaging memory', Tamara Cohen, *Daily Mail*, October 2011

119 'Do You Live Next to a Skunk Factory?', Paul Bracchi, *Daily Mail*, 19 October 2007

120 'Portsmouth, Lincoln, Doncaster': Patrick Barkham, *Guardian*, June 2008

120 Allen Morgan: Interview with authors

122 'In 2005 *Bizarre*': *Bizarre* Readers Offer 2005

122 'in 2008, Tom': Bill 136, October 2008

123 'Three Derbyshire hydrophonics': 'Appeal Court Quashes Hydroponic Cannabis Convictions', Duncan Campbell, *Guardian*, 14 July 2008

123 Gary Potter: Interview with authors

125 'On publishing': UK National Problem Profile: Commercial Cultivation of Cannabis, ACPO, 2010

125 '8,000 cannabis farms': UK National Problem Profile: Commercial Cannabis Cultivation, ACPO, 2012

125 'previous two years': UK National Problem Profile: Commercial Cultivation of Cannabis . . . Three Years On. ACPO 2010

126 'indicating that the': ibid

127 Recman: Interview with authors (searches and products available relate to that time period before the mephedrone ban in 2010)

129 'Interpol's loose-fit': 'Internet Drug Trafficking Skyrockets, Experts Warn', AFP, 10 September 2008

129 Tim Hollis, ACPO press release, April 2012

130 'There's this feeling': 'Internet Drug Trafficking Skyrockets, Experts Warn', AFP, 10 September 2008

130 'One man who's': 'World Wired Web', Mike Power, *Druglink*, January, 2010

131 'Under the headline': 'The Chinese laboratories where scientists are already at work on the new 'meow meow', Mike Power and Simon Parry, *Mail on Sunday*, October 2010

132 'forty new drugs': Press release, EMCDDA, January 2011

134 'service went viral': 'The Underground Website Where You Can Buy any Drug Imaginable': Gawker, 1 June 2011

134 'Because of the': '"Silk Road" website called the Amazon or Ebay of Drug Trafficking', Michael George, ABC News, 8 October 2011

135 'genie had been': 'Open Secrets: How the Government Lost the Drug War in Cyberspace', *Reason*, October 2004

135 Mike Slocombe: Interview with authors

137 Judith Aldridge: Interview with authors

138 'Mephedrone sales teams': Judith Aldridge, unpublished research

138 *Youth in Crisis: Gangs, Territoriality and Violence*, Judith Aldridge, Juanjo Medina, Robert Ralphs, Routledge

4: Pursuit: A Game of Cat and Mouse

143 'extremely successful operation': Press Release, HM Customs & Excise, 10 December 2004

143 'Chatting in a bar': Interview with authors

144 *Urban Smuggler*, Andrew Pritchard and Norman Parker, Mainstream Publishing, 2008

144 '1 per cent': Heroin Seizures and Heroin Use in Scotland, Centre for Drug Misuse Research, University of Glasgow, 2009

145 'drug cases a week': Crime in England and Wales 2010/2011, Home Office

145 'half of all prisoners': Bromley Briefings Prison Factfile, 2011, Prison Reform Trust

145 'acquisitive crime': Drug Strategy, Home Office

145 'sustain their habit': DrugScope

145 'stolen goods fetch': ibid

145 *Dope Girls: The Birth of the British Drug Underground*, Marek Kohn, Granta

146 Dick Hobbs: interview with authors

147 'In the days': ibid

147 'police gardening club': 'Torquay's Other History: 1970: Hippies say Police are Leaning on Us', The People's Republic of South Devon website, December 2011

148 Graeme Pearson: Interview with authors

149 'four handshakes': 'Market Forces', Harry Shapiro, *Druglink*, November 2009

150 'What we're trying': 'G8 backs Blair Summit on Drugs', BBC Online, 22 July 2000

150 'Blue sky' document: No.10 Strategy Unit Drugs Project, Phase 2 Report: 'Diagnosis and Recommendations', John Birt, 2003.

151 '£1 from gangs': Home Affairs Select Committee report on SOCA, 2008, House of Commons

152 'only 2 per cent': Seizures of drugs in England and Wales, 2010/11, HomeOffice

153 'Police Destroy Ipswich's Drug Network', *Eastern Daily Press*, 8 October 2007

154 'Detectives estimate': 'Boom and Bust', Max Daly, *Druglink*, November 2007

5: Money: The Most Addictive Drug of All

Notes

188 '$120 billion of': FATF Forty Recommendations, April 1990

189 'FATF conceded': ibid

189 'In 1998 the': 'The Company File City Firms in Money Laundering Probe', BBC News Business, 24 November 1998

189 'Where organised crime': ibid

189 'Blair's "drugs czar"': 'Target Banks Call on Drug Money', Paul Kelso, *Guardian*, 28 November 2000

190 'NCIS expressed concern': ibid

190 'As one former London': Interview with authors

190 'French parliamentary report': 'City "Haven" for Terrorist Money Laundering', John Henley, *Guardian*, 10 October 2001

191 'Peter Lilley, author': *Dirty Dealing: The Untold Truth About Money Laundering, International Crime and Terrorism*, Peter Lilley, Kogan Page, 2002

191 '$2.1 trillion in dirty money': UNODC press release, October 2011

191 'describing the profits': Philip Parham, UK Deputy Permanent Representative at the Security Council, UN UK Mission to New York, ukun.fco.gov.uk/en/news, 24 June 2011

192 'The World Bank': World Development Report 2011: Conflict, Security, and Development

192 'telecoms, insurance and recruitment: 'CIFAS Confirms Link Between Staff Fraud and Organised Crime', cifas.org.uk, 7 November 2011

192 'Organised criminals have': Infosecurity 200 conference in London, Tony Neate, e-crime liaison, SOCA

192 'Organised crime costs': Theresa May, New Strategy to Strike at the Heart of Organised Crime, Home Office, 28 July 2011

192 'the FSA conceded': Banks' management of high money laundering risk situations: How banks deal with high-risk customers, correspondent banking relationships and wire transfers, June 2011 (FSA)

193 'made a full apology': 'HSBC "sorry" for aiding Mexican drugs lords, rogue states and terrorists', Dominic Rushe, *Guardian*, July 2012

193 'Senator Carl Levin': 'HSBC "acted as financier to drug gangs" – US Senate report', *Daily Telegraph*, July 2102

193 'The story of': 'Britain's Biggest Banking Scandal', BBC News Business, 13 January 2004

194 Robert Mazur: Interview with authors

196 'Until leaders of' 'The Man Who Infiltrated Pablo Escobar's Cartel Explains What's Wrong With The Global Banking System, Michael Kelly, Business Insider, September 2012

196 '20,000 bank accounts': 'HSBC used by "drug kingpins", says US Senate', BBC Online, July 2012

196 'They are watertight': Interview with authors

197 'Shaxson says that': 'The City of London and its Offshore Empire', the *Occupied Times* website, 10 February 2012

197 '150 cases of corruption': The Puppet Masters How the Corrupt Use Legal Structures to Hide Stolen Assets and What to Do About It, star.worldbank.org

197 'mystery-shopping exercise': Global Shell Games: Testing Money Launderers' and Terrorist Financiers' Access to Shell Companies, Michael Findley, University of Texas at Austin, Daniel Nielson, Brigham Young University, Jason Sharman, Griffith University, September 2012

198 'Jack Straw highlighted': 'Once the Biggest Drug Dealers in the World', Jack Straw, *Lancashire Telegraph*, 12 June 2008

199 'In 1839, Lin': *China's Response to the West*, J. Fairbank and S. Teng, Harvard University Press, 1979

200 'In 1999, Carl': *Opium, Empire and the Global Political Economy: A Study of the Asian Opium Trade 1750-1950* Carl Trocki, Routledge

200 'The legacy of': *The Chinese Opium Wars*, Jack Beeching, Harcourt Brace Jonanovich

200 'shippers P&O' *Flagships of Imperialism: The P&O Company and the Politics of Empire from its Origins to 1867*, Freda Harcourt, Manchester University Press

201 'SOCA was granted': Annual Report and Accounts, SOCA, 2010/11

202 'Everyone involved': 'Bradford crime gang "dismantled from the top man down"', Steve Wright, *Bradford Telegraph & Argus*, March 2010

202 'new crime squad': 'There's One Recession-Proof Industry . . . Organised Crime', *Scotsman*, 25 October 2008

203 'It's the lawyers': 'War on the Suits: New Crime Unit will Target the Middle Class Professionals Helping Scotland's Gangsters', *Daily Record*, 17 March 2011

203 'The Care Commission': Strathclyde Police and Care Commission Probe Money, STV, 12 March 2011

203 Graeme Pearson: Interview with authors

204 'The global reach': 'Jailed: Money Laundering Accountant from Wilmslow who Led Life of Luxury', Charlotte Cox, *Wilmslow Express*, 1 December 2011

204 'Malcolm Carle': 'Unmasked: The "English gent" behind the UK's biggest ever drugs racket worth £300MILLION who splashed his cash on fast

cars, mansions and a race horse', Chris Greenwood, *Daily Mail*, March 2013

204 'Professor Hamid Ghodse': 'UN: Drugs gangs creating "no-go" areas in UK cities', Channel 4, February 2012

205 'senior police officers': 'Police and politicians reject United Nations professor claims of Manchester "no-go areas controlled by drug gangs"', Neal Keeling, *Manchester Evening News*, February 2012

205 'An undercover police officer': Interview with authors

205 'He Jia Jin': 'Money Laundering Drugs Gang Boss Jia Jin He Jailed', BBC News Online, 8 March 2012

206 'A walk-in recording': 'Gangsters Caught Selling Guns to undercover Police Officers in Boombox shop in Edmonton', Tristran Kirk, *Enfield Independent*, 12 September 2011

206 'thirteen kilos of': '500k "Cocaine" Haul was Actually Dental Power', *Telegraph*, 24 July 2009

206 'In 2008 the': 'Thousand Police Raid Drug Gangs in North London', Mail Online, 27 March 2008

207 'expressed the difficulties': 'Blackstock Road Raid: A Top Cop Responds', Rachel From North London blogspot, 2008

207 'Four years after': Operation Condor, Metropolitan Police press office, 2012

207 Yusuf: Interview with authors

209 'write a tongue-in-cheek': 'Local drugs for local people', Daniel Davies, Comment is Free, *Guardian*, September 2006

210 'hosted an exhibition': 'High Society', Wellcome Collection, November 2010 – February 2011

210 'Nicholas Dorn': 'Functions and Varieties of Explanations of Recreational Drug Use', N Dorn, Vol. 70 Issue 1, British Journal of Addiction, March 1975

212 'former ecstasy user': *Altered State: The Story of Ecstasy Culture and Acid House*, Matthew Collin, Serpent's Tail, 1997

212 Jennifer Ward: Interview with authors

212 'Demos, outlined a plan': *BritainTM: Renewing Our Identity*, Mark Leonard, Demos, 1997

212 'In 2005, Blair': The Licensing Act 2003, came into force 2005

213 'one high-ranking police detective': Interview with authors

213 'Under the headline': 'E is for England', *The Economist*, 4 June 1998

213 'the Henley Centre': *Illegal Leisure: The Normalization of Adolescent Recreational Drug Use*, Howard J. Parker, Judith Aldridge, Fiona Measham, Routledge

214 'Project Edge': 'Cannabis Economy Brings in £11 Billion', Ben Summerskill, *Observer*, 2 February 2003

214 'Cannabis users spend': ibid

215 'unpublished piece of': study for Home Office seen by authors

215 'Youngsters can get ecstasy': *Altered State: The Story of Ecstasy Culture and Acid House*; Matthew Collin, Serpent's Tail, 1997

216 'In 1999 publisher': 'Posters for men's magazine banned', Janine Gibson, Media Correspondent, *Guardian*, 7 July 1999

216 'radio station VH1': 'Sex, drugs and rock'n'roll argument fails to save cocaine ad', Jennifer Whitehead, brandrepublic.com, 13 March 2002

216 'Golden Wonder crisps': Golden Wonder poster campaign, BBC, 11 December 2002

216 'Brain Reserve Forecast': Polly Popcorn Brain Reserve, www.faithpopcorn.com/ 2008

217 Fiona Measham: Interview with authors

217 'Until society as': '"Drugs Culture" Attacked after Lakota Ecstasy Death', Bristol 24-7 website, 3 February 2012

217 '"Opium" scent': Estée Lauder, Advertising Standards Authority

218 'In 2011, MSN': 'Nike Plans Cheech & Chong Shoe (Don't Smoke the Laces)', Al Olson, msnbc.com, 4 January 2011

218 'harmless brand promotion': ibid

219 'In 2003 an advert': 'Rizla under fire over "drug" ads', Claire Cozens, *Guardian*, November 2003

219 'Four years later': News, *Druglink* , 2007

220 'A trip to': 'Golden Ticket Holder to Win Drugs', Sky News, February 2009

220 'with police reporting': 'Relaxed Licensing Laws Led to Rise in Cocaine, Warns Officer', Tom Whitehead, *Telegraph*, 2 December 2011

220 '*Daily Mail* revealed': 'Fast-Living: Three Out of Four Youngsters "Rely on Energy Drinks" To Keep Them Going', *Daily Mail*, 26 October 2011

220 'It highlights a': 'Generation Zzz', John Forsyth, Mintel Oxygen Reports, October 2011

221 'automated Google adverts': 'World Wired Web', Mike Power, *Druglink*, January 2010

221 'a really powerful thing': 'Bitcoin: Dawn of a new currency or destined to fail?', Romi Levine, BBC World Service, April 2013

6: Omertà: The Haunted House

224 'a threefold rise': *A Land Fit for Heroin*, Eds. Dorn/South, Macmillan, 1983

224 'forty-six lives': 'Acquired Immune Deficiency Syndrome, general information for doctors', 1985, (Department of Health & Social Security)

225 'fifty-five confirmed HIV': *A History of Drugs*, Toby Seddon, Routledge, 2010

225 Royal College of Nursing report: 'AIDS: A Plague in Us, A Social Perspective', Vass, 1986

225 'all available means': Aids and Drug Misuse, ACMD, 1988

226 'The result stands': 'Haunted House', Mike Trace, *Druglink*, 2004

227 'British taxpayer': 'A Comparison of the Cost-Effectiveness of Prohibition and Regulation of Drugs', Stephen Rolles, Transform, 2009

227 'makes up £739 million': ibid

228 'Tackling Drugs Together', Home Office, 1995

229 'hideous monster Frankenstein': The American, Hearst, 1938

230 'Drugs: Facing Facts: the Report of the RSA Commission on Illegal Drugs, Communities and Public Policy', RSA, 2007

231 'Having a pint': 'The Power of Culture', Marcus Roberts, *Druglink*, May 2009

231 'Runciman Report': Drugs and the Law: Report of the Inquiry into the Misuse of Drugs Act 1971, Runcimann, Police Foundation, 2000

233 'leaked Strategy Unit report': No.10 Strategy Unit Drugs Project, Phase 2 Report: 'Diagnosis and Recommendations', John Birt, 2003.

233 'An Analysis of Drug Policy', Reuter/Stevens, UKDPC, 2007

234 'Drug Classification: Making a Hash of It?', House of Commons Science and Technology Committee, 2006

235 'Why We Won't be Going Soft on Cannabis', Jack Straw, *News of the World*, March 2000

236 'We Should All Join the Drugs Debate', Editorial, *Mail on Sunday*, 27 March 2000

236 'Equasy: An Overlooked Addiction with Implications for the Current Debate on Drug Harms', *Journal of Psychopharmacology*, January 2009

236 'Ecstasy "No More Dangerous than Horse Riding"', Christopher Hope, *Daily Telegraph*, 7 February 2009

238 'the "Nutty professor"': Editorial, *Sun*, 2 November 2009

238 'issue an apology': Press Complaints Commission, Mr Stephen Nutt (Complainant)

238 'Fatuous, Dangerous, Utterly Irresponsible: the Nutty Professor Who's Distorting the Truth About Drugs', Melanie Phillips, *Daily Mail*, 4 November 2009

238 Alan Johnson letter: 'Why Professor David Nutt was Shown the Door', Jack Straw, *Guardian*, 2 November 2009

239 'vote catching exercise': 'Drugs Adviser Says Politics Rules', BBC Online, 11 November 2009

239 'detailed analysis of cannabis': 'Cannabis: Classification and Public Health (2008), ACMD, Home Office

239 'DrugScope Extremely Disappointed by Cannabis Reclassification Decision', press release, DrugScope, 7 May 2008

240 'half of all property crime': 'Drug Addicts "Commit Half of Property Crimes"', Heather Mills, *Independent*, 12 February 1994

240 'crumbles to dust': 'The Blair experiment', Alex Stevens, *Druglink*, July 2010

242 'more than £50 million': 'The Drug Treatment and Testing Order: Early Lessons', National Audit Office, 2004

243 'a "good light"': 'Home Office Rebuked for "Highly Selective" Briefing on Drugs Seizures', Alan Travis, *Guardian*, 15 November 2011

243 'In June 2003': No.10 Strategy Unit Drugs Project: Phase 1 Report: 'Understanding the Issues', Strategy Unit, 2003

243 'evaluative framework': *Tackling Problem Drug Use*, 2010 National Audit Office

243 Drugs Value for Money Review, Home Office, 2007

244 HM Customs and Excise: The Prevention of Drug Smuggling, House of Commons Committee of Public Accounts: Fifteenth Report of Session UK Parliament, 1998–1999

244 'fresh-faced Tory': 'The Government's Drugs Policy: Is It Working? Home Affairs Committee, UK Parliament, 2002

244 'failing for decades': 'Tory Contender Calls for More Liberal Drug Laws', Marie Woolf, *Independent*, 7 September 2005

245 'a startled crab': Interview with authors

246 'Our political culture': 'The War on Drugs has Failed', Bob Ainsworth, LabourList, 16 December 2010

247 'While this suppression': 'Ed Miliband Rebukes Bob Ainsworth over "Legalise Drugs" Call', Helene Mulholland, *Guardian*, 16 December 2010

247 'When David became': Interview with authors

248 Drug Futures 2025, Foresight Brain Science, Addiction and Drugs Project, Government Office for Science, 2005

249 'leaving drug-free': 'Drug Treatment: Success or Failure?' Mark Easton, BBC News, 3 October 2008

249 'Governments do not give': 'Haunted House', Mike Trace, *Druglink*, November 2004

250 'seductive political message': 'Drug Policy: Lessons Learnt, and Options for the Future', Mike Trace, Global Commission on Drugs, 2012

252 Peter Hitchens: *The War We Never Fought: Britain's Non-Existent War on Drugs*, Peter Hitchens, Continuum, 2012

258 'creating failed states': 'How to Stop the Drug Wars', Editorial, *The Economist*, 5 March 2009

7: Warped: Media, Myth and Propaganda

260 'The spectre of': 'Police Warn Someone Could Die from Legal High Sweeping Region', *Northern Echo*, 20 November 2009

260 Gabrielle Price: 'Schoolgirl, 14, Dies After Taking Dangerous New Drug "Meow Meow" at House Party, James Mills, *Daily Mail*, 24 November 2009

260 'User Rips Off Scrotum On Legal Drug', Press Association, 26 November 2009

261 'revealed that 180 pupils': 'Meow Meow: 180 Pupils at One School Off Sick After Taking Legal High' (*Daily Mail*), 'Meow Meow Drug Blamed for 180 School Children Off Sick' (*Metro*), 'Meow Meow Kids Go Off Sick' (*Sun*), 8 March 2009

261 'telling the BBC': 'Scunthorpe Parents Call for Mephedrone Ban', BBC Online, 17 March 2010

261 'Kids' Deadly Cocktail Mix', Emma Morton, *Sun*, 12 January 2009

261 'Powder of Death UK's Fave Drug', Ross Kaniuk, *Daily Star*, 14 January 2009

261 '90 per cent of Liverpool are on it . . . everyone takes it', Scott Hesketh, *Daily Star*, 21 March 2009

261 'Mephedrone at World Cup', Stewart MacLean, *Daily Star*, 22 March 2010

261 'Ban Meow Now', Antonella Lazzeri, Alastair Taylor And Kevin Schofield, *Sun*, 8 April 2010

262 'the ACMD, reported': 'Legal High Mephedrone Linked with 26 Deaths in UK', Martin Evans, *Daily Telegraph*, 29 March 2010

262 'major victory': 'Meow is Banned from Bidnight', Editorial, *Sun*, 16 April 2010

262 'spokeswoman for Leicestershire': 'Mephedrone and the Media', Nic Fleming, *Palladium* magazine, Issue 6, 2010

262 'blamed each other': ibid

262 'just six deaths': 'Evidence based policy? Why Banning Mephedrone May Not have Reduced Harms to Users', online article by Dr Les King, 19 September 2011

263 'hysterical journalism': 'Mephedrone and the Media', Nic Fleming, *Palladium* magazine, Issue 6, 2010

263 'Eric Carlin': 'Mephedrone Ban Prompts Latest Drugs Council Resignation', Peter Walker, *Guardian*, 2 April 2010

263 Jon Silverman: *Crime, Policy and the Media: The Shaping of Criminal Justice, 1989-2010*, Jon Silverman, Routledge, 2011

263 'analysis of Google': 'Feline Frenzy', Andrew McNicoll, *Druglink*, May 2010

264 'music magazine *Mixmag*': 'Mephedrone: Meet The UK's Favourite New Drug', *Mixmag*, 12 January 2010

264 'NRG-1 is 25p a Hit and Will Kill Many More than Meow', Virginia Wheeler, *Sun*, 31 March 2010

264 'twelve million newspapers': 'ABC Newspaper Circulation', *Press Gazette*, May 2012

266 Tim Luckhurst quote: Leveson Inquiry, transcript, (Levesoninquiry.org.uk), 6 February 2012

266 'drug pornography': 'Exclusive? Celebrity Drug Scandals Exposed', Lena Corner, *Druglink*, November 2009

267 'just one puff': 'Police Issue Warning About Super Strength Cannabis', Ben Rossington, *Liverpool Echo*, 20 March 2007

267 'smoking just one': 'Smoking Just One Cannabis Joint Raises Danger of Mental Illness by 40%', Fiona Macrae And Emily Andrews, *Daily Mail*, 26 July 2007

267 'The Vampire Murderer Whose Mind was Warped by Cannabis', Jaya Narain, *Daily Mail*, 3 August 2002

268 'probable but weak': 'Cannabis: Classification and Public Health (2008), ACMD, (Home Office)

268 'Psychologically, use of cannabis': DrugScope website

268 New Zealand studies: 'Mental Disorders and Violence in a Total Birth Cohort: Results from the Dunedin Study', Arseneault et al, Archives of General Psychiatry, 2000; 'The Targets of Violence Committed by Young Offenders with Alcohol Dependence, Marijuana Dependence, and Schizophrenia-Spectrum Disorders: Findings from a Birth Cohort', Arseneault et al, Criminal Behavior and Mental Health, 2002

268 Louise Arseneault: 'Killer Cannabis: The Return of Reefer Madness', Max Daly, *Druglink*, March 2004

269 'Cannabis: An Apology', Jonathan Owen, *Independent on Sunday*, 18 March 2007

269 'average cannabis joint': 'Skunk: Potency Doubles', Max Daly, *Druglink*, September 2007

270 'fill column inches': Source: *Sun* journalist call to drug charity press officer in June 2011

270 'Crystal Meth: Britain's Deadliest Drug Problem', Jason Bennetto and Maxine Frith, *Independent*, 21 November 2006

270 'less than fifty': Seizures of Drugs in England and Wales 2007/8, Home Office

270 'falling to zero': Drug Misuse Declared: Findings from the British Crime Survey, England and Wales, 2008/9, 2010/2011, Home Office

270 Sean Hoare interview: 'Sean Hoare Knew How Destructive the *News of the World* Could Be', Nick Davies, *Guardian*, 18 July 2011

271 'He grabs Jimmy's left arm': 'Jimmy's World', Janet Cooke, *Washington Post*, 28 September 1980

272 'Dominant Ideology and Drugs in the Media', Craig Reinarman and Ceres Duskin, *International Journal on Drug Policy*, 1992

273 'Most tabloids have': Interview with authors

274 Roy Greenslade: 'Myth Representation', Roy Greenslade, *Druglink*, Mar 2006

274 'ICM research poll': ICM/*Observer* Drugs Poll 2008

276 Danny Kushlick: 'Mephedrone and the Media', Nic Fleming, *Palladium* magazine, Issue 6, 2010

277 'lines of attack': *Shooting Stars: Drugs, Hollywood and the Movies*, Harry Shapiro, Serpent's Tail, 2003

278 'a moral panic': *Dope Girls: The Birth of the British Drug Underground*, Marek Kohn, Granta

278 'From the middle': 'Myth Representation', Roy Greenslade, *Druglink*, Mar 2006

278 *Drugs and Popular Culture: Drugs, Media and Identity in Contemporary Society*, Paul Manning, Willan, 2007

279 Information is Beautiful: 'Deadliest Drugs: UK Drug Poisoning Deaths 2008 vs Popular Press Coverage', David McCandless, Information is Beautiful website, 6 November 2009

279 'drug-death reporting': 'Representation of Illegal Drug Case Stories in the Scottish Press', Alasdair Forsyth, *Scottish Journal of Criminal Justice Studies*, 2005

279 Richard Peppiatt: Leveson Inquiry, Richard Peppiatt, (Levesoninquiry.org.uk), 6 October 2011

280 'In 2001 nearly': British Social Attitudes, annual survey, NatCen

280 'overwhelming the policy': Submission to the Leveson Inquiry: press reporting of illicit drug use, UKDPC, 2012

280 Tony Blair article: *News of the World*, February 2004

281 'six-month drug-testing': 'Tabloid Funds First School Drug Tests', Max Daly, *Druglink*, January 2005

281 'Purge on Pushers at the School Gate', Jane Merrick, *Daily Mail*, 26 November 2004

282 'On Sale At School's Gates . . . Kiddie Coke at 50p A Go', Stewart Fowler, *People*, 6 April 2003

282 'made up stories': 'People Sued Over Drug Dealer Picture Fake', Claire Cozens, *Guardian*, 14 March 2005

282 'Since the law', 'West Yorkshire Police': 'Chasing Shadows', Max Daly, *Druglink*, May 2009

283 'touched by the mantle': 'Paul Dacre: the zeal thing', Bill Hagerty, British Journalism Review, Vol 13 No3, 2002

283 'head and shoulders': Editorial, *Daily Mail*, 23 February 2007

284 'personal instinct of Mr Brown': 'Brown Ditches Disastrous Softly-Softly Policy on Cannabis', *Daily Mail*, 19 July 2007

284 '"brave, justified" decision': 'Gordon Brown Made a Brave and Justified Decision on Cannabis', *Daily Mail*, 9 May 2008

284 'To our surprise': Crime, Policy and the Media: The Shaping of Criminal Justice, 1989-2010, Jon Silverman, Routledge, 2011

284 'Ipsos MORI in 2008': ACMD General Public Polling: Public views on Cannabis, Rhonda Wake, ACMD

285 'Science and Technology Committee': 'Drug classification: Making a Hash of It?', House of Commons Science and Technology Committee, UK Parliament, 2006

286 'There is no field': 'Addicted to getting drugs wrong', Jon Silverman, *British Journalism Review*, Vol 21, No4, 2010

287 'Much of the': 'Drugs: Facing Facts: The Report of the RSA Commission on Illegal Drugs, Communities and Public Policy', RSA, 2007

287 'soap opera *Hollyoaks*': 'Viewing habits', Andrew McNicoll, *Druglink*, July 2009

288 'Sterilising Junkies: May Seem Harsh, but it Does Make Sense', Ian O'Doherty, *Irish Independent*, 18 February 2011

289 'ridiculous newspaper stories': 'Mephedrone and the Media', Nic Fleming, *Palladium* magazine, Issue 6, 2010

Notes

8: Overworld: Closer Than You Think

292 'If you sit': Interview with authors

293 Amber: Interview with authors

298 'leading global consumer': World Drug Report 2011, UNODC

298 'the top three': 2010 Annual Report on the State of the Drugs Problem in Europe, EMCDDA

298 'per-head cocaine': World Drug Report 2011, UNODC

301 'House of Commons report': *Drugs: Breaking the Cycle*, Home Affairs Committee – Ninth Report, December 2012, UK Parliament

302 '*Wall Street Journal*': 'Have We Lost the War on Drugs?', Becker & Murphy, *Wall Street Journal*, January 2013

302 'abstain from using': 'Why Say No? Reasons given by young people for not using drugs, Fountain et al, Addiction Research, 1999

303 'at least £16.7 billion': 'A Comparison of the Cost-Effectiveness of Prohibition and Regulation of Drugs', Stephen Rolles, Transform, 2009

303 '£40 billion a year': National crime agency: oral statement by Theresa May on recognising organised crime as a threat to national security, June, 2011

303 'acquisitive crime': The economic and social costs of Class A drug use in England and Wales 2003–04, Home Office

303 'need to raise': NEW ADAM survey of arrestees 1999–2002, Home Office

303 'Six people every day': Drug-related deaths in the UK Annual Report 2010, National Programme on Substance Abuse Deaths, St George's, University of London

304 'fourth drive': *Intoxication: Life in Pursuit of Artificial Paradise*, Ronald K. Siegel, EP Dutton, 1989

310 'The statutory amount': 'Personal, social, health and economic (PSHE) education: a mapping study of the prevalent models of delivery and their effectiveness', Department for Education, January 2011

Select Bibliography

Bancroft, A., *Drugs, Intoxication and Society*, Polity, 2008

Beeching, J. *The Chinese Opium Wars*, Harvest/HBJ, 1977

Carnwath, T. & Smith, I., *Heroin Century*, Routledge, 2002

Collin, M., *Altered State: The Story of Ecstasy Culture and Acid House*, Serpent's Tail, 1997

Collison, M., *Police, Drugs and Community*, Free Association Books, 1995

Coomber, R., *Pusher Myths: Re-Situating the Drug Dealer*, Free Association Books, 2006

Fairbank, J. & Teng, S., *China's Response to the West*, Harvard University Press, 1979

Feiling, T., *The Candy Machine: How Cocaine Took Over the World*, Penguin, 2009

Jay, M., *High Society: Mind Altering Drugs in History and Culture*, Thames & Hudson, 2010

Kerr, N., *Inebriety or Narcomania: Its Etiology, Pathology, Treatment and Jurisprudence*, HK Lewis, 1894

Kohn, M., *Dope Girls: The Birth of the British Drug Underground*, Granta, 2001

McKeganey, N., *Controversies in Drugs Policy and Practice*, Palgrave Macmillan, 2010

Pritchard, A & Parker, N., *Urban Smuggler*, Mainstream Publishing, 2008

Shapiro, H., *The Media Guide to Drugs*, DrugScope, 2011

Shapiro, H., *Shooting Stars: Drugs, Hollywood and the Movies*, Serpent's Tail, 2003

Shapiro, H., *Waiting for the Man: The Story of Drugs and Popular Music*, Helter Skelter, 2003

Shiner, M., *Drug Use and Social Change: The Distortion of History*, Palgrave Macmillan, 2009

Siegel, R. K., *Intoxication; The Universal Drive for Mind-Altering Substances*, E.P Dutton , 1989

Silverman, J., *Crack of Doom*, Headline, 1994

Simpson, M. et al., *Drugs in Britain: Supply, Consumption and Control*, Palgrave Macmillan, 2006

Streatfeild, D., *Cocaine*, Virgin Books, 2003

Walton, S., *Out of It*, Penguin, 2001

Young, J., *The Drugtakers*, Granada Publishing, 1971

Other

Druglink magazine

Various articles

DrugScope

DS Daily

Daily email news service on the drugs world

Urban75, Online Brixton-based community, www.urban75.com

Erowid, Online drugs library, www.erowid.org

Bluelight, Online drugs discussion forum, www.bluelight.ru

Acknowledgements

Our thanks go to Tom Avery and Laurie Ip Fung Chun, our editors at William Heinemann and Windmill, whose contributions to this book have been awe-inspiring. To our agent, Jonny Pegg and the editor who commissioned this book, Drummond Moir, for their leap of faith in turning *Narcomania* into a reality.

There are many friends and professionals who have offered us invaluable guidance, feedback and advice during the writing of this book. Particular thanks go to: Andy McNicoll, Catherine Sampson, Lena Corner, Allen Morgan, Dick Hobbs, Martin Woods, Gary Sutton, Gary Potter, Fiona Measham, Karenza Moore, Jennifer Ward, Judith Aldridge, James Bluemel, Gordon Wilson, Mike Power, Michael and Judy Daly, Ilyas Lorgat, Tiggey May, Mike Hough, Suffolk Police Force, Metropolitan Police Force, Andy Sellers, Alex Stevens, Toby Seddon, the staff at DrugScope, Elliot Elam, Niamh Eastwood, Jane Fountain and Steve Rolles.

Thanks to the many people who helped us who cannot be named.